David Mitchell Aird

Blackstone Economized: A Compendium of the

LAWS OF ENGLAND TO THE PRESENT TIME

Elibron Classics
www.elibron.com

Elibron Classics series.

ISBN 0-543-90214-5 (paperback)
ISBN 0-543-90213-7 (hardcover)

This Elibron Classics book contains the complete text of the edition published in 1873 by Longmans, Green, and Co., London.

PREFACE

MANY years have passed since I began this work. I was then a diligent attendant at the public and private lectures of the respective Readers of the Inns of Court, from which I and others profited much; and I strongly advise students to disregard the invidious remarks that may still be made upon those lectures, for not a few young men who then listened and laboured with delight under those talented lecturers have attained distinguished positions in their profession; and, what is more, if stimulated by DUTY, brighter prospects are before them. Oral tuition not only amplifies the mind, but it attunes the ear, and guides the tongue to fluency of speech. Slight not these public or private lectures of the Readers of the Inns of Court. The advantage is of apparently slow growth; but it grows.

As I said, many years have passed since I first entertained the idea of burdening the mind of the legal student by adding another work upon Blackstone, to whose *Commentaries so* many talented jurists have since his time done ample justice; nor would I have transgressed in the present instance, had I not been fully convinced that a voluminous work should not at first be given to the student — that the immature understanding ought not to be loaded at the outset with a mass of technical details which involves much labour and delay; and, indeed, often causes him to desert his studies. My object is to place before the student the "PRINCIPLES OF THE LAWS OF ENGLAND," adapted to the present state of the law, in the simplest form, excluding all extraneous matter, leaving abstract speculations on the early origin of our laws, old and obsolete enactments, and any discussion thereon, as an after-study for the student; for when he is well grounded in the fundamental principles of English Law and of our Constitution, antiquarian research will then be a source of infinite pleasure to him, instead of a hindrance and a drawback.

In order to fix the attention of the student by exciting thought, I have adopted the *interrogatory system;* and for facility of reference, have divided the work into Four Books, each Book embracing all the legal points and practical information contained in the respective four volumes of Blackstone as originally written, supplemented by subsequent statutory enactments and important legal decisions. The changes that have taken place in English jurisprudence are concisely explained; and the jurisdiction of our Courts of Law, which has been lately modified and much enlarged, is carefully noted, so as to render BLACKSTONE ECONOMIZED a solid foundation on which the student may build a legal edifice.

If I have succeeded in placing before students preparing for the Legal Profession an elementary work of utility, I shall deem myself well rewarded for the leisure hours of years which I have bestowed upon it; and I sincerely trust that it will aid them in prosecuting a profession which, when followed with dignity and sincerity, is as ennobling as it is useful and advantageous; a profession which, when guided by the conscientiousness of DUTY, elevates man to the highest position that honourable ambition can attain.

I also trust that the present work may be, from its practical nature, useful to all interested in the study of English law, which ought to be universal; for it is an undeniable fact that a knowledge of the laws of that society in which we live is not only a desirable, but a useful accomplishment; indeed, an essential part of a liberal and polite education; and it is an equally established fact, that the study of the science of law is the best kind of mental training, conducing to logical precision of thought, to accuracy of language, and to vigour of the reasoning faculty.

I must here acknowledge the kind suggestions I received, when I began this work of labour and of love, from my dear departed friend, John Grady, Esq., of the Middle Temple; and to my esteemed friends, William Heath Bennet, Esq., of the Equity Bar, and W. Cockerell, Esq., of the Norfolk Circuit, I am also indebted for a careful revision of the whole work as it passed through the press.

DAVID MITCHELL AIRD.

3, PUMP COURT, TEMPLE.

July 14, 1873.

BOOK I
NATURE OF THE LAWS OF ENGLAND

INTRODUCTORY CHAPTER
IMPORTANCE OF A GENERAL KNOWLEDGE OF THE LAWS OF ENGLAND

THERE are few studies more important to Englishmen than that of the Law, and yet the science of the Laws and Constitution of our country — those legal and equitable rules of action by which the meanest individual is protected from the insults and oppression of the greatest — is a species of knowledge in which Englishmen are remarkably deficient; and the want of a general knowledge of the English Constitution, a Constitution built upon the soundest foundations, approved by the experience of ages, and now made the exemplar or model for the constitutions of most of the European nations, as well as of the newly constituted governments of our colonies, has always been a defect in the education of Englishmen.

As every subject is interested in the preservation of the laws of the realm, it is incumbent upon every man to be acquainted with those rules of conduct with which he is immediately concerned, lest he suffer for his ignorance, and incur the censure as well as inconvenience of living in society without being aware of the obligations which the law imposes.

For example, every man possessed of landed property, of whatever extent or value, is primarily interested in a knowledge of the leading principles of the law relating to estates and conveyances, as a guard against fraud and imposition. Besides, the policy of all laws has made some forms necessary in the wording of *wills* as to the bequests of *real* and *personal* estates, and the manner of attesting them, an ignorance of which must always be of dangerous consequence to such as by choice or necessity compile their own testaments without any technical assistance. A knowledge of these forms may also be of considerable use to medical men, called in, as they sometimes are, suddenly to a patient in a dangerous state, when they may assist in giving a right direction to a testator's intentions as to the disposition of his property. Those who attend our courts of justice are witnesses of the confusion and distress often occasioned in families, and of the difficulties that arise in discerning the true meaning of a testator, or sometimes in discovering any meaning at all in that which he has written, so that in the end, his property often passes away contrary to his intentions, because he has omitted one or two formal words which are necessary to ascertain the sense with indisputable legal precision, or has not executed his will in the presence of such witnesses as the law requires.

A very large portion of the community are liable to be called upon to establish the rights, to estimate the injuries, to weigh the accusations, and sometimes to dispose of the lives of their fellow-subjects, by serving upon juries. In this situation they have frequently to decide, and that upon their oaths, questions of great importance, in the solution of which some legal knowledge is required, especially where the law and the fact as it often happens, are intimately blended together. In Blackstone's time the general incapacity of juries to do this with any tolerable propriety had greatly depreciated their authority, and unavoidably threw, and, indeed, does now throw, more power into the hands of the judges to direct, control, and even reverse their verdicts, than, perhaps, the Constitution intended.

It is true that all jurymen cannot be expected to be able to examine with close application the critical niceties of the Law, but one of our most eminent judges and early legal writers, Sir John Fortescue, gave it as his opinion, "that a person of ordinary capacity might attain an adequate knowledge of law, consistent with the *status* of a gentleman, within the brief period of one year, without neglecting his other avocations."

It is not as a juror only that an Englishman is called upon to determine questions of right and distribute justice to his fellow-subjects. A very ample field is opened for a gentleman who is in the Commission of the Peace to exert his talents by maintaining good order in his neighbourhood, by punishing the dissolute and idle, by protecting the peaceable and industrious; and, above all, by healing petty differences and preventing vexatious prosecutions; but in order to attain these desirable ends it is necessary that he should not only have the will, but possess the capability of administering legal and effectual justice; else, when he has mistaken his authority through ignorance or obtuseness, he will be the object of censure from those to whom he is accountable for his conduct.

Gentlemen of fortune, indeed others in a more humble sphere of life, may *now* — and the probabilities are, that this privilege and duty will be extended — be called upon to represent important constituencies as members of Parliament. When elected, they ought to consider that they are then the guardians of the English Constitution; the makers, the repealers, and interpreters of English laws, delegated to watch, to check, and to avert any dangerous innovation, to propose and to adopt any solid and well-weighed improvement, and bound by every tie of honour and religion to transmit that Constitution and those Laws to their posterity, amended if possible, but at least without any derogation.

CHAPTER II
THE NATURE OF LAWS IN GENERAL

Let us first consider Laws in general — Laws that denote the *rules* of human action or conduct; that is, the precepts which man — a creature endowed with both reason and free-will — is commanded to observe in the general regulation of his behaviour; then, secondly, Laws in their more limited sense, being the *rules* which regulate our civil conduct as Englishmen.

What is Law; and explain the Foundations upon which all Human Laws depend.

LAW, in its most general and comprehensive sense, signifies a *rule of action* prescribed by a *superior* to an *inferior* being, and is applied indiscriminately to all kinds of action, whether animate or inanimate, rational or irrational; and it is that rule of action which the inferior is bound, to obey.

LAW comprises the LAW OF NATURE; REVEALED LAW; the LAW of NATIONS; and MUNICIPAL LAW.

The *Law of Nature* is the *Will* of our Maker; for God, when He created man and endowed him with free-will, not only laid down certain immutable laws of human nature, whereby that free-will is in some degree regulated and restrained, but He gave him the faculty of reason to discover the purport of those laws; and He has so intimately connected, so inseparably interwoven, the laws of eternal justice with the happiness of each individual, that the latter cannot be secured but by observing the former. Also, in compassion to the frailty, the imperfection, and the blindness of human reason, Divine Providence has been pleased, at sundry times and in divers manners, to discover and enforce his laws by an immediate and direct *revelation,* which we call the DIVINE or REVEALED LAW. These laws are to be found in the Holy Scriptures; and upon the Law of Nature and the Law of Revelation depend all human laws.

The *Law of Nations* is what is termed *International Law,* a law to regulate the intercourse of nations — the offspring of Civilization — a moral obligation of justice and humanity from one State to another, and which entirely depends upon mutual compacts, treaties, and agreements between the several communities.

Municipal Law is "a *rule* of civil conduct, prescribed by the supreme power in a State, commanding what is *right,* prohibiting what is *wrong,* and regulating matters in themselves indifferent."

It is a *rule;* not a transient sudden order from a superior to or concerning a particular person; but something permanent, uniform, and universal. It is called a *rule* to distinguish it from advice or counsel, which we are at liberty to follow or not, and to judge upon the reasonableness or unreasonableness of the advice tendered; whereas our obedience to the law depends not upon our approbation, but upon the enactments of the legislature.

It is also called a *rule,* to distinguish it from a contract or agreement; for a contract is a *promise* proceeding from us; law is a *command* directed to us.

Municipal Law is also a *rule* of "civil conduct," which regards man as a citizen, and binds him to contribute on his part to the subsistence and peace of the society in which he is placed.

It is likewise a *rule* "prescribed," because a bare resolution confined in the breast of the legislator, without manifesting itself by some external sign, can never be properly a law. It is requisite that this resolution be notified to the people who are to obey it, and when this *rule* is in the usual manner notified or prescribed, the law holds that it is then the subject's duty to be thoroughly acquainted therewith; for if ignorance of what he might know were admitted as a legitimate excuse for a breach of law, the laws would be of no effect, but might be eluded with impunity.

But further, Municipal Law is a *rule* of civil conduct "prescribed by the supreme power in a State;" in other words, the British Legislature. When civil society is once formed, government at the same time results, as a necessary consequence, to preserve and keep that society in order; therefore it is requisite to the very essence of a municipal law that it be made by the supreme power.

Explain the Origin and Forms of Government.

How the several forms of Government originated, is a matter of great uncertainty, which has occasioned infinite discussion. However they began, or by what right soever they subsist, there must be in all of them a supreme, irresistible, absolute authority, in which the *jura summa imperii,* or the rights of sovereignty, reside; and this authority is placed in those hands wherein, according to the opinion of the majority of such respective States, either expressly given or collected from their tacit approbation, the qualities requisite for supremacy, wisdom, goodness, and power are to be found.

The political writers of antiquity do not acknowledge more than *three* regular forms of Government; the first, when the supreme power is lodged in an aggregate assembly, consisting of all the free members of a community, which is a DEMOCRACY; the second, when it is lodged in a council, composed of select members, and then it is styled an ARISTOCRACY; the third, when it is intrusted to the hands of a single person, and then it takes the name of a MONARCHY. These *three* forms are embodied in the British Constitution, — first, the Queen; secondly, the Lords spiritual and temporal; thirdly, the House of Commons, freely chosen by the people; and in no other shape could we be so certain of finding the great qualities of government so well and so happily blended.

What are the Duties of Government?

One of the duties of supreme power is to make laws; in other words, *to prescribe the rules of civil action* — "commanding what is right, prohibiting what is wrong, and regulating matters in themselves indifferent." Now, in order to do this completely, it is first of all necessary that the boundaries of *right* and *wrong* should be established and ascertained by law.

In what manner does the Law ascertain the Boundaries of Right and Wrong? Explain the method it takes to command the one and prohibit the other.

Every law consists of several parts; one *Declaratory,* whereby the rights to be observed and the wrongs to be avoided are clearly defined and laid down; another *Directory,* whereby the subject is instructed and enjoined to observe those rights, and to abstain from the commission of those wrongs; a third *Remedial,* whereby a method is pointed out to recover a man's private rights or redress his private wrongs; to which may be added a fourth, usually termed the *sanction,* or *vindicatory* branch of the law; whereby it is signified what punishment or penalty shall be incurred by such persons as commit public wrongs by transgressing or neglecting their duty.

With regard to the first of these — the *Declaratory* part of the municipal law — this depends upon the wisdom and will of the Legislature; for those rights which God and nature have established, called *natural rights,* such as life and liberty, need not the aid of human laws to be more effectually possessed by man. On the contrary, no human legislature has power to abridge or destroy them, unless the owner shall himself commit some act that amounts to a forfeiture. The case is the same as to crimes and misdemeanors that are forbidden by the superior laws, and therefore styled *mala in se,* such as murder, theft, and perjury, which contract no additional turpitude from being declared unlawful by the inferior legislature. But with regard to *things* which are said to be *in themselves indifferent,* the case is otherwise. These become either right or wrong, just or unjust, duties or misdemeanors, according as the Legislature enacts for promoting the welfare of society, and more effectually carrying on the purposes of civil life. Thus by our own common law, as at present interpreted, the goods of the wife do instantly upon marriage become the property and right of the husband, and our statute law has declared all monopolies a public offence; yet that right and this offence have no foundation in nature, but are merely created by the law for the purpose of civil society.

Thus much for the *declaratory* part of the municipal law; and the *directory* stands upon the same footing; for this virtually includes the former. The law that says "Thou shalt not steal" implies a *declaration* that stealing is a crime. And we have seen that, in things *naturally indifferent,* the very essence of RIGHT and WRONG depends upon the direction of the laws to *do* or to *omit* them.

The *remedial* part of a law is so necessary a consequence of the former two, that a law must be very vague and imperfect without it; for in vain would rights be declared, in vain directed to be observed, if there were no method of recovering and asserting those rights, when wrongfully withheld or invaded. This is the PROTECTION of the law. When, for instance, the *declaratory* part of the law has said "that the field or inheritance which belonged to a man is vested by his death in his son;" and the *directory* part has "forbidden any one to enter on another's property, without the leave of the owner;" if a stranger, after this, will presume to take possession of the land, the *remedial* part of the law will then interpose its office, and make the stranger not only restore possession to the son, but also make him pay damages for the invasion.

With regard to the *sanction* of laws, or the evil that may attend the breach of public duties, it is observed, that human legislators have for the most part chosen to make the *sanction* of their laws rather *vindicatory* than *remuneratory,* or to consist rather in punishments than in rewards. Because, in the first place, the quiet enjoyment and protection of all our civil rights and liberties, which are the sure and general consequence of obedience to the municipal law, are in themselves the best and most valuable of all rewards; and farther, because the dread of evil is a much more forcible principle of human action than the prospect of good. For which reasons, though a prudent bestowing of rewards is sometimes beneficial, yet we find that those civil laws which enjoin and enforce our duty do seldom, if ever, propose any privilege or gift to such as obey the law, but do constantly come armed with a penalty denounced against transgressors, either expressly defining the nature and quantity of the punishment, or else leaving it to the discretion of the judges, and those who are entrusted with the care of putting the laws in execution. Unquestionably of all parts of a law, the most effectual is the *vindicatory;* for it is but lost labour to say "Do this," or "Avoid that," unless we also declare, "This shall be the consequence of your non-compliance."

It is true that human laws are binding upon men's consciences. But if that were the only or most forcible obligation, the good only would regard the laws, and the bad would set them at defiance. So also in regard to *natural duties,* and such offences as are *mala in se;* here we are bound in conscience; because we are bound by superior laws, revealed before those human laws were propounded, to perform the one and abstain from the other. But in relation to those laws which enjoin *positive duties,* annexing a penalty to non-compliance, conscience is no farther concerned, than in yielding obedience and submission to the penalty, in case of the breach of those laws.

The main strength and force of a law consists in *the penalty* annexed to it. Herein is to be found the principal obligation of human laws.

CHAPTER III
THE LAWS OF ENGLAND

Next under our consideration is the *Municipal Law of England,* defined, as the "rule of civil conduct prescribed to the inhabitants of this kingdom," which comprises in its highest and widest sense all those rules, written or customary, which have been laid down for the guidance of the community, and to which its members must, if they would avoid penal consequences or civil liabilities, necessarily conform. It is divided into two classes — the *Lex non Scripta,* the unwritten or Common Law; and the *Lex Scripta,* the written or Statute Law.

Explain the "Lex non Scripta."

The *lex non scripta,* or *unwritten* law, is not literally unwritten, but is contained in. the records of our courts of justice, in books of reports, and in the treatises of learned lawyers handed down from times of great antiquity.

The *lex non scripta* includes not only *general customs,* called the Common Law, but also the *particular customs* of certain parts of the kingdom; and likewise those *particular laws* that are by custom observed only in certain courts and jurisdictions.

Our ancient lawyers, and particularly Fortescue, insist that these *customs* are as old as the primitive Britons, and continued down, through the several mutations of government and inhabitants, to the present time, unchanged and unadulterated. This may be the case as to some; but in general, as Mr. Selden observes, "this assertion must be understood with many grains of allowance, and ought only to signify, as the truth seems to be, that there never was any formal exchange of one system of laws for another; though, doubtless, by the intermixture of adventitious nations, the Romans, the Picts, the Saxons, the Danes, and the Normans, they must have insensibly introduced and incorporated many of their own customs with those that were before established; thereby, in all probability, improving the texture and wisdom of the whole, by the accumulated wisdom of divers particular countries."

However that may be, it is certain that these *laws* and *customs* are of higher antiquity than memory or history can reach, nothing being more difficult than to ascertain the precise beginning and first spring of an ancient and long-established custom; whence it is that in our law the goodness of a custom depends upon its having been used time out of mind; or, in the solemnity of our legal phrase, "time whereof the memory of man runneth not to the contrary." This it is that gives it its weight and authority, and of this nature are the maxims and customs which compose the common law, or *lex non scripta,* of this kingdom.

Explain these General Customs of the Common Law.

The unwritten or Common' Law is distinguishable into two kinds: — 1. GENERAL CUSTOMS; which are the universal *rule.* of the whole kingdom, and form the COMMON LAW in its stricter and more usual signification. — 2. PARTICULAR CUSTOMS; which, for the most part, affect only the inhabitants *of particular districts.*

First, as to *general customs,* by which proceedings and determinations in the Queen's ordinary courts of justice are guided and directed. These, for the most part, settle the course in which lands descend by inheritance — the manner and form of acquiring and transferring property — the solemnities and obligations of contracts — the rules for expounding wills, deeds, and Acts of Parliament — the respective remedies for civil injuries — the several species of temporal offences, and an infinite number of more minute particulars which diffuse themselves as extensively as the ordinary distribution of common justice requires. Thus, for example, that there shall be four superior courts of record — the Courts of Chancery, the Queen's Bench, Common Pleas, and Exchequer — that the eldest son alone is heir to his ancestor — that a deed is of no validity unless sealed and delivered — that *wills* shall be construed more favourably, and deeds more strictly — that money lent upon a bond is recoverable by action of debt — that breaking the public peace is an offence, and punishable by fine and imprisonment. All these are doctrines that are not set down in any written statute or ordinance, but depend upon immemorial usage; that is, upon common law for their support.

The SECOND BRANCH of the unwritten laws of England are *particular customs,* or laws which affect only the inhabitants of particular districts. These particular customs, or some of them, are without doubt the remains of that multitude of local customs, out of which the common law as it now stands was collected, at first by King Alfred, and afterwards by King Edgar and Edward the Confessor; each district mutually sacrificing some of its own special usages, in order that the whole kingdom might enjoy the benefit of one uniform and universal system of laws; but for reasons that have been long forgotten, particular counties, cities, towns, manors, and lordships were indulged with the privilege of abiding by their own customs, in contradistinction to the rest of the nation at large, which is confirmed to them by several Acts of Parliament.

1. Such is the custom of *gavelkind,* in Kent, and some other parts of the kingdom, which ordains, among other things, that the eldest son of the father shall *not* succeed to the inheritance, but *all the sons* alike; and that though the ancestor be attainted and executed, yet the heirs shall succeed to his estate without any escheat to his lord.

2. Such is the custom that prevails in divers ancient boroughs, called *borough-English* — that the youngest son shall inherit the estate, in preference to his elder brothers.

3. Such is the custom in other boroughs, that a widow shall be entitled for her dower to all her husband's lands; whereas, at the common law she shall be endowed of one-third part only.

4. Such also are the special and particular customs of manors, which bind all the copyhold and customary tenants that hold of the said manors.

5. Such likewise is the custom of holding divers inferior courts, with power of trying causes in cities and trading towns; the right of holding which, when no Royal grant can be shown, depends entirely upon immemorial and established usage.

6. Such, lastly, are many particular customs within the City of London, with regard to trade, apprentices, widows, orphans, and a variety of other matters.

All these are contrary to the general law of the land, and are good only by special usage. The customs of London are however, confirmed by Act of Parliament.

To this head may be referred a particular system of customs which comprises certain rules relative to bills of exchange and other mercantile matters, and which is generally denominated the custom of merchants — *Lex Mercatoria,* and allowed for the benefit of trade. It forms a portion of the general law of England, and is composed of European usages in matters relative to commerce.

What are the Rules with regard to "Particular" Customs?

Proof of their existence; their *legality* when proved; the *legal* construction to be put upon them.

To make a particular custom good, the following are necessary requisites: —

1. The custom must have been used so long that the memory of man runneth not to the contrary. Legal memory dates from the first year of the reign of Richard I.; but stat. 2 & 3, Wm. IV., c. 71, and subsequent statutes materially qualify this rule, and in a large class of cases shorten

the legal time of prescription to twenty years, making undisturbed usage for that period a bar or title in itself, unless enjoyed in virtue of an agreement between the parties.

2. A *custom,* in order to be valid, must have been *continued.* Any interruption of the right would cause a temporary ceasing: the revival gives it a new beginning, which, if within time of memory, the custom will be void. This must be understood only with regard to an *interruption* of the *right;* for an interruption of the *possession* for ten or twelve years will not destroy the custom.

3. It must have been *peaceable* and acquiesced in, not subject to contention and dispute.

4. A custom must be *reasonable;* it being sufficient that no good reason can be assigned against it.

5. A custom must be *certain,* for a custom admits of no caprice or fancy.

6. A custom must be *compulsory,* not left to the option of every man whether he will use it or not.

7. Customs must be *consistent* with each other; for one custom cannot be set up in opposition to another.

How are Customs Construed?

Customs in derogation of the common law must be construed strictly, but not necessarily confined to literal interpretation. Thus, by the custom of *gavelkind,* an infant of fifteen years may, by one species of conveyance, called a deed of feoffment, convey away his lands in fee simple or for life; yet this custom does not empower the use of any other conveyance, for the custom must be strictly pursued; but if there is a custom in a manor that a man may convey his copyhold in fee-simple, it will also enable him to convey for life, or any other estate, for the *less* is implied in the *greater.*

No custom, however, can prevail against an express Act of Parliament.

Besides *local customs,* there are in different parts of the country certain *usages* which, unless expressly excluded by agreement, regulate the contract. For instance, the reciprocal rights of incoming and outgoing tenants; *usages* of trade which exist in certain places; but they cannot in strictness be considered as forming part of our customary law[1].

Explain the Laws which, by "Custom," are adopted and used only in certain peculiar Courts and Jurisdictions.

These are the *Civil* and *Canon* Laws.

The *Civil Law is* generally understood to be the civil or municipal law of the Roman Empire, as comprised in the *Institutes,* the *Code,* and the *Digest* of the Emperor Justinian, and the *Novel Constitutions* of himself and some of his successors; but all the force that either the Imperial or Papal laws have attained in this realm, is because they have been admitted and received by immemorial usage and custom in some particular cases and some particular courts, where they form a branch of the *leges non scriptæ;* or else, in some other cases, introduced by consent of Parliament, and then they owe their validity to the *leges scriptæ,* or statute law.

The *Canon Law* is a body of Roman *ecclesiastical law* relative to matters over which that Church either has, or pretends to have, the proper jurisdiction. It is compiled from the opinions of the ancient Latin fathers, the decrees of general councils, and the decretal epistles and bulls of

[1] The validity of these customs and usages is determined by the Judges in the several courts of justice, who are bound by oath to decide according to the law of the land, viz., the judicial decisions of their predecessors.

the Holy See. Besides these pontifical collections, there is also a kind of national law, composed of *legatine* and *provincial constitutions,* and adapted only to the exigencies of this Church.

There are three species of courts in which the civil or canon laws are permitted, under different restrictions, to be used.

The Courts of Common Law have the superintendency over these courts, to keep them within their respective jurisdiction, to determine wherein they exceed them, to restrain and prohibit such excess; and, in case of contumacy, to punish the officer who executes, and in some cases the judge who enforces the sentence so declared to be illegal.

The common law has also reserved to itself the exposition of all such Acts of Parliament as concern either the extent of these courts or the matters depending before them.

An appeal lies from all these courts to certain superior courts hereafter discussed, and to the Sovereign in the last resort.

CHAPTER IV
STATUTE LAW

Let us next proceed to the *Leges Scripts,* the written laws of the kingdom.

Explain the Written or Statute Laws, and state briefly the different kinds of Statutes, and the general rules with regard to their construction.

The *written laws* of the kingdom are Statutes, Acts, or Edicts, made by the Sovereign, by and with the advice and consent of the Lords Spiritual and Temporal and Commons in Parliament assembled. The oldest of these, now extant and printed in our Statute-book, is the famous *Magna Charta,* as confirmed in Parliament in the ninth year of Henry III.

Statutes are either *public* or *private.* A public Act is a universal rule that regards the whole community. Private Acts are rather exceptions than rules, being those which only operate upon particular persons and private concerns.

Statutes are either *declaratory* of the common law, or *remedial* of some defects therein. Declaratory, where the old custom of the kingdom is almost fallen into disuse, or become disputable; in which case Parliament has thought proper, *in perpetuum rei testimonium,* and for avoiding all doubts and difficulties, to declare what the common law is and ever has been. *Remedial* statutes are those which are made to supply such defects and abridge such superfluities in the common law as arise from the general imperfection of all human laws; or from change of time and circumstances, or the mistakes and unadvised determinations of unlearned or even learned judges, or from any other cause whatsoever.

There is also a subdivision of these Acts of Parliament into *enlarging* and *restraining* Acts, and this is done either by enlarging the common law where it was too narrow and circumscribed, or by restraining it where it was too lax. A *repealing* Act revokes and cancels a former statutory law.

Parliament is presumed to legislate prospectively, not retrospectively; and statutes are therefore to be construed as prospective, unless they are expressly made applicable to transactions past or pending.

An Act of Parliament begins to operate when it receives the Royal assent, unless some other time is fixed by the Act itself.

What are the Rules for the Construction of Acts of Parliament?

1. To consider how the law stood at the time of passing the Act; what the mischief was for which the law did not provide; what remedy the Parliament provided to cure the mischief.

2. A statute which treats of things or persons of an inferior rank cannot, by general *words,* be extended to those of a superior degree.

3. Penal statutes must be construed strictly, but not too literally.

4. Statutes against frauds are to be liberally and beneficially expounded; this difference to be remembered, that where the statute inflicts a penalty or fine, it is then to be taken strictly; but where the statute acts upon the *offence,* as by setting aside a fraudulent transaction, here it is to be construed liberally.

5. One part of a statute must be construed by another, so that the whole may be valid rather than perish: *ut res magis vulcat quam pereat.*

6. A saving totally repugnant to the body of the Act is void.

7. Where the common law and a statute differ, the common law gives place to the statute, and an old statute gives place to a new one.

8. Where an Act repealing in whole or in part any former statute is itself repealed, such last repeal shall not

revive the act or provisions before repealed, unless *words be added for that purpose.*

9. Acts of Parliament derogatory from the power of subsequent Parliaments bind not.

10. Acts of Parliament that are impossible to be performed are of no validity, and if there arise out of them collaterally any absurd consequences manifestly contradictory to common reason, they are with regard to those collateral circumstances void.

In addition to these rules of interpretation and construction, EQUITY is sometimes called in to assist, to moderate, and to explain them. Courts of Equity[2] are, however, only cognizant of matters of *property;* for the freedom of our Constitution will not permit that, in *criminal* cases, a power should be lodged in any judge to construe the law otherwise than according to the letter. A man cannot suffer *more* punishment than the law assigns, but he may suffer *less;* for the law cannot be strained by partiality to inflict a penalty beyond what the letter will warrant; and in cases where the letter induces any apparent hardship, the Crown has the power to pardon.

CHAPTER V
THE COUNTRIES SUBJECT TO THE LAWS OF ENGLAND

Having considered. the nature of laws in general, let us now direct our inquiries respecting the countries that are under the jurisdiction of the Laws of England.

---

[2] The powers, business, and jurisdiction of the Equity Courts will, in due course, be discussed.

State the Countries to which the Laws of England extend.

The Kingdom of England, over which our municipal laws have jurisdiction, does not, by the common law, include Wales, Scotland, or Ireland, Berwick-upon-Tweed, or any other part of the Queen's dominions, except the territory of England only; and yet the civil laws and local customs of this territory now prevail in part, or in all, with more or less restrictions, in these and in many other adjacent countries.

By stat. 27, Henry VIII. it is enacted that all Welshmen born shall have the same liberties as other the Queen's subjects; that lands in Wales shall be inheritable according to the English tenures and rules of descent; and that the laws of England, and no other, shall be used in Wales. Wales and Berwick-upon-Tweed are comprehended in the word "England," when used in any Act of Parliament.

Since the Union with Scotland, May 1, 1707, all statutes of a general nature extend to that kingdom; or if not included, the method is expressly to declare that the Act does not extend to Scotland. The Municipal Laws of Scotland continue in full force, unless altered by the Imperial Legislature.

In like manner, since the Union with Ireland, January 1,1801, all statutes of a general nature extend to that kingdom, unless expressly excepted, or the intention to except it be otherwise plainly shown.

The Isle of Wight, the Isle of Portland, the Isle of Thanet, &c., are comprised within some neighbouring county, and are, therefore, to be looked upon as annexed to the mother island, and part of the kingdom of England.

The Isle of Man is a distinct territory from England, and is not in general governed by our laws; neither does any Act of Parliament extend to it, unless specially named therein; nor does any ordinary process run there from the English courts, except the writ of *habeas corpus*.

Guernsey, Jersey, Alderney, Sark, and their appendages are not comprehended in a statute, unless specially mentioned. They are governed by their own laws, which are, for the most part, the Ducal Customs of Normandy, being collected in an ancient book of very great authority, entitled *Le Grand Coustumier*.

Besides these adjacent islands, our more distant settlements or colonies in America, Australia, the West Indies, and elsewhere are also, in some respects, subject to the English laws, but this must be understood with very many and very great restrictions. Such colonists carry with them only so much of the English law as is applicable to their own situation and condition of an infant colony; but in conquered or ceded countries that have already laws of their own, Parliament may alter and change those laws; but the ancient laws of the country remain, unless such of them as are against the laws of God, as in the case of an infidel country.

The main or high seas are in one sense part of the realm of England, over which our Courts of Admiralty have jurisdiction. The main sea begins at the low-water mark, but between the high-water mark and the low-water mark, where the sea ebbs and flows, the common law and Admiralty have alternate jurisdiction, one upon the water when it is full tide, the other upon the land when it is an ebb.

INDIA

Give a brief account of the Past and Present Forms of the Indian Government, and explain also our Territorial Possessions in India.

Previously to 1708, two trading associations existed in England, and in that year they were amalgamated and consolidated by Act of Parliament, and thenceforth, traded under the name of "The United Company of Merchants of England Trading to the East Indies." Very exclusive commercial privileges were thereby granted, to the Company.

The East India Company from time to time acquired, by treaty and conquest, vast territorial dominions, subject, it is true, to the supremacy of the British Crown; but it was virtually the sovereign of the greater part of India. Great abuses crept in, till at length its constitution was rearranged in 1781, by Act of Parliament (24 Geo. III., c. 25). which considerably restricted the powers of the Company.

Before that time there were three supreme courts of law constituted at the three Presidencies — Bombay, Calcutta, and Madras — presided over by English judges sent out from England.

The laws promulgated by the Company from time to time were termed "Regulations," and were collected in Codes appertaining to each of these Presidencies, which had the force of laws. Courts had also been created for the administration of law between natives, presided over by judges appointed by the Company, generally chosen from their civil servants, assisted by natives skilled in the Hindoo and Mohammedan law.

These exclusive privileges, modified by degrees, continued until their total abolition in 1832, by stat. 3 & 4 Wm. IV., c. 85; and the administration of law in India is now regulated by 21 & 22 Vict., c. 26, by which the Crown is now entrusted with the sole dominion over the territories acquired and possessed by the East India Company, and the administration of affairs is regulated by its various provisions.[3]

The Territory of England being liable to two divisions, the one "Ecclesiastical," and the other "Civil," give a brief outline of each.

The ECCLESIASTICAL division is primarily divided into two provinces, those of Canterbury and York. A province is the circuit of an archbishop's jurisdiction, and each province contains divers dioceses or sees of suffragan bishops, whereof Canterbury includes twenty, and York six, besides the bishopric of the Isle of Man, which was annexed to the province of York by King Henry VIII. Every diocese is divided into archdeaconries, whereof there are sixty in all; each archdeaconry into rural deaneries, which are the circuit of the archdeacons' and rural deans' jurisdiction. Every deanery is divided into parishes.

A *Parish is* that circuit of ground the inhabitants of which are committed to the charge of one parson or vicar, or other minister having cure of souls therein. How ancient the division of parishes is may at present be difficult to ascertain. Mr. Camden says that England was divided into parishes by Archbishop Honoring, about the year 630; but Sir Henry Hobart lays it down that parishes were first erected by the Council of Lateran, which was held in 1179. These parishes were gradually formed, and parish

[3] See 33 & 34 Vict., c. 3, an Act to make better provision for making laws and regulations for certain parts of India; also chapter 69, an Act to render valid contracts informally executed in India.

churches endowed with the tithes that arose within the circuit assigned[4].

The CIVIL division of the territory of England is into counties, counties into hundreds, hundreds into tithings or towns. Tithings, towns, or vills have the same signification in law, and are said to have had each originally a church, and celebration of divine service, sacraments, and burials. The word *town* or *vill* is now become a generic term, comprehending the several species of cities, boroughs, and common towns. A *City* is a town incorporated, which usually is or has been the see of a bishop. A *Borough* is now understood to be a town either corporate or not, that sends burgesses to Parliament. These towns contained each originally but one parish and one tithing; but now by the increase of the inhabitants many of them are divided into several parishes and tithings.

Shire is a Saxon word signifying a division. England is divided into forty counties or shires, Wales into twelve and Scotland into thirty. Three of these counties, Chester, Durham, and Lancaster, are called counties palatine. The two former are such by prescription, or immemorial custom, or at least as old as the Norman Conquest; the latter was created by King Edward III. in favour of Henry Plantagenet, first Earl and then Duke of Lancaster, whose heiress being married to John of Gaunt, the King's son, the franchise was greatly enlarged and confirmed in Parliament, to honour John of Gaunt himself, whom, on the death of his father-in-law, the King had also created Duke of Lancaster.

The distribution into counties or shires is at present materially connected with the administration of justice; for

[4] The affairs of a Parish, the mode of conducting the business of the Vestry, and other matters relating thereto, are now regulated by the General Vestry Act, 58 Geo. III., c. 69, amended by 68 Geo. III., c. 85, and by 16 & 17 Vict., c. 65.

trials both civil and criminal are periodically heard before the justices of the assizes which are held in each county twice a year, or oftener if necessary. In the Parliamentary representation of the people, each county sends county members, called knights of the shire; and where the county is divided, each portion forms a separate county, and each sends its separate representative. Each county is subject to a particular rate for the relief of the poor and purposes connected with prisons and criminal offenders.

Counties Palatine are so called *a palatio;* because the owners thereof, the Earl of Chester, the Bishop of Durham, and the Duke of Lancaster, had in those counties *jura regalia,* as fully as the King had in his palace. They appointed all judges and justices of the peace, and might pardon all treasons, felonies, and even murders. The proceedings and practice of the Courts of Durham and of Lancaster are now in general assimilated to those of the Courts of Westminster.

The Isle of Ely is not a county palatine, but only a royal franchise, whereby the bishop exercised a jurisdiction over all causes, criminal as well as civil. By 6 & 7 Win. IV., c. 87, the jurisdiction has been entirely taken from the bishop, and is now vested in the Crown.

There are also *Counties Corporate,* which are certain cities and towns to which, out of special grace, the Kings of England granted the privilege to be counties in themselves, governed by their own sheriffs and other magistrates, so that no officers of the county at large have any power to intermeddle therein. Such were London, York, Bristol, Norwich, Coventry, and many others; but the regulation of those places is now provided for by the Municipal Corporation Act, 5 & 6 Win. IV., c. 76; 2 & 3 Vict., c. 72; 24 & 25 Vict., c.. 75; and 32 & 33 Vict, c. 55.

CHAPTER VI
THE RIGHTS OF PERSONS

In order to consider with perspicuity the numerous and diverse laws of England, it will be necessary to lay down a suitable arrangement of the subject, to distribute it methodically under proper and distinct heads, and to avoid as much as possible divisions too large and comprehensive on the one hand, and too trifling and minute on the other. Having seen that Municipal Law is "a rule of civil conduct, commanding what is right and prohibiting what is wrong," let us first, then, consider the *rights* that are *commanded,* and the *wrongs* that are *forbidden* by the Laws of England.

Explain the "Rights" that are "commanded" and the "Wrongs" that are "forbidden" by the laws of England.

RIGHTS are, first, those which concern and are annexed to the persons of men, and are then called *jura personarum,* or the rights of persons; or they are, secondly, such as a man may acquire over external objects or things unconnected with his person, and are designated *jura rerum,* or the rights of things.

WRONGS also are divisible into, first, *private wrongs,* which, being an infringement of particular rights concerning individuals, are called *civil injuries;* and, secondly, *public wrongs,* which being a breach of general and public rights, affect the whole community, and are called *crimes* and *misdemeanors.* Thus the objects of the laws of England fall into this fourfold division: —

1. The RIGHTS OF PERSONS, with the means whereby such rights may be either acquired or lost.

2. The RIGHTS OF THINGS, with the means also of acquiring and losing them.

3. PRIVATE WRONGS, or civil injuries, with the means of redressing them by law.

4. PUBLIC WRONGS, or crimes and misdemeanors, with the means of prevention and punishment.

First, then, as to the *rights of persons,* with the means of acquiring and losing them.

The rights of persons that are commanded to be observed by the municipal law are of two sorts; first, such as are due *from* every citizen, which are usually called *civil duties;* and, secondly, such as belong *to* him, which is the more popular acceptation of *rights* or *jura.* Both may, indeed, be comprised in this latter division, for as all social duties are of a relative nature, at the same time they are due *from* one man or set of men, they must also be due *to* another. Thus, for instance, *allegiance* is considered the duty of the people, and *protection* as the duty of the magistrate; and yet they are reciprocally the rights as well as the duties of each other.

Persons also, are divided by the law into either *natural* or *artificial* persons. Natural persons are such as God has formed us; artificial are such as are created and devised by human laws for the purposes of society and government, which are called *corporations,* or *bodies politic.*

The rights of persons, considered in their *natural* capacities, are also of two sorts, *absolute* and *relative.* Absolute, which are such rights as appertain and belong to particular men merely as individuals or single persons; relative, which are incident to them as members of society, and standing in various relations to each other.

Absolute rights of individuals are those which are so in their primary and strictest sense, such as would belong to their persons merely in a state of nature, and which every man is entitled to enjoy whether out of society or in it; but with absolute *duties* which man is bound to perform, considered as a mere individual, it is not to be expected that any human municipal law should at all explain or enforce them, for the end and intent of such laws being only to regulate the behaviour of mankind as they are members of society and stand in various relations to each other, they have consequently no concern with any other but social or relative duties. Let a man therefore be ever so abandoned in his principles or vicious in his practice, provided he keeps his wickedness to himself and does not offend against the rules of public decency, he is out of the reach of human laws; but if he makes his vices public, though they be such as seem principally to affect himself, they then become, by the bad example they set, offensive to society, and therefore it is thus the business of human laws to correct them. Hero the circumstance of *publicity* alters the nature of the case. *Public* sobriety is a *relative* duty, and therefore enjoined by our laws; *private* sobriety is an *absolute* duty, which, whether it be performed or not, human tribunals can never know. But with respect to *rights* the case is different; for human laws define and enforce as well those rights which belong to a man considered as an individual, as those which belong to him considered as related to others. The principal aim of society is to protect individuals in the enjoyment of those *absolute rights* which are the first and primary end of human laws; but which could not be preserved in peace without that mutual assistance and intercourse which are gained by the institution of friendly and social communities. Hence it follows, that the first and primary end of human laws is to maintain and regulate these *absolute* rights of individuals.

These *absolute* rights of every Englishman (usually called *liberties),* as they are founded on nature and reason, so they are coeval with our form of government. Subject at times to fluctuations and change, their establishment being human, they have been depressed by overbearing and tyrannical princes: but the vigour of our free Constitution has ultimately delivered the nation from these embarrassments, and as soon as the convulsions consequent on the struggle have been over, the balance of our rights and liberties has settled to its proper level, and their fundamental articles have been asserted in Parliament whenever these rights were thought to be in danger.

Explain the Rights of the People.

The *rights* of the people of England may be reduced to three principal or primary articles: —

1. THE RIGHT OF PERSONAL SECURITY.

2. THE RIGHT OF PERSONAL LIBERTY.

3. THE RIGHT OF PRIVATE PROPERTY.

I. The right of *personal security* consists in a person's legal and uninterrupted enjoyment of his life, his limbs, his body, his health, and his reputation.

Life is the immediate gift of God, a right inherent by nature in every individual, and it begins in contemplation of law as soon as an infant is able to stir in the mother's womb; so if a woman is quick with child, and by a potion or otherwise designedly kills it in her womb; or, if anyone else gives it to her, or beats her with a like design, whereby the child dies in her body, and she is delivered of a dead child, it is treated in law as if actually born.

An infant in *ventre sa mere* (in the mother's womb) is supposed in law to be born for many purposes. It takes land by descent. It may have a guardian assigned to it; and it is enabled to have an estate limited to its use, and to take afterwards by which limitation, as if it were then actually born.

A man's limbs are also the gift of the Creator, to enable him to protect himself from external in juries in a state of nature; and a man's life and limbs are held of such value by our law, that it pardons even homicide if committed *se defendendo,* or in order to preserve them; for whatever is done by a man to save either life or member, is looked upon as done upon the highest necessity and compulsion. If a man, through fear of death or mayhem, is prevailed upon to execute a deed, or do any other legal act, this may afterwards be avoided, if forced upon him by a well-grounded apprehension of losing his life, or even his limbs, in case of his non-compliance.

The law not only regards life and member, and protects every man in the enjoyment of them, but also furnishes him with everything necessary for their support; for there is no man so indigent or wretched but he may demand a supply sufficient for all the necessities of life from the more opulent part of the community, by means of the several statutes enacted for the relief of the poor.

Besides limbs and members that may be necessary to a man in order to defend himself or annoy his enemy, a man is entitled by the same natural right to security from corporal insults or injuries, whether by menaces, assaults, beating, and wounding. The preservation of health from such practices as may prejudice or annoy it, is his absolute right, also the security of his reputation or good name from slander.

II. Next to *personal security* the law of England regards, asserts, and preserves the *personal liberty* of individuals. This personal liberty consists in the power of locomotion, of changing situation, or moving one's person to whatsoever place one's own inclination may direct, without imprisonment or restraint, unless by due course of law. The language of the Great Charter is, "that no freeman shall be taken or imprisoned but by the lawful judgment of his equals, or by the law of the land;" and subsequent statutes expressly direct that no man shall be taken or imprisoned by suggestion, or petition to the King or his Council, unless it be by legal indictment, or by the process of the common law.[5] To make imprisonment lawful, it must be either by process from the courts of judicature, or by warrant from some legal officer having authority to commit to prison which warrant must be in writing under the hand and seal of the magistrate, with the cause of the commitment, expressed, in order to be examined, if necessary, upon a *habeas corpus*. By 16 Carl. I., c. 10, if any person be restrained of his liberty by order or decree of any illegal court, or by command of the king's majesty in person, or by warrant of the council board, or of any of the privy council, who shall, upon demand of his counsel, have a writ of *habeas corpus to* bring his body before the Court of King's Bench or Common Pleas, who shall determine whether the cause of his commitment be just, and thereupon do as to justice shall appertain; and, by the Habeas Corpus Act, the methods of obtaining this writ are so plainly pointed out and enforced, that so long as this statute remains unimpeached, no subject in England can be long detained in prison, except in those cases in which the law requires and justifies such detainer.

III. The third *absolute right* inherent in every Englishman is that of *property,* which consists in the free use enjoyment, and disposal of all his acquisitions, without any control or diminution, save only by the laws of the

---

[5] Parliament only, when the State is in danger, can suspend the *Habeas Corpus Act* for a short and limited time, to enable the Crown to imprison suspected persons without the possibility of their obtaining their discharge during that period by any interference of the courts of law.

land. The laws of England are, in point of justice, extremely watchful in ascertaining and protecting this right. Upon this principle the Great Charter has declared that no freeman shall be deprived or divested of his freehold, or of his liberties or free customs, but by the judgment of his peers, or by the law of the land. So great is the regard of the law for private property that it will not authorize the least violation of it. Every invasion of private property, be it ever so minute, is a trespass. If, for instance, a new road or line of railway were proposed to be made through the grounds of a private person, which might be for the benefit of the public, the law will not allow the road or line of railway to be made without the consent of the owner of the land. In this and similar cases the Legislature alone can and does interpose, and it compels the individual to acquiesce; but in doing so, it gives the owner of the property an indemnification and equivalent for the injury thereby sustained.

Another right which appertains to every Englishman, is the right to apply to the courts of justice for redress of injuries; for since the *law* in England is the supreme arbiter of every man's *life, liberty,* and *property,* courts of justice must at all prescribed times be open and available to the subject, and the law must be duly administered therein; and if there should happen any uncommon injury or infringement of rights which the ordinary course of law is too defective to reach, there still remains a further right appertaining to every individual, namely, that of petitioning the Sovereign or either House of Parliament for the redress of grievances.

Such rights and liberties belong to every Englishman: they are his birthright, and they give him the power to do anything that a good man would desire to do, and only restrain him from doing that which would be pernicious to himself or his fellow-citizens.

CHAPTER VII
PARLIAMENT

We are next to treat of the *rights* and *duties* of persons, as they are members of society and stand in various relations to each other, which relations are either *public* or *private.* First, then, let us examine those that are public.

State the most universal public relation by which men are connected together, and explain the relationship.

The most universal relation by which men are connected is that of government — the governors and the governed; or in other words, magistrates and people. Of magistrates, in our constitution, one is *supreme,* in whom the sovereign power of the State resides; others are *subordinate,* deriving their authority from the supreme magistrate, accountable to him for their conduct, and acting in an inferior secondary sphere.

In all tyrannical governments the supreme magistracy, or the right both of *making* and *enforcing* laws, is vested in one and the same man, or in one and the same body of men; and whenever these two powers are united together, there can be no public liberty. The magistrate may enact tyrannical laws and execute them in a tyrannical manner, since he possesses, in quality of dispenser of justice, all the power which he as legislator thinks proper to give himself; but when the legislative and executive authority are in distinct hands, the former will take care not to entrust the latter with so large a power as may tend to the subversion of its own independence, and therewith of the liberty of the subject. With us, therefore, in England, this supreme power is divided into two branches; the one *legislative,* that is, the Parliament, consisting of King, Lords, and Commons; the other *executive,* consisting of the Sovereign alone.

Give a brief outline of Parliament, its Origin, and its Constituent Parts.

The origin or first institution of Parliaments is one of those matters which lie so far hidden in the dark ages of antiquity that the tracing it out is a thing equally difficult and uncertain. The word *Parliament* is comparatively of modern date, and was first applied to general assemblies of the States under Louis VII., in France, about the middle of the twelfth century. In England this General Council has been held immemorially under the several names of *michel-synoth,* or great council; *michel-gemote,* or great meeting; and more frequently, *witena-gemote,* or the meeting of wise men. It was also styled in Latin, *commune consilium regni — magnum concilium regis — curia, magna — conventus magnatum vel procerum — assisa generalis* and sometimes *communitas Regni Angliæ.*

As to the manner and time of assembling, the Parliament is regularly to be summoned by the Sovereign's writ or letter, issued out of Chancery not less than thirty-five days before it begins to sit.

The constituent parts of a Parliament are the King or Queen sitting there in the royal political capacity; the Lords Spiritual and Temporal, who sit in one House; and the Commons, who sit by themselves in another; and these three Estates form the great corporation or body politic of the kingdom, of which the Crown is said to be *caput, principium, et finis.* The consent of all three is required to make any new law that shall bind the subject.

The CROWN cannot of itself make laws or inaugurate alterations in the present established laws; but it may approve or disapprove of the alterations suggested and consented to by the two Houses. The Crown has not any power of doing wrong, but merely of preventing wrong from being done. In the Legislature the people are a check upon the nobility, and the nobility a check upon the people, whilst the Sovereign is a check upon both, and may preserve the executive power from encroachments.

The LORDS SPIRITUAL consist of two archbishops and twenty-four bishops for England and Wales. Though the lords spiritual are, in the eye of the law, a distinct estate from the lords temporal, they are usually blended together under the one name of "the Lords," they intermix in their votes, and a majority of votes so intermixed decides the specific question before the House.

The LORDS TEMPORAL consist exclusively of the Peers of the realm, by whatever title of nobility distinguished — dukes, marquises, earls, viscounts, or barons. Some sit in the HOUSE OF LORDS by descent, some by creation, others by election, as do the sixteen peers who represent the body of the Scottish nobility, who are elected for one Parliament only, and the twenty-eight representative Irish peers, who are elected for. life. The number of Peers in the United Kingdom is indefinite, may be increased at will by the power of the Crown, and is by new creations gradually increasing.

The COMMONALTY are divided into two classes, those who have and those who have not the elective franchise.

The counties are represented in the HOUSE OF COMMONS by knights (called Knights of the Shire), duly elected by the proprietors and occupiers of land; the cities and boroughs by burgesses chosen by the supposed trading interests of the nation.

The Universities of Oxford, Cambridge, and London are represented by persons chosen by their respective graduates; and the four Universities of Scotland and that of Dublin are also duly represented in the House of Commons.

The Sovereign, the Lords Spiritual and Temporal, and the Commons, who have uncontrollable authority in the making, confirming, enlarging, restraining, abrogating, repealing, and reviving laws, are the constituent parts of a Parliament, and all mischiefs and grievances, operations, and remedies that transcend the ordinary course of the laws, are within the reach of this high tribunal.

Give a brief Explanation of the method of Making Laws.

The Speaker of the House of Lords, whose office it is to preside there, is the Lord Chancellor; the Speaker of the House of Commons is chosen by the House, but must be approved of by the Sovereign.

In the House of Commons the Speaker never votes, except when the numbers are equal, and in such case his vote determines the majority; but the Speaker of the House of Lords has his vote counted with the votes of the Peers, and when there is an equality of votes the rule is that the negative opinion prevails.

The mode of introducing and passing Bills into Statutes is almost the same in each House of Parliament; but the exclusive right of the House of Commons to grant supplies and impose pecuniary charges on the people, accounts for the vastly greater proportion of bills being originated in that House.

A bill is brought in by a member upon motion made to the House for leave to bring it in. The bill is read throe times at specific intervals before it can pass. After it has been read a first time, it is ordered to be printed. On the second reading, the principle and policy of the proposed enactment are discussed; and if opposed, it is then determined by the majority of votes whether it shall be proceeded with any further.

After the second reading of the bill it is referred to a committee, which is either selected by the House in matters of a private nature, or else, upon a bill of a public character, when the House resolves itself into a Committee of the whole House. A Committee of the whole House is composed of every member; and to form it the Speaker vacates the chair (another member being appointed chairman), but he may sit and debate as a private member. In these committees the bill is debated clause by clause, amendments made, the blanks filled up, and sometimes the bill is entirely remodelled. After it has gone through the committee, the chairman reports it to the House with such amendments as the committee have made; and it is subsequently read a third time. The Speaker then puts the question, whether the bill shall pass. If this is agreed to, the title to it is then settled. After this it is sent to the Lords for their concurrence. It there passes through the same forms as in the House of Commons [except engrossing, which is previously done], and if rejected, no more notice is taken; and the matter passes *sub silentio,* to prevent unbecoming altercations. If it is agreed to, the Lords send a message to the other House that they have agreed *to* the bill; and, if they have made no amendment on it, the bill remains with the Lords; but if any amendments are made, such amendments are sent down with the bill to receive the cuncurrence of the Commons. If the Commons disagree to the amendments, a conference usually follows between members deputed from each House; who, for the most part, settle and adjust the difference but if both Houses remain inflexible, the bill is lost.

The Royal assent to bills may be given in person, when the Queen comes to the House of Peers with crown and royal robes. Sending for the Commons to the bar, the titles of all the bills that have passed both Houses are read, and the Queen's answer is declared by the clerk of the Parliament in Norman-French. If the Queen consents to a public bill, the clerk usually declares, "*La Regne le vent,*" "The Queen wills it so to be;" if to a private bill, "*Soit fait comme il est desiré,*" "Be it as it is desired." If the Queen refuses her assent, it is in the gentle language of "*La Regne s'avisera,*" "The Queen will advise upon it." When a bill of supply is passed, it is carried up and presented to the Queen by the Speaker of the House of Commons, and the Royal assent is thus expressed, "*La Regne remercie ses loyal subjects, accepts leur benevolence, et ainsi le veui,*" "The Queen thanks her loyal subjects, accepts their benevolence, and wills it so to be. "

The Royal assent to bills is, however, usually given by commissioners appointed by a Royal Commission directed to three or more Peers for that purpose, and the same formalities of assent are made by the chief commissioner.

An Act of Parliament thus made is the exercise of the highest authority that this kingdom acknowledges upon earth. It binds every subject in the land, and the dominions thereunto belonging; nay, even the Sovereign herself, if particularly named therein. It cannot be altered, amended, dispensed with, suspended, or repealed, but in the same forms and by the same authority of Parliament; for it is a maxim in law, that it requires the same strength to *dissolve* as to *create* an obligation. It requires no formal promulgation to give it the force of law; it is printed by the Queen's printer by virtue of Ids office, and copies at a small charge are sold to the public.[6]

[6] [NOTE. — STUDENTS desirous of examining any particular Statute referred to in "BLACKSTONE ECONOMIZED" may procure the same at a trifling cost from Messrs. Eyre and Spottiswoode, East Harding Street, E.G.]

Explain the modes of Adjourning, Proroguing, and Dissolving Parliament.

An ADJOURNMENT is the continuance of the Session from one day to another, and this is done by the authority of each house.

A PROROGATION is the continuation of the Parliament from one session to another, as an adjournment is a continuation of the session from day to day.

A DISSOLUTION is the civil death of the Parliament, which may be effected in two ways: — 1. By the Sovereign's *will* expressed either in person or by proclamation. — 2. By *efflux of time.*

By stat. 6 Wm. & Mary, c. 22, the duration of a Parliament was three years; but by stat. 1 Geo. I., stat. 2, c. 38, known as the *Septennial Act,* seven years is the fixed period, if not sooner dissolved by the Royal prerogative.

What are the Qualifications and Disqualifications for serving in the Commons House of Parliament?

The property qualification of members of the House of Commons is abolished by 21 & 22 Vict., c. 26.

Any person may now be elected a Member of the House of Commons except the following, who are either disqualified by the law and custom of Parliament, or upon the statute law: — An alien born, or naturalised — an idiot, or lunatic, if incurable — a person attainted of treason or convicted of felony — a peer of the realm of Scotland, or a representative peer of Ireland — a judge of a superior court in England *[except the Master of the Rolls],* or of the Court of Admiralty, or in bankruptcy, or of a county court. The following officers are likewise disqualified: — a metropolitan police magistrate — a recorder for the borough for which he is appointed — a revising barrister[7] [for eighteen months from appointment] — a judge of Scotland or Ireland — any one ordained to the office of priest or deacon of the Church of England — a minister of the Church of Scotland — or any one in holy orders of the Church of Rome. No Government contractor nor any person having a pension under the Crown during pleasure or for any term of years is qualified; nor is any person holding an office under the Crown created since 1705.

Innovations on the above rule have, however, been made by successive statutes, with a view to the requirements of the Government and the conduct of the public service.

How are Persons now Elected to be Members of the House of Commons?

The recent Act of Parliament known as the Ballot Act, 1872[8], has caused a material change in the mode of electing members of the House of Commons. Instead of the practice which existed for upwards of 300 years of open voting, the Ballot is now introduced. It is a temporary measure, which expires in the year 1880; but if the beneficial effects which are expected — (that is, to render corruption, intimidation, personation, &c., improbable) — are realized, the new Ballot Act will, no doubt, be made a permanent measure.

By the new Act, candidates to serve in Parliament for a county or borough shall be nominated in writing, sub-

---

[7] See 6 Vict., c. 18, s. 28, by which no barrister so appointed shall for eighteen months from the time of his appointment be eligible to serve in Parliament. The duty of a revising barrister is to revise the list of voters for members of Parliament. It the decision is disputed, the Court of Common Pleas decides the point.

[8] 35 & 36 Vict., c. 33, an Act to amend the law relating to procedure at Parliamentary and Municipal elections.

scribed by two registered electors, as proposer and seconder, and by eight other registered electors of the same county or borough, and delivered to the returning officer by the candidate, or his proposer or seconder.

A candidate may withdraw from his candidature during the time appointed for the election, but not afterwards.

Any ballot paper which has not on its back the official mark, or on which anything is written or marked by which the voter can be identified, is void.

Every person who forges, or fraudulently defaces, or fraudulently destroys any nomination paper, or delivers to the returning officer any nomination paper knowing the same to be forged; or destroys, takes, opens, or otherwise interferes with any ballot-box or packet of ballot papers then in use for the purposes of the election, shall be guilty of a misdemeanor, and be liable, if he is a returning officer, or an officer or clerk in attendance at the polling station, to imprisonment for any term not exceeding two years with or without hard labour; and if he is any other person, to imprisonment for any term not exceeding six months, with or without hard labour.

By 31 & 32 Vict., c. 125 (an Act for the prevention of Corrupt Practices at Parliamentary Elections), it is enacted that where it is proved that bribery has been committed by, or with the knowledge and consent of, any candidate at an election, such election shall be void, and the candidate shall be incapable of being elected to sit in the House of Commons for seven years, or of holding any judicial or municipal office during that term.

The poll at any contested *municipal election* shall, so far as circumstances admit, be conducted in the manner in which the poll is by this Act directed to be conducted at a contested Parliamentary election; but if not contested, the election shall be conducted in the same manner as if the Act had not passed.[9]

What are the Qualifications of the Electors?

In boroughs occupation of a house or warehouse gives the right of voting. The occupation must be as sole owner or tenant only, and the claimant must have been rated, and have paid the rates for the space of twelve months from the preceding last day of July in any year, and must be of full age and legal capacity.

The Reform Act of 1867 creates the lodger-voters as follows: — "Every man shall in and after the year 1868 be entitled to be registered as a voter who is of full age and not subject to any incapacity, who has occupied as sole tenant for the twelve months preceding the last day of July, in any year, the same lodgings, being part of one and the same dwelling-house, and of a clear value of £10 and upwards." As previously, freemen, or burgesses by servitude, freemen and liverymen of London by birth, servitude, or purchase, have the right of voting.

Voters for counties comprise the 40s. Freeholders — persons possessing a freehold estate for life or lives of 40s., but under £5, who, if they do not actually occupy the premises which qualify them, must either have possessed the estate before June 7, 1832, or must have acquired it by marriage-settlement, devise, or by virtue of some benefit or office — Persons possessing an estate for life or lives of tenure (copyhold, for instance), of the annual value of £5 — Lessees and their assignees for a term originally created for not less than sixty years of the annual value of £5; or for a term not less than twenty years of the annual

---

[9] The persons of members are free from arrest or imprisonment in civil actions, but their property is as liable to all legal claims as that of any private individual.

value of £50 — Sub-lessees of these persons are also entitled to the franchise, if they actually occupy the premises in question — Also, the occupiers of lands rented at £12 per annum.

At a contested election for a county or borough returning three members, no person shall vote for more than two candidates; and in London, which returns four members, only three votes are allowed.

CHAPTER VIII
THE SOVEREIGN AND THE NATURE OF THE SOVEREIGN'S TITLE

The supreme Executive power of the kingdom is vested by our laws in a single person, the King or Queen; for it matters not to which sex the Crown descends, and the person entitled to it is immediately invested with all the ensigns, rights, and prerogatives of Sovereign power, let us, therefore, in this chapter investigate the Sovereign's right of succession, and inquire into the Royal right from the days of Egbert, the first sole monarch of the kingdom, to our present gracious Sovereign, Queen Victoria.

Explain the Sovereign's Eight of Succession.

The grand fundamental maxim upon which *the jus coronæ,* or right of succession to the Throne of these kingdoms depends, is this: — That the Crown is, by common law and constitutional custom hereditary, and this in a manner peculiar to itself; but that the right of inheritance may, from time to time, be changed or limited by Act of Parliament, under which limitations the Crown still continues hereditary.

The hereditary right which the laws of England acknowledge owes its origin to the founders of our Constitution, and to them only; for it has no relation to, nor does it depend upon, the civil laws of the Jews, the Greeks, the Romans, nor upon any other nation. The founders of our English Monarchy might, perhaps, if they had thought proper, have made it an elective monarchy; but they rather chose to establish originally a succession by inheritance, which has been acquiesced in by general consent, and ripened by degrees into common law, being the very same title that every private man has to his own estate. Lands are not naturally descendible, any more than thrones; but the law has thought proper, for the benefit and peace of the public, to establish hereditary succession, in the one as well as the other. An hereditary succession to the Crown is therefore now established in this and most other countries, in order to prevent the periodical bloodshed and misery which the history of ancient Imperial Rome, and the more modern experience of Poland and elsewhere, show are the consequences of elective kingdoms.

It is true, this succession, through fraud or force, or sometimes through necessity, when in hostile times the Crown descended on a minor or the like, has been very frequently suspended, but it has generally at last returned into the old hereditary channel, though sometimes a very considerable period has intervened. And, even in those instances where the succession has been violated, the Crown has ever been looked upon as hereditary in the wearer of it; of which fact the usurpers themselves were so sensible that they, for the most part, endeavoured to establish some feeble show of a title by descent in order to amuse the people, while they gained the possession of the kingdom; and, when possession was once gained, they considered it as the purchase or acquisition of a new estate of inheritance, and transmitted, or endeavoured to transmit it, to their own posterity, by a kind of hereditary right of usurpation.

Give a brief History of the Succession of the Crown from King Egbert to Queen Victoria.

King Egbert, about the year 800, found himself in possession of the throne of the West Saxons, by a long and undisturbed descent from his ancestors of above three hundred years; and from Egbert to the death of Edmund Ironside, a period of above two hundred years, the Crown descended regularly through a succession of fifteen princes without any deviation or interruption, save only that the sons of King Ethelwulf succeeded to each other without regard to the children of the elder branches, according to the rule of succession prescribed by their father, and confirmed by the Witena-gemote, in the heat of the Danish invasions; and also that King Edred, the uncle of Edwy, mounted the throne for about nine years in the right of his nephew, a minor, the times being very troublesome and dangerous. But this was with a view to preserve, and not to destroy the succession, and accordingly Edwy succeeded him.

King Edmund Ironside was obliged by the hostile irruption of the Danes, at first to divide his kingdom with Canute, King of Denmark; and Canute, after his death, seized the whole of it, Edmund's sons being driven into foreign countries. Here the succession was suspended by actual force, and after three reigns, upon the death of Hardikanute, the ancient line was restored in the person of Edward the Confessor.

On his decease without issue, Harold II. usurped the throne, and almost at the same time came the Norman invasion, when William the Conqueror succeeded by force, which transferred the Crown of England into a new family, and all the inherent properties of the Crown were transferred with it. The Crown descended from him to his sons William II., and afterwards to Henry I. Stephen of Blois, grandson of William I., succeeded him; and Henry, the second of that name, the heir of William the Conqueror, and lineally descended from Edmund Ironside, the last of the Saxon race, succeeded. Then followed Richard I., who, dying childless, the right vested in his nephew, Arthur; but John, the youngest son of King Henry, seized the throne, claiming the Crown by hereditary right. Henry III., the son of John, succeeded, and from him to Richard II., a succession of six generations, the Crown descended in the true hereditary line. Upon Richard II.'s resignation of the Crown, he having no children, the right resulted to the issue of his grandfather, Edward III. Henry IV. succeeded by usurpation; then the Crown descended to his son and grandson, Henry V., and Henry VI., in the latter of whose reign the House of York asserted their dormant title, and after imbruing the kingdom in blood and confusion for seven years, the Crown at last was established in the person of Edward IV.

Edward IV. left two sons and a daughter, the eldest of which sons, King Edward V., enjoyed the regal dignity for a very short time. He was deposed by Richard III., his unnatural uncle. The tyrannical reign of Richard III. gave occasion to Henry, Earl of Richmond, to assert a title to the Crown, and after the battle of Bosworth Field he assumed the regal dignity as Henry VII. Soon after he married the undoubted heiress of the Conqueror, Elizabeth of York. Henry VIII., the issue of this marriage, succeeded to the Crown by clear indisputable hereditary right, and transmitted it to his three children in successive order; but in his reign we at several times find the Parliament busy in regulating the succession to the kingdom. Ultimately, by stat. 35 Henry VIII., c. 1, the Crown was limited to Prince

Edward by name (Edward VI.), after that to the Lady Mary, and then to the Lady Elizabeth, and the heirs of their respective bodies.

On the death of Queen Elizabeth, who survived them, and died without issue, the line of Henry VIII. became extinct. It therefore became necessary to recur to the other issue of Henry VII. by Elizabeth of York, his queen, whose eldest daughter Margaret, having married James IV. of Scotland, King James VI. of Scotland and I. of England was indisputably the lineal heir of the Conqueror; and, what is still more remarkable, in his person also centred the right of the Saxon monarchs which had been suspended from the Conquest till, his accession. His unfortunate son Charles I. succeeded; and after dire calamities, that lasted for twenty years, a solemn Parliamentary Convention of the Estates restored the right heir of the Crown in the person of Charles II., son of Charles I.

At the end of the reign of Charles II. the famous Bill of Exclusion was introduced. The purport of this bill was to set aside the King's brother and presumptive heir, the Duke of York, from the succession, on the ground of his being a Papist. The bill passed the House of Commons, but the Lords rejected it; and the King also declared that it would never have his consent. The bill therefore took no effect, and King James II. succeeded to the throne of his ancestors, and might have enjoyed it during the remainder of his life, but for his own misconduct, which, with other concurring circumstances, brought on the Revolution in 1688 and his consequent abdication. The abdication of James II. ended the old line of succession, which, from the Conquest, had lasted above six hundred years, and from the Union of the Heptarchy in King Egbert, almost nine hundred years.

The Lords and Commons in a convention thereupon determined that there was a vacancy of the Throne, and proceeded to fill up that vacancy in such manner as they judged most proper; and this was done by their Declaration of February 12, 1688, in the following manner: — "That William and Mary, Prince and Princess of Orange, be declared, King and Queen of England, to hold the Crown and the Royal dignity during their lives, and the life of the survivor of them; and that the sole and full exercise of the regal power be only in, and executed by, the said Prince of Orange, in the names of the said Prince and Princess, during their joint lives; and after their deceases the said Crown and Royal dignity to be to the heirs of the body of the said Princess, and for default of such issue to the Princess Anne of Denmark and the heirs of her body, and for default of such issue to the heirs of the body of the said Prince of Orange."

King William, Queen Mary, and Queen Anne did not take the Crown by hereditary right or *descent,* but by way of donation or by *purchase,* as the lawyers call it, by which word "purchase" they mean any method of acquiring an estate otherwise than by descent.

The new settlement did not merely consist in excluding King James and the person pretending to be Prince of Wales, and then suffering the Crown to descend in the old hereditary channel — (for the usual course of descent was in some instances broken through) — yet the Convention kept it before them, and paid a great, though not exclusive, regard to it.

Towards the end of King William's reign, when all hopes of any surviving issue from any of these princes died with the Duke of Gloucester, the King and Parliament thought it necessary again to exert their power of limiting and appointing the succession, in order to prevent another vacancy to the Throne, which must have ensued upon their deaths, as no farther provision was made at the Revolution than for the issue of Queen Mary, Queen Anne and King William. The Parliament had previously, by 1 Win. & Mary, stat. 2, c. 2, enacted that every person who should be reconciled to, or hold communion with, the See of Rome, or profess the Popish religion, or marry a Papist, should be excluded and for ever incapable to inherit, possess, or enjoy the Crown; and hat in such case the people should be absolved, from their allegiance, and the Crown should descend to such persons, being Protestants, as would have inherited the same, in case the person so reconciled, holding communion, professing, or marrying were naturally dead. To act, therefore, consistently with themselves, and at the same time render as much regard to the old hereditary line as their former resolutions would admit, they turned their attention to the Princess Sophia, Electress and Duchess-Dowager of Hanover, the most accomplished princess of her age; for, upon the impending extinction of the Protestant posterity of Charles I., the old law of regal descent directed them to recur to the descendants of James I.; and the Princess Sophia, the youngest daughter of Elizabeth, Queen of Bohemia, and the daughter of James I., was the nearest of the ancient blood royal who was not incapacitated by professing the Popish religion. On her, therefore, and the heirs of her body, being Protestants, the Crown, expectant on the death of King William and Queen Anne without issue, was settled by stat. 12 & 13 Wm. III., c. 2; and at the same time it was enacted that whosoever should hereafter come to the possession of the Crown should join in the communion of the Church, of England as by law established.

The Princess Sophia dying before Queen Anne, the inheritance thus limited descended on her son and heir, King George I., and having on the death of the Queen taken effect in his person, from him it descended to George II., and from him to his grandson and heir, George III. From George III. the Crown descended to his eldest son, George IV., who, dying without leaving issue, was succeeded by William IV., the third son of George III.; the second son, Frederick Augustus, Duke of York, having previously died without lawful issue. On the death of William IV., the Crown descended to the only child of Edward Duke of Kent, fourth son of George III., our present gracious Sovereign, Queen Victoria.

CHAPTER IX
THE QUEEN AND THE ROYAL FAMILY

Let us now direct our attention to the Sovereign and the Members of the Royal Family, in the order which seems natural and proper; then to the consideration of the divers Councils of the Sovereign who assist her in the discharge of her duties, the maintenance of her dignity, and the execution of her prerogative.

Give a brief Description of the Queen and the Royal Family, and slate the Duties of the Sovereign.

The Queen of England is either *queen-regent, queen-consort,* or *queen-dowager*. The queen-regent, *regnant,* or sovereign, is she who holds the Crown in her own right, as the first Queen Mary, Queen Elizabeth, Queen Anne, and Queen Victoria; and such a one has the same powers, prerogatives, rights, dignities, and duties as a king would have.

The principal duty of the Crown is to govern the people according to law; and this is not only consonant to the principles of liberty, reason, and of society, but has always been esteemed, an express part of the common law of England, even when *prerogative* was at the highest. "The King," says Bracton, who wrote under Henry III., "ought not to be subject to man, but to God and to the law; for the law maketh the King, and he is not truly King where *will* rules, and not the law," and Fortescue, two centuries later, lays it down as a principle "that the King of England must rule his people according to the decrees of the laws thereof, inasmuch that he is bound by an oath at his coronation to the observance and keeping of his own laws." Stat. 12 & 13 Wm. III., c. 2, also declares that the laws of England are the birthright of the people thereof; and all the kings and queens who shall ascend the throne of this realm ought to administer the government of the same according to the said laws, and all their officers and ministers ought to serve them respectively according to the same; and, therefore, all the laws and statutes of this realm, for securing the established religion, and the rights and liberties of the people thereof, and all other laws and statutes of the same now in force, are ratified and confirmed accordingly.

Besides the attribute of sovereignty, the law also ascribes to the Queen in her political capacity absolute perfection; for the Sovereign is not only incapable of *doing* wrong, but even of *thinking* wrong, which ancient and fundamental maxim is not to be understood as if everything transacted by the Government was just and lawful, but means two things. First, that whatever is exceptionable in the conduct of public affairs, is not to be imputed to the Sovereign, nor is she answerable for it personally to the people; for that would totally destroy that constitutional independence of the Crown which is necessary for the balance of power in our free and active and compounded Constitutions, and secondly, it means that the prerogative of the Crown extends not to do any injury; it is created for the benefit of the people and therefore cannot be exerted to their prejudice.

The law also determines that on the part of the Sovereign there can be no negligence, or *lâches. Nullum tempus occurrit regi* has been the standing maxim; for the law intends that the Crown is always busied for the public good. In the eye of the law the Sovereign is always present in all the courts; the judges are the mirrors by which the Sovereign's image is reflected. The Sovereign is the fountain of justice, of honour, of office, and of privilege — the *arbiter* of commerce, the head of the Church, and the *dernier ressort* in all ecclesiastical causes.

The husband of a Queen Regent is her subject, and may be guilty of high treason against her.

The QUEEN CONSORT, or wife of the reigning king, is a notable person enjoying peculiar privileges, exemptions, and pecuniary advantages. She can purchase land without the concurrence of her lord, and convey it; may grant leases, and do other acts of ownership. She is also capable of taking a grant from the King, which no other wife can from her husband. She may likewise sue and be sued alone, without joining her husband; in short, she is in all legal proceedings looked upon as a *feme sole,* and not as *a feme covert* — as a single, not as a married woman. The common law established this to prevent the King being troubled with his wife's private affairs.

A QUEEN DOWAGER is the widow of the King, and as such enjoys most of the privileges belonging to her as Queen Consort; but it is not high treason to conspire her death or to violate her chastity, because the succession to the Crown is not thereby endangered. Yet still, *pro dignitate regali,* no man can marry a Queen Dowager without special licence from the Crown, on pain of the forfeiture of his lands and goods.

The Prince of Wales, or heir apparent to the Crown, and also his royal consort, and the Princess Royal, or eldest daughter of the Queen, are likewise peculiarly regarded by the laws; to compass or conspire the death of the former, or to violate the chastity of the latter, is high treason. The Prince of Wales is by inheritance Duke of Cornwall, and the payments to his Royal Highness's use from the Duchy of Cornwall were, in the year ended 31st December, 1872, £62,348 16s. 11d.[10]

The rest of the Royal Family — the younger sons and daughters, and other branches of the Royal Family who are not in the immediate line of succession — were little further regarded by the ancient law than to give them a certain degree of precedence before all peers and public officers, as well ecclesiastical as temporal. In 1718, upon a question referred to all the Judges by King George I., it was resolved by the opinion of ten against the other two that the education and care of all the King's children, while minors, belonged of right to the Crown. And no Prince of the Blood can marry without the Sovereign's consent, unless he be twenty-five years old; nor even then, without twelve months' notice being given to the Privy Council. A marriage otherwise will be void, and persons assisting or being present will incur the penalties of *præmunire.*

Explain the Royal Prerogative, and specify its particular extent and restrictions.

By the word "prerogative" we usually understand that special pre-eminence which the King has over and above all other persons in right of his regal dignity.

---

[10] See Duchy of Cornwall Management Act, 26 & 27 Vict, c. 49, an Act giving a power to sell and dispose of lands, parcel of the Duchy of Cornwall, to purchase other lands annexed thereto, and to regulate future grants of leases, *&c.* See also 31 and 32 Vict., c. 35.

The limitation of the Sovereign's prerogative is by bounds so certain, that it is impossible he should ever exceed them without the consent of the people on the one hand; or without, on the other, a violation of that original contract which subsists between the throne and the subject, which is one of the principal bulwarks of civil liberty; or, in other words, of the British Constitution; and the power of discussing and examining with decency and respect the limits of the sovereign prerogative, is one of the strongest proofs of that genuine freedom which is the boast of this age and country.

Prerogatives are either *direct* or *incidental.* The *direct* are such positive substantial parts of the royal character and authority as are rooted in and spring from the Sovereign's political person, as the right of sending ambassadors, of creating peers, and of making war or peace. But such prerogatives as are *incidental* bear always a relation to something else distinct from the Sovereign's person, and are indeed only exceptions in favour of the Crown to those general rules, the are established for the rest of the community; such as "that the King can never be a joint-tenant;" "that his debt shall be preferred before a debt to any of his subjects."

The law ascribes to the wearer of the Crown the attributes of sovereignty or pre-eminence. Besides the attribute of sovereignty, the law also imputes to the Sovereign in his or her political capacity absolute perfection, as the "King can do no wrong;" nor can *lâches* be imputed to the Sovereign. The law also ascribes to the Sovereign, in his political capacity, an absolute immortality. *Rex nunquam moritur* — the King never dies; for immediately upon the decease of the reigning prince in his natural capacity, his kingship or imperial dignity by act of law, without any *interregnum,* is vested at once in his heir, who is *eo instante* king to all intents and purposes.

It is the Sovereign's prerogative to make treaties, leagues, and alliances with foreign states and princes, and also to make war and peace; and whatever contracts he engages in, no power in the kingdom can legally delay, resist, or annul. The Sovereign is also a constituent part of the supreme legislative power; and, as such, has the prerogative of rejecting such provisions in Parliament as he judges improper to pass.

What is the amount of the Queen's Revenues?

Before the Revolution the Sovereign had the uncontrolled disposal of the revenues of the Crown, both taxes and hereditary revenues, and whatever remained, after defraying the necessary expenses of the Government, was at his absolute disposal for the maintenance of his dignity and for private purposes; but George III., soon after his accession, spontaneously signified his consent that his own hereditary and other revenues might be so disposed of as best to conduce to the utility and satisfaction of the public; and having graciously accepted the limited sum of £800,000 per annum for the support of his civil list, the hereditary and other revenues were carried into and made a part of the aggregate fund, which was charged with the payment of the whole annuity to the Crown of £800,000; but this being found insufficient, it was increased several times during his reign. Hereby the revenues themselves, being put under the same care and management as the other branches of the public patrimony, produce more and are better collected than heretofore, and the public is still a gainer of near £100,000 per annum by this disinterested conduct of his Majesty. Since this period, in lieu of the hereditary and other revenues of the Crown, a fixed annual sum for the support of the Sovereign and the Royal household has been granted by Parliament at the commencement of a new reign.

The net yearly grant to her present Majesty is fixed at the sum of £385,000, which includes the salaries of her Majesty's household and retired allowances, expenses of her Majesty's household, Royal bounty, alms, pensions, donations to distinguished individuals, and grants to charitable institutions. Besides these, when the Income-Tax was imposed by stat. 5 & 6 Vict., c. 25, her Majesty graciously signified to Parliament that she wished her own income to be subject to the tax imposed upon her subjects.

The Sovereigns of England, from the accession of Henry IV., have enjoyed the possession of the Duchy of Lancaster, as an inheritance separate from the Crown, and the revenue from the duchy is now received by her Majesty. In 1872 it amounted to 640,000.

Specify the Councils belonging to the Sovereign, and explain the Duties of a Privy Councillor.

The first of these is the High Court of Parliament, which we have already discussed.

The Peers of the Realm, by their birth, are hereditary Councillors of the Crown, and maybe summoned to impart their advice at all times in all matters of importance to the kingdom. The Judges are the Queen's Councillors in matters of law, but the principal Council belonging to the Queen is her Privy Council.

Privy Councillors are made by the Sovereign's nomination, without either patent or grant; and, on taking the necessary oaths, they become immediately Privy Councillors during the life of the Sovereign who chooses them, but subject to removal at her discretion.

The *duty* of a Privy Councillor appears, from the oath of office, to consist of seven functions. — 1. To advise the Sovereign to the best of his wisdom and discretion. — 2. To advise for the Sovereign's honour and the good of the public, without partiality. — 3. To keep the Sovereign's counsel secret. — 4.To avoid corruption. — 5. To help and strengthen the execution of what shall be there resolved. — 6. To withstand all persons who would attempt the contrary. — 7. To observe, keep, and do all that a good and true councillor ought to do to his sovereign.

By certain members of the Privy Council — called the Cabinet — the government of the country and the general administration of affairs are conducted, subject to the approval of the Sovereign. The Cabinet consists of the highest officers of the State. 1. The first Lord of the Treasury, who in general is entrusted with the formation of the Ministry, and who is its premier and head. — 2. The Lord Chancellor. — 3. The Chancellor of the Exchequer, who is especially charged with the management of the national finances. — 4. The President of the Council. — 5. The Lord Privy Seal. — 6. The Home Secretary, who exercises a general surveillance over the administration of the law, extends the Royal prerogative of mercy in regard to convicted persons, and likewise superintends the magistracy and police. — 7. The Foreign Secretary, who has exclusive charge of the interests of the British Empire abroad, and extends protection to subjects of the Grown in foreign countries. — 8. The Secretary for the Colonies. — 9. The Secretary for War. — 10. The Secretary for India. — 11. The First Lord of the Admiralty. — 12. The President of the Board of Trade. — 13. The President of the Local Government Board. — 14. The Chief Secretary for Ireland. — 15. The Vice-President of the Council on Education.

The dissolution of the Privy Council depends upon the Sovereign's pleasure; and he may, whenever he thinks proper, discharge any particular member; or he may discharge the whole Council and appoint another. By the common law the Council was dissolved *ipso facto* by the demise of the King, as deriving all its authority from the Crown; but by stat. 6 Anne, c. 7, it is enacted that the Privy Council shall continue for six months after the demise of the Sovereign, unless sooner determined by the successor.

Who are the Subordinate Magistrates under the Crown, and state shortly their Rights and Duties.

First, the SHERIFF, who is an officer of very great antiquity. He is called in Latin, *Vice-Comes,* as being the deputy of the Earl or *Comes,* to whom the custody of the shire is said to have been committed at the first division of the kingdom into counties.

The mode of appointment of sheriffs of counties, whose term of office is annual, or *durante bene placito,* is by the judges proposing three persons to be reported, if approved of, to the Sovereign, who afterwards appoints one of them to be sheriff. His powers and duties are various. *Judicially* he superintends the election, of knights of the shire, coroners, and verderers, and proclaims outlawries and the like. As keeper of the peace he may apprehend and commit to prison all persons breaking it, and may bind them by recognizance to keep it. He is bound to execute process issuing out of the superior courts of justice — attend the judges at the assizes — summon and return, juries — gee the judgment of the court carried into execution — must levy all fines and forfeitures, and seize and keep all waifs, wrecks, &c.

For the execution of these various duties he has under him an under-sheriff, bailiffs, and gaolers, the under-sheriff performing the chief functions of the office.

The CORONER is also a very ancient officer, called *coronator,* because he has principally to do with pleas of the Crown; and, in this light, the Lord Chief Justice of the

Queen's Bench is the principal coroner in the kingdom; but there are coroners for every county of England. The coroner is chosen for life by the freeholders of the county, but is removable for incapacity, extortion, neglect, or misdemeanor. By 7 & 8 Vict., c. 92, coroners may be appointed for districts within counties, and the manner of the election and the salaries to be allowed are prescribed by 28 & 24 Vict., c. 116.

The principal duties of a coroner are to inquire into the cause by which any person came to a violent or unnatural death; and this must be "*super visum corporis,*" "on view of the body," for, if the body be not found, the coroner cannot sit, except by virtue of a special commission issued for that purpose. The coroner must also sit at the place where the death happened. A jury is empanelled from the neighbourhood, over whom he is to preside, and if any one be found guilty of murder or homicide, the coroner commits the person to prison for further trial. By 7 Geo. II., c. 64, all coroners on inquisition for manslaughter or murder are required, under penalty, to take the evidence in writing, and are empowered to bind witnesses by recognizance to appear at the trial. The 22 Vict., c. 33, enables coroners to admit to bail persons charged with manslaughter.

JUSTICES OF THE PEACE are officers deputed by the Crown to administer justice, and do right by way of judgment. The common law has always had a special care and regard for the conservation of the peace, for peace is the very end and foundation of civil society; and therefore, before the present constitution of justices was invented, there were peculiar officers appointed by the common law for the maintenance of the public peace. These justices are usually selected on the recommendation of the Lord-Lieutenant of the county, and appointed by special commission of the Crown under the Great Seal, the form of which was settled by all the Judges, in 1590. By this commission they are appointed, jointly and severally, to keep the peace, and any two or more of them to inquire of and determine felonies and other misdemeanors. When any person named in the commission intends to act under it, he sues out a writ of *dedimus potestatem,* from the Clerk of the Crown in Chancery, empowering certain persons therein named to administer the usual oaths to him pointed out by 31 & 32 Vict., c. 72; which done, he is at liberty to act. These justices, with the exception of particular classes, act gratuitously, receiving neither salary nor fees.

CONSTABLES are of three sorts — high constables, petty constables, and special constables. Their general duty is to keep the Queen's peace in their several districts. High constables are appointed at Courts Leet, or by the provisions of stat. 7 & 8 Vict., c. 8. The duties of petty constables are very much altered by recent statutes, by which a Police Force or County Constabulary is created.

SURVEYORS of the highways are constituted by various Acts of Parliament, and their duty consists in putting in execution a variety of laws for the repairs of the public highways. They may remove all annoyances in the highways, or give notice to the owner to remove them, and take measures as prescribed by Acts of Parliament for the sustentation and repair of highways, &c.

OVERSEERS OR THE POOR. — Public officers created by 43 Eliz., c. 2, to provide for the poor by raising competent sums for the necessary relief of the impotent, old, blind, and such other, being poor, and not able to work; and secondly, to provide work for such as are able, and cannot otherwise get employment. Churchwardens are by virtue of their office overseers of the poor. By stat. 12 &

13 Vict., c. 103, the management of the poor is entrusted to a central authority in London, called "The Commissioners for Administering the Laws for the Relief of the Poor in England," since called the Local Government Board,[11] who are empowered to issue general rules, subject to specified supervision. By the Poor Law Amendment Act, in connection with the new Act of 10 & 11 Vict., c. 109, the Commissioners are empowered, when they think it desirable, to direct that the relief of the poor in any parish shall be administered by a Board of Guardians, to be elected by the owners of property and ratepayers in such parish, in such manner as the Acts particularize; and they are directed to appoint Inspectors, for the purpose of exercising a visitorial power over workhouses, and of being present at meetings of guardians, or other local meetings held for the relief of the poor.

By 12 & 13 Vict., c. 2, the Poor Law Board are empowered to consolidate any number of parishes into one Union for the relief of the poor, when each parish has to elect one or more guardians, who act for the relief of the poor in the Union, subject to the rules of the Board.

CHAPTER X
THE PEOPLE

Having treated of *persons* as they stand, in the public relations of magistrates, let us now proceed to consider such persons as fall under the denomination of the *people.*

---

[11] See Local Government Board Act, 1871, 34 & 36 Vict., c. 70; and for provision for giving shelter to the casual poor at night, see 27 & 28 Vict., c. 116; also 34 & 35& Vict., c. 108.

Explain briefly the People — whether Aliens, Denizens, or Natives.

The first and most obvious division of the people is into *natural-born subjects* and *aliens*. Natural-born subjects are such as are born within the dominions of the Crown of England; that is, within the legiance, or, as it is generally called, the allegiance of the Sovereign; and aliens are such as are born out of it. Allegiance is the tie, or *ligamen,* which binds the subject to the Sovereign, in return for that protection which the Sovereign affords the subject.

Allegiance is both *expressed* and *implied,* and is distinguished by the law into two sorts or species; the one *natural,* the other *local.* Local allegiance is such as is due from an alien or stranger-born, for so long time as he continues within the dominion and protection of the Crown. Natural allegiance is such as is due from all men born within the dominions of the Crown immediately upon their birth.

By the Naturalization Act, 33 Vict., c. 14, an Act to amend the law relating to the legal condition of aliens and British subjects, real and personal property of every description may be taken, acquired, held, and disposed of by an alien in the same manner in all respects as by a natural-born British subject; and a title to real and personal property of every description may be derived through, from, or in succession to an alien, in the same manner in all respects as through, from, or in succession to a natural-born British subject.

An alien is not qualified for any Government office, or for any municipal, parliamentary, or other franchise, and is not entitled to any right or privilege as a British subject, except such rights and privileges in respect of property, as are hereby expressly given.

A married woman shall be deemed to be a subject of the State of which her husband is for the time being a subject.

Where the father — or the mother being a widow — has obtained a certificate of naturalization in the United Kingdom, every child of such father or mother, who during infancy has become resident with such father or mother in any part of the United Kingdom, shall be deemed to be a naturalized British subject.

The Act abolishes the jury *de medietate linguæ,* and an alien is now triable in the same manner as if he were a natural-born subject.

Nemo potest exuere patriam is no longer a maxim of English law. By this Act, a natural-born subject may, if of full age and not under any disability, make a *declaration of alienage,* as prescribed by the Act, and from and after the making of such declaration of alienage, such person shall cease to be a British subject, and be regarded as an alien; but mere residence abroad for any length of time will not convert a British subject into an alien.

What is a Denizen?

A *denizen* is an alien born, but who has obtained, *ex donatione regis,* letters-patent to make him an English subject, a high and incommunicable branch of the Royal Prerogative. A denizen is in a kind of middle state between an alien and a natural-born subject. These letters-patent gave to aliens, amongst other privileges, that of holding lands by purchase or devise — a privilege now extended in an enlarged degree by the Naturalization Act to all aliens. This Act, however, does not affect the granting of letters of denization by Her Majesty.[12]

---

[12] For Naturalization Oath Act, see 33 & 34 Vict., c. 102.

What is a Jew?

One who professes Judaism. Our treatment of the Jews in early ages reflects little credit upon our humanity; but, as education progressed, a more liberal state of things has been introduced. Various statutes of Queen Victoria give the Jews relief as to municipal offices, and they remove disabilities in regard to religions opinions, marriages, making declarations a qualification for office, and sitting in Parliament.[13]

By 34 Vict., c. 19, persons professing the Jewish religion are exempted from penalties in respect of young persons and females professing the said religion working on Sundays.

Give a brief explanation of that Body of the People called the Clergy.

The *Clergy* comprehend all persons in Holy Orders and in ecclesiastical offices, and are separate and set apart from the rest of the people, or laity. In order that they may attend more closely to the service of Almighty God, they have large privileges allowed them by our municipal laws. They cannot be compelled to serve in war, or on a jury; nor can they be chosen to any secular office, such as members of Parliament, sheriffs, bailiffs, constables, or the like.

The clergy are divided into various ranks and degrees, as archbishops, bishops, deans, canons, and prebendaries; archdeacons, rectors, vicars, and curates.

---

[13] See 10 & 11 Vict., c. 58, and 19 & 20 Vict., c. 119, as to their marriages; 21 & 22 Vict., c. 48, amended by 23 & 24 Vict., c. 63, as to their declarations as a qualification for office; 21 & 22 Vict., c. 49, admitting them to sit in the House of Commons; and the Promissory Oath Act, 31 it 32 Vict., c 72.

An ARCHBISHOP is the chief of the clergy in his province, has supreme power under the Crown in all ecclesiastical causes, and it is his province to superintend the conduct of other bishops, his suffragans or assistants. He is elected by the chapter of his cathedral church, by virtue of a licence from the Crown called a *congé d'elire.* The selection is generally exercised by the government of the day. After election he sues to the Crown for an investiture of the temporalities of the bishopric, which, as a matter of course, follows. The archbishops are said to be *enthroned* when they are invested in the archbishopric, whereas bishops are said to be *installed.* England has two archbishops, Canterbury and York. The Archbishop of Canterbury is styled Primate of All England, and the Archbishop of York Primate of England.

A BISHOP is the chief of the clergy within a diocese, but is subordinate to the archbishop, to whom he is sworn to pay due obedience. The mode of his appointment is similar to that of an archbishop.

The DEAN AND CHAPTER are the council of the bishop, to assist him with their advice in affairs of religion, and also in the temporal affairs of his See. Deaneries and prebends may become void, like a bishopric, by death, by deprivation, or by resignation to either the Crown or the bishop.

An ARCHDEACON has an ecclesiastical jurisdiction immediately subordinate to the bishop. He is usually appointed by the bishop himself, and hath a kind of episcopal authority, originally derived from the bishop, but now independent and distinct from his.

RURAL DEANS are deputies of the bishop, planted all round his diocese, the better to inspect the conduct of the parochial clergy, to inquire into and report dilapidations, and to examine the candidates for confirmation; and are armed, in minuter matters, with an inferior degree of judicial and coercive authority.

A PARSON — *persona ecclesiæ* — is one that hath full possession of all the rights of a parochial church; has, during his life, the freehold in himself of the parsonage house, the glebe, the tithes, and various customary dues; but these are sometimes *appropriated;* that is to say, the benefice is perpetually annexed to some spiritual corporation, either sole or aggregate, and patron of the living, which the law esteems equally capable of providing for the service of the Church as any single private clergyman. Many appropriations, however, are now in the hands of lay persons, who are usually styled, by way of distinction, *lay impropriators.* In all appropriations there is generally a spiritual person attached to the church, under the name of VICAR, to whom the spiritual duty belongs; and to whom a fixed stipend, out of the emoluments enjoyed by the appropriator, is assigned.

A CURATE is the lowest degree in the Church, being an officiating temporary minister regularly employed by the spiritual rector or vicar, either to serve in his absence or as his assistant, and must be licensed by the bishop. By 1 & 2 Vict., c. 106, numerous provisions are made as to the appointment and payment of curates during an incumbency. Where an incumbent does not duly reside, the bishop is empowered to grant a satisfactory fixed salary to the curate out of the proceeds of the benefice.

CHURCHWARDENS are the guardians or keepers of the church, and representatives of the body of the parish. They are annually appointed in Easter week, sometimes by the minister, sometimes by the parish, and sometimes by both, as custom may direct, and are, by virtue of their office, overseers of the poor.

PARISH CLERKS are regarded by the common law as persons who have freeholds in their offices; but by stat. 7 & 8 Vict., c. 59, they may be suspended by the archdeacon for misconduct or neglect.

The SEXTON is chosen by the incumbent, unless custom has given the right to the parishioners. His duties are to superintend the church, preserve order, and to dig graves when necessary.

The BEADLE is chosen by the vestry, principally to attend upon them in vestry meetings, and to give notice of them to the parishioners, and to assist in the apprehension of vagrants.

CHAPTER XI
THE CIVIL STATE

We shall now direct our attention to the *lay* part of Her Majesty's subjects, or such of the people as are not comprehended under the denomination of Clergy, and which may be divided into three distinct states: — 1. The Civil. — 2. The Military. — 3. The Maritime.

Explain these Three Distinct Estates.

The CIVIL STATE includes all orders of men, from the highest nobleman to the meanest peasant, who are not included either under the clergy, or under one of the two latter divisions, viz., the Military and Maritime States. It may, indeed, include individuals of the other three orders, for a nobleman, a knight, a gentleman, or a peasant may become a divine, a soldier, or a seaman.

The Civil State consists of the NOBILITY and the COMMONALTY. All degrees of nobility or honour are derived from the Crown as their fountain, and the Sovereign may at pleasure institute new titles. Hence it is that all degrees of nobility are not of equal antiquity. Those now in use are dukes, marquises, earls, viscounts, and barons.[14] — A DUKE is the first title of dignity after the Royal Family. — A MARQUIS, *marchio,* is the next degree of nobility, which was first conferred upon Robert do Vere, Earl of Oxford, whom Richard II., in the year 1386, created Marquis of Dublin. — An EARL is a title of nobility so ancient that its origin cannot be clearly traced. — VISCOUNT, or *Vice-Comes,* first conferred by Henry VI., when he created John Beaumont a peer, by the name of Viscount Beaumont. — A BARON'S is the most general and universal title of nobility, for originally every one of the peers of superior rank had a barony annexed to his other titles. — PEERS are now created by either writ or patent. The creation by writ, or the Sovereign's letter, is a summons to attend the House of Peers by the style and title of that barony which the Sovereign is pleased to confer. Creation by writ has an advantage over that by patent; for a person created by writ holds the dignity to him and his heirs, without any words to that purport in the writ; but in letters patent there must be words to direct the inheritance, otherwise the dignity enures only to the grantee for life.

The COMMONALTY, like the nobility, are divided into several degrees; and as the lords, though different in rank, yet all of them are peers in respect of their nobility; so the commoners, though some are greatly superior to others, yet all are in law equals in respect of their want of nobility.

The first personal dignity after the nobility is a knight of the Order of St. George, or of the *Garter,* instituted by

---

[14] For the origin of these titles and their introduction into England, see Selden's "Titles of Honour."

Edward III. in 1344. Next, after certain official dignitaries, follows a knight-banneret, who is ranked, next to barons. The Baronets are the next order, which title is a dignity of *inheritance* usually descendible to the issue male. Then follow Knights of the Bath; Military Knights Grand Cross, and Civil Knights Grand Cross; Knights of the Thistle and Knights of St. Patrick. There are also the orders of Knights Grand Commanders and Knights of the Exalted Order of the Star of India.

ESQUIRES AND GENTLEMEN.— Every esquire is a gentleman, defined to be one *qui arma gerit.* Esquires by law may be such by virtue of their offices, as justices of the peace, or those who bear offices of trust under the Crown — barristers-at-law and doctors in the learned professions.

A YEOMAN is one having free land of forty shillings by the year, who was anciently thereby qualified to serve on juries, vote for knights of the shire, and do any other act for which the law requires one who is *probus et legalic homo.*

The MILITARY STATE[15] includes the whole of the soldiery, or such persons as are peculiarly appointed from among the rest of the people for the safeguard and defence of the realm. The Militia, Volunteers, and irregular forces of all kinds, are regulated by various Acts of Parliament.[16] Soldiers in actual military service may make nuncupative wills, and dispose of their goods, wages, and other personal chattels without those forms, solemnities, and ex-

---

[15] See for Army regulations, 10 & 11 Vict., c. 37; and for the Navy, 10 & 11 Vict.. e. 63; also 34 & 36 Vict., c. 86, an Act for the better regulation of the regular and auxiliary land forces of the Crown, for compensation, to officers holding saleable commissions, and other purposes.

[16] See General Militia Act, 42 Geo. III., c. 90; and 14 & 15 Vict., c. 32; 15 & 16 Vict., cc. 50,74, & 75. For Volunteer, Rifle, and Artillery Corps, see 26 & 27 Vict., c. 65.

penses which the law requires in other cases. The Royal Hospital at Chelsea is appropriated for the maimed soldiers, and such as are worn out in their duty.

The MARITIME STATE is nearly related to the former. The Royal Navy of England has ever been England's greatest defence and ornament, its ancient and natural strength — the floating bulwark of the island. With regard to the privileges conferred on sailors, they are pretty much the same as those conferred on soldiers, provision being made for their relief when maimed or wounded, or superannuated. They have also the same power of making nuncupative testaments.

CHAPTER XII
THE THREE GREAT RELATIONS IN PRIVATE LIFE

Having briefly commented on the rights and duties of parsons as standing in the public relations of magistrates and people, let us now consider their rights and duties in private relations.

What are the Three Great Relations in Private Life?

1. MASTER and SERVANT, which is founded on convenience, whereby a man is obliged to call in the assistance of others, where his own skill and labour are not sufficient to answer the duties incumbent upon him. — 2. HUSBAND and WIFE, which is founded in nature, but modified by civil society; the one directing man to continue and multiply his species, the other prescribing the manner in which that natural impulse must be confined and regulated. — 3. PARENT and CHILD, which is consequential to that of marriage, being its principal end and

design; and it is by virtue of this relation that infants by law are protected, maintained, and educated.

But, since the parents, on whom this care is primarily incumbent, may be snatched away by death before they have completed this duty, the law has therefore provided a fourth relation, that of GUARDIAN and WARD, which is a kind of artificial parentage.

Explain the Relative Rights and Duties of Master and Servant.

There are several sorts of *servants* acknowledged by the laws of England. The first are MENIAL SERVANTS or DOMESTICS. The contract of a menial *servant* arises upon the hiring, and if the hiring be general, without and particular time limited, the law construes it to be a hiring by the year. It is, however, the custom that either party may determine the contract upon giving a month's notice or warning; but a servant may be discharged without notice for moral misconduct, wilful disobedience, or habitual neglect of a master's lawful demands. A master is not bound to give his servant a character to any one applying for it, but if he gives one it must be a true and just one. To protect masters from the consequences of being imposed upon by false characters, stat. 32 Geo. III., c. 56, renders both the giver and the obtainer liable to fine or imprisonment. A master cannot, without express stipulation, deduct from the wages the value of articles broken or lost by a servant for want of care.

If an innkeeper's servants rob his guests, the master is bound to make restitution or compensation; for, as there is a confidence reposed in him that he will take care to provide honest servants, his negligence is a kind of implied consent to the robbery.

There are other servants who are called APPRENTICES, from *apprendre,* to learn, who are usually bound for a term of years by written indentures, to serve their masters, and be maintained and instructed by them. The contract of apprenticeship is one of those by which a person under age is permitted to bind himself, on the general ground, that if an agreement be for the *benefit* of an infant it is binding. There are also what are termed *out-door* apprentices who receive a given sum per week, and who, in every respect, learn and do the work of an *in-door* apprentice.[17]

A third species of servants are LABOURERS and WORKMEN, whether in husbandry, manufactures, or otherwise, who are only hired by the day or week, not living as part of the family. The huring depends upon the *expressed* will of the parties.

There is a fourth species of servants, if they may be so called, of a superior order — STEWARDS, FACTORS, and BAILIFFS, whom, however, the law considers as servants *pro tempore.* In these cases a general engagement is usually entered into at a given rate.

If any person *knowingly* entices away a servant and retains him in his service after due notice that he is under an *unexpired* contract of service, he is liable to an action at the suit of the master.

In all cases, the master may be frequently a loser by the trust reposed in his servant; for he is answerable for his servant's misbehaviour, and never can shelter himself by laying the blame on the agent. A master, however, is not liable for the *misfeasance* of his servant who has

[17] For enactments by which justices of the peace may settle disputes between masters and their apprentices and servants, see 7 & 8 Vict., c. 101; 14 & 15 Vict., c. 11; 17 & 18 Vict., c. 104; 30 & 31 Vict., c. 141. See also recent Act [1872], 35 & 36 Vict., c. 46.

wholly lost sight of his duty; that is, not engaged in the service of his master. For instance, no liability attaches to the master if the servant, without his leave or knowledge, takes his carriage and with it commits an injury; because in this case the master has not entrusted the servant with the carriage, or commissioned him to perform any service; he must be in the *employ* of his master at the time of committing the act.

It is now settled that in general a servant takes his employment with its ordinary risks, and cannot claim compensation for any accident that befalls him whilst engaged in it, unless such accident is caused by the master's negligence.

Explain the Second Private Relation of Persons.

It is that of MARRIAGE, which includes the reciprocal rights and duties of MAN and WIFE — of *baron* and *feme* — a solemn contract, dictated by nature and instituted by Providence, whereby a man is united to a woman for the lawful purposes of civilized society.

The common law treats this contract as a civil institution, and deems it to be good and valid where it is entered into by persons *willing* and *able* to *contract,* and who actually did contract in the proper forms and solemnities required by law. Each party must exercise *free will;* for it is the *consent* and not the mere *union* of the parties which constitutes the marriage; and the parties must be *able,* that is, not labouring under any legal disability, such as having another husband or wife living, want of age, want of reason, or proximity of relationship within the prohibited degrees of consanguinity.

By 5 & 6 Win. IV., c. 54, all marriages thereafter solemnized between persons within the prohibited degrees of consanguinity or affinity shall be absolutely void to all purposes whatever.

The marriages now prohibited are those between parties related to each other, either by consanguinity or affinity, within the third degree inclusive.

A man's parents are counted as one degree in collaterals; his brothers and sisters, grandfather and grandmother, are in the second degree; and his uncles, aunts, nephews, and nieces in the third degree. Cousins-german, or first cousins, being in the fourth degree of collaterals, may marry; a nephew and great aunt, or a niece and great-uncle, are also in the fourth degree, and may marry, and although a man cannot marry his grandmother, he can, if he likes, marry his grandmother's sister. But a man can neither marry his sister nor his wife's sister, for both are related to him in the second degree; nor his sister's daughter, nor wife's sister's daughter, for both are in the third degree. Two brothers may marry two sisters, or father and son may marry mother and daughter. If a brother and sister marry two persons not related, and the brother and sister die, the widow and widower may intermarry; for though a man is related to his wife's brother by affinity, he is not so to his wife's brother's wife, whom it would not be unlawful for him to marry.

With respect to the marriages of minors, stat. 26, Geo. II., c. 33, enacts that all marriages celebrated by licence without the consent of the father, or if he be not living, of the mother or guardian, shall be absolutely void; but this Act was so prejudicial that the law was, by stat. 3 Geo. IV., c. 75, and 4 Geo. IV., c. 76, relaxed to this extent, that though consent is still required for the marriage of minors, yet marriages without such consent are valid.[18]

[18] See 6 & 7 Wm. IV., c. 85, s. 25; 19 & 20 Vict., c. 119, s. 17.

For the legal constitution of any marriage solemnized according to the forms of the Established Church, it must either be preceded by the publication of banns for three Sundays in the parish church, or public chapel of the parish or chapelry in which the parties reside, and churches or chapels specially authorized by episcopal licence or order in Council; or be authorized by a licence or registrar's certificate with or without licence.

There are two kinds of licences, one a *common* licence, which is granted by the ordinary through his chancellor and surrogates; the other a *special* licence, granted only by the Archbishop of Canterbury, for which no fixed period of residence is necessary; and which authorizes marriage at any hour of the day or night, and in any place, whether consecrated or not. It is granted only on special grounds, and for a pecuniary payment so large as to be prohibitory to persons who are not affluent. A common licence may be obtained by any person on the payment of the fees, and declaring on oath that one of the parties to be married has for the preceding fifteen, days had his or her usual place of abode within the parish or district in the church or chapel of which the marriage is to be solemnized; that there is no lawful impediment to the marriage known to the deponent; and if either party be a minor, that the consent of the proper parent or guardian (if any) has been obtained.[19]

For marriages other than. those solemnized by clergymen of the Established Church certain proceedings, required to be taken in the office of the superintendent registrar, which stand in place of the banns or licence, are fully detailed in the Acts referred to; and the presence of a civil registrar at the solemnization of the marriage is in all

---

[19] See 4 Geo. IV, c. 76, ss. 10,14; 6 & 7 Wm. IV., c. 85, s. 1; and 19 & 20 Vict., c. 119, a. 11.

cases required, except when the marriage is according to the usages of Quakers or of Jews.

By marriage, the husband and wife are one person in law; that is, the legal existence of the woman is suspended during the marriage, and she is called a *feme covert,* is under the protection and influence of her husband, her *baron,* or lord; and her condition during her marriage is called her *coverture.* Upon this principle of a union of person in husband and wife depend almost all the legal rights, duties, and disabilities that either of them acquires by the marriage. For this reason, a man cannot grant anything to his wife, or enter into covenant with her; for the grant would be to suppose her separate existence, and to covenant with her would be only to covenant with himself; and therefore it is also generally true, that all compacts made between husband and wife when single are made void by the inter-marriage. The husband, however, may grant to or contract with a third person as trustee for the wife; and if he conveys land to a third person *to her use,* that will be an effectual conveyance under the "Statute of Uses."

A woman may be an agent for her husband, for that implies no separation from, but is rather a representation of, her husband; and a husband may also bequeath anything to his wife by *will,* for that cannot take effect till the coverture is determined by his death. The husband is bound to provide his wife *necessaries* by law, and if she contracts debts for them he is obliged to pay them; but, for anything besides necessaries, he is not chargeable.[20] He is also liable to the payment of *necessaries* for his wife's children (if any) born before marriage, whether legitimate or illegitimate, until they have attained the age of sixteen, or till the death of the mother, and by recent statutes the

[20] See "Titles to Things Personal"; also the "Married Women's Property Act".

parents of such children as are detained in a reformatory or industrial school shall contribute to their support a sum. not exceeding five shillings a week.

Marriage is dissolved by death, by judicial separation, and by judicial divorce. In cases of judicial separation and judicial divorce,[21] the law allows alimony to the wife, which is generally proportioned to the rank and quality of the parties and other circumstances; but in cases of elopement and living in adultery, the law allows no alimony.

What is considered the nearest Relation in Nature?

PARENT and CHILD, of which there are two sorts — *Legitimate* and *Illegitimate.* A legitimate child is one that is born in lawful wedlock; for with us in England the nuptials must be *precedent* to the birth. A bastard is one born out of wedlock.

The duties of parents to legitimate children consist in three particulars: their *maintenance,* their *protection,* their *education.*[22]

1. As to MAINTENANCE, it is now provided that if any parent shall wilfully neglect to provide adequate food, clothing, medical aid, or lodging for his child, being in his custody, under the age of fourteen years, whereby the health of such child shall have been or shall be likely to be seriously injured, he shall be guilty of an offence punishable on summary conviction; and shall be liable to six months' imprisonment. — 2. PROTECTION is a natural duty, permitted rather than enjoined by municipal laws. —

[21] Till 1857 the ecclesiastical courts had the sole jurisdiction in matrimonial causes and possessed the exclusive power of annulling marriages; but that power was taken from them by the stat. 20 & 21 Vict., c. 85, which established the Court for *"Divorce and Matrimonial Causes."* The jurisdiction of that court will be duly considered in a forthcoming chapter.

[22] See for duty of parents, &c., 18 & 19 Vict., c. 24; 24 & 25 Vict., c. 113; 25 & 26 Vict., c. 10; 31 & 32 Vict, c. 122, ss. 16, 17, 22.

3. The last and very important duty of parents is that of EDUCATION; for a parent confers little benefit upon his child if he neglect his CULTURE and EDUCATION.

By the Elementary Education Act, 1870,[23] an Act to provide for public elementary education in England and Wales, provision is made for the establishment of school districts, providing for every district a sufficient amount of accommodation in public elementary schools available for all the children resident in such district, for whose elementary education efficient and suitable provision is not otherwise made. These schools are managed by district school boards, appointed by the Education Department, that is, "the Lords of the Committee of the Privy Council on Education." The expenses are paid out of a fund called the school fund, moneys received as fees from scholars, that is, from those who are able to pay, — moneys provided by Parliament and moneys raised by the School Board as provided by the Act. Any sum required to meet any deficiency in the school fund shall be paid by the rating authority out of the local rates.

Thus the Elementary Education Act not only affords the means of establishing in every parish a good elementary school, but provides that every child shall be taught to read and write, and enforces the attendance of all children who are not otherwise educated.[24]

The POWER of parents over their children is given them partly to enable the parent more effectually to perform his duty, and partly as a recompense for his care and trouble in the faithful discharge of it. The consent or concurrence of the parent to the marriage of his child under age is a means which the law has put into the parent's

---

[23] See 33 & 34 Vict., c. 75; also recent stat. 35 & 36 Vict., c. 54, which amends the Public Schools Act of 1870.

[24] As to the education of criminal children, see 3 & 4 Vict., c. 90; and 29 &. 30 Vict., c. 117.

hands in order the better to discharge his duty of protecting his child from the snares of artful and designing persons, and of settling it properly in life by preventing the ill consequences of too early and precipitate a marriage.

The father may, by will, appoint a guardian to such of his unmarried children as are infants, called a *testamentary* guardian, who has the same legal powers as the parent.

The mother has no legal power over the children in the father's lifetime, except by Talfourd's Act, 2 & 3 Vict., c. 51, by which a court of equity is empowered, on petition by the mother, to order the custody by her of children under seven years of age.

What are the Duties of Children to their Parents?

They arise from a principle of natural justice, for to that — the closest and dearest tie — we naturally owe subjection and obedience during our minority, and honour and reverence ever after. They who protected the weakness of our infancy are entitled to our protection in the infirmity of their age: they who by SUSTENANCE, CARE, and EDUCATION have enabled their offspring to prosper, ought in return to be supported by that offspring, in case they stand in need of assistance. Upon this principle proceed all the duties of children to their parents which are enjoined by positive laws; and, by the Acts relating to the poor, the children of poor parents not able to work are compelled, if of sufficient ability, to relieve and maintain their parents, as the justices of the peace may direct.

Explain the general Private Relation of Guardian and Ward.

A GUARDIAN is a temporary parent of an infant; but when the ward comes of age, he is bound to give him an account of all that he has transacted on his behalf, and must answer for all losses by his wilful default or negligence. The Lord Chancellor is, by right derived from the Crown, the general and supreme guardian of all infants; and, in the event of any guardian abusing his trust, the Court of Chancery will check and punish him, and may remove him and appoint another in his stead.[25]

GUARDIANS are of five kinds: — 1. *Testamentary,* where the father by will or deed executed disposes of the custody and tuition of his children until they attain twenty-one years. — 2. *Customary,* which depends upon the law of the particular place where it exists. — 3. *Ad liten,* where any court before which the infant is a suitor has power to appoint a guardian to protect such infant's particular interest in the particular proceedings instituted. — 4. By appointment of *Chancery;* where the court has power to appoint a guardian as its instrument to protect the general interests of its infant ward. — 5. *Guardian in Trust;* an implied, indirect guardianship, arising from a person intruding himself into an infant's property, who must account for his acts in Chancery, being regarded as the infant's trustee.

An infant may contract for his *benefit* — may bind himself apprentice, because it is for his advantage: so, also, he may be bound after he attains twenty-one, to pay for NECESSARIES furnished during his infancy; and likewise for good TEACHING and instruction, whereby he may profit himself afterwards.

An infant cannot be sued but under the protection and joining the name of his guardian, who is to defend him against all attacks, as well by law as otherwise; but an infant may sue either by his guardian, or *prochein amy,* his next friend who is not his guardian. This *prochein amy*

[25] See 13 & 14 Vict., c. 60, ss.7, 20.

may be any person who will undertake the infant's cause, and undertaking to pay the necessary costs; and it frequently happens that an infant, by his *prochein amy,* institutes a suit in equity against a fraudulent guardian.

By stats. 7 Wm. IV., and 1 Vict., c. 26, s. 7, an infant cannot make a valid will, nor act as a sole executor.

In criminal cases, an infant of the age *of fourteen* years may be capitally punished for any capital offence; but under the age of *seven* he cannot. The period between *seven* and *fourteen is* subject to much uncertainty; for the infant shall, generally speaking, be judged *primâ facie* innocent; yet, if he was *doli capax,* and could discern between good and evil at the time of the offence committed, he may be convicted and undergo judgment and execution, though he hath not attained to years of puberty or discretion.

An infant may be sworn as a witness, however young, provided he understands the nature of an oath.

Who are Bastards? What are the Legal Duties of the Parents towards a Bastard Child? What are the Rights and Incapacities attending Bastard Children?

A *bastard,* by our English laws, is born out of lawful wedlock. The civil and canon laws do not allow a child to remain a bastard if the parents afterwards intermarry; and herein they differ most materially from our common law, which though not so strict as to require that the child shall be *begotten,* yet makes it an indispensable condition to make it legitimate, that it shall be born *after* lawful wedlock. The rights of an illegitimate child are very few, being only such as he can acquire; for he can inherit nothing, being looked upon as the son of nobody —*filius nullius.*

The duty of parents to their bastard children is principally that of maintenance. The mother is primarily liable to support it; but, if unable to do so, she may summon the putative father before justices in petty sessions, who can, by the recent Act to amend the Bastardy Laws, make an order on the putative father of such bastard child for the payment to the mother, or to any person who may be appointed to have the custody of such child, of a sum of money weekly, not exceeding five shillings a week for the maintenance and education of the child, and of the expenses incidental to the birth. This order continues till the child attains the age of thirteen years, or till its mother marries, whereupon the husband will be liable to support the child. If the putative father neglects to pay the sum in pursuance of such order, he may be committed to gaol, or to the House of Correction, for a period not exceeding three calendar months, unless the sum is paid sooner, with the costs and charges attending the commitment.

The rights which appertain to a bastard were only such as he could acquire; but now he is entitled to have a birth settlement of his mother until he attains the age of sixteen.

The incapacity of a bastard consists in this, that he can neither *be* heir to any one or *have* heirs, except the issue of his own body; because, being *nullius filius,* ho has neither ancestors nor collateral relations. If he die intestate and without lawful issue, his personal or real property will escheat to the Crown. Upon petition to the Crown the right will generally be transferred to the nearest member of the family.

CHAPTER XIII
CORPORATIONS AND COMPANIES

We have hitherto considered persons in their natural capacities, and have treated of their *rights* and *duties;* but as all personal rights die with the person, and as the necessary forms of investing a series of individuals, one after another, with the same rights would he very inconvenient, if not impracticable, it has been found necessary, when it is for the advantage of the public to have particular rights kept on foot and continued, to constitute certain abstract bodies or *artificial persons* (a number of persons associated together), who may maintain a perpetual succession and enjoy a kind of legal immortality. These "artificial persons" are called *bodies politic, bodies corporate,* or *corporations,* of which, for the advancement of religion, of learning, and of commerce, a great variety subsist.

What are these "Corporations" or "Bodies Politic," and explain their Purposes and Advantages.

Artificial persons established as a body for preserving in perpetual succession certain rights, which, being conferred on natural persons only, would, fail in process of time by their successive deaths.

When these persons are consolidated and united into a corporation, they and their successors are then in law considered as one person, and have only one will, which is collected from the votes of the majority upon any given subject affecting the general body.

When a corporation, is instituted, a name must be given to it, and by that name alone it must sue and be sued, and perform all legal acts. A corporation aggregate must appear by attorney, for it cannot appear in person, being invisible, and existing only in intendment and consideration of law. It must have a common seal; for a corporation cannot manifest its intention by any personal act or verbal order. It has power to purchase lands, and hold them for the benefit of themselves and their successors; also to make byelaws for the government of the corporation.

Corporations — being composed of individuals subject to human frailties — are liable to deviate from the end of their institution, and for that reason the law has provided proper persons to visit, inquire into, and has given them power to correct all irregularities that arise in such corporations.

Corporations, as regarded by the laws of England, may be divided into four classes: — 1. Corporations existing at common law, irrespective and exclusive of statute. — 2. Municipal corporations. — 3. Railway companies, canal companies, gas companies, and other companies which require special Parliamentary powers. — 4. Joint-stock companies, formed under the Joint-Stock Companies' Acts.

One division of corporations is into *aggregate* and *sole.* A corporation *aggregate* consists of many persons united together into one society, and is kept up by a perpetual succession of members so as to continue for ever, of which kind are the mayor and commonalty of a city; the head and fellows of a college; the dean and chapter of a cathedral.

A corporation *sole* consists of one person only and his successors, who are incorporated by law in order to give them some legal capacities and advantages, particularly that of perpetuity, which in their natural persons they would not have had. In this sense, the Sovereign is a sole corporation; so is a bishop, and so is a parson or vicar.

Another division of corporations, either sole or aggregate, is that *of ecclesiastical* and *lay*. Ecclesiastical corporations are those where not only the members that compose them are entirely spiritual persons, but where the objects of the institutions are spiritual. These are for the furtherance of religion, and perpetuating the rights of the Church. Lay corporations are of two sorts, *civil* and *eleemosynary*. The civil are such as are instituted for various temporal purposes. The Sovereign, for instance, is made a corporation, to prevent the possibility of an *interregnum* or vacancy of the Throne, and to preserve the possessions of the Crown entire. A lay corporation may be created for the good government of a town or particular district, as a mayor or commonalty, bailiff and burgesses, and the like. Some lay corporations have been instituted for the advancement and regulation of manufactures and commerce, and some for better carrying on of divers special purposes; as churchwardens, who are incorporated for the preservation of the goods of the parish; the Royal College of Physicians and Royal College of Surgeons in London, for the improvement of the medical science, &c. Among others, the general corporate bodies of the Universities of Oxford, Cambridge, and Durham must be ranked, for it is clear they are not purely spiritual or ecclesiastical corporations, not having been established for spiritual purposes, and being composed of more laymen than clergymen.

An *eleemosynary* corporation is such as has been constituted for the perpetual distribution of the free alms or bounty of its founder to such persona as he may have directed. Of this kind are hospitals, colleges for the promotion of education and learning, and others of a like nature.

The consent of the Crown, either impliedly or expressly given, is necessary to the establishment of any of these corporations; but all or most of them are regulated by legislative enactments.

A corporation may be dissolved by Act of Parliament; by the natural death of all its members in case of an aggregate corporation; by surrender of its franchises into the hands of the Crown; and by forfeiture of its charter through negligence or abuse of its franchises.

Municipal corporations, consisting of a mayor and commonalty, are institutions intended for the government of towns, for the preservation of order, and for the liberties of their inhabitants.

Railway companies, gas, canal, and other companies require for their constitution special Parliamentary powers, to obtain by compulsory process the possession of land, houses, &c., and to hold them for the purposes of the corporation.

Joint-stock companies, a modern creation, are *quasi*-corporations, and are regulated by the Companies' Act, 1862, and the Companies' Act, 1867.

These companies differ from corporations, inasmuch as the property of the company is divided into shares, of which each member holds one or more, and which he may transfer to any other person, who, on the completion of the transfer, becomes a member of the association. Each member of the company is liable for its debts, unless the company be *limited,* in which case he is only liable to the amount of capital not called up on the shares which he holds in it. There are statutory provisions for the dissolution of the company by winding it up voluntarily, or compulsorily in the Court of Chancery, when it fails to meet its obligations.

The general duties of all bodies politic, considered in their corporate capacity, may, like those of natural persons, be reduced to this single one — that of acting up to the end or design, whatever it may be, for which they were created by their founders or by Parliament. Where this, from the altered state of circumstances or other causes, cannot be done, the Court of Chancery will administer the property on the doctrine of *cy près;* that is, will direct a reference to inquire what objects are nearest to such express objects, and will direct the application of the trust funds to such objects.

Partnership is the result of a contract whereby two or more persons agree to combine property or labour or both for the purpose of a common undertaking and the acquisition of a common profit. Each partner is a principal, and each is an agent for the other, and each is bound by the other's contract in connection with the business. The test of liability of a person as a partner is a *participation in the profits* of the concern.[26] To obviate difficulties that frequently arose, stat. 28 & 29 Vict., c. 86, enacts, *inter alia,* that no person shall be constituted a partner by advancing to a trader a sum of money as a loan, with the understanding that he shall receive a share of the profits; and that no servants or agents shall be accounted a partner, because his remuneration consists of a specified share of the profits. A partner retiring remains liable in respect of previous engagements, and his liability continues for subsequent engagements, if he does not bring to the creditor's knowledge the fact of his retirement.

[26] By stat. 31 & 32 Vict., c. 116, partners stealing or embezzling money or other property belonging to the co-partnership may be convicted and punished as if they had not been such partners.

BOOK II
THE RIGHTS OF THINGS

CHAPTER I
OF PROPERTY IN GENERAL

Having explained the *Jura Personarum,* or such *Rights* and *Duties* as are annexed to the persons of men, let us next inquire into the *Jura Rerum,* or those *Rights* which a man may acquire in and to such external things as are unconnected with his person. These are what writers on natural law style "the rights of dominion, or property." Before proceeding to classify and consider their several objects let us make a few inquiries respecting the nature and origin of such rights.

Explain the Origin and Foundation of the Rights to Property.

There is nothing which so generally strikes the imagination, and engages the solicitude of mankind, as the right of property; or that sole and despotic dominion which a man claims and exercises over the external things of the world, in total exclusion of the right of other men; yet few consider the origin and foundation of this right. Pleased with the possession, we seem afraid to look back to the means by which it was acquired, as if fearful of some defect in our title; or at best we rest satisfied with the decision of the laws in our favour, without examining the reason or authority upon which those laws have been founded. These inquiries would be useless and even troublesome in common life, but when law is considered not only as a matter of practice, but also as a rational science, it cannot be improper or useless to examine the rudiments and grounds of these positive constitutions of society.

In the beginning of the world, we are informed by Holy Writ, the all-bountiful Creator gave to man "dominion, over all the earth; and over the fish of the sea, and over the fowl of the air, and over every living thing that moveth upon the earth." This is the only true and solid foundation of man's dominion over external things. The earth, therefore, and all things therein, are the general property of all mankind, exclusive of other beings, from the immediate gift of the Creator; and, while the earth continued bare of inhabitants, it is reasonable to suppose that all was in common among them, and that every one took from the public stock to his own use such things as his immediate necessities required.

As the world by degrees grew populous, it daily became more difficult to find out new spots to inhabit, without encroaching upon former occupants; and, by constantly occupying the same individual spot, the fruits of the earth were consumed, and its spontaneous produce destroyed, without any provision for a future supply or succession. It therefore became necessary to pursue some regular method of providing a constant subsistence; and this necessity produced, or, at least, promoted and encouraged, the art of agriculture; and the art of agriculture, by a regular connection and consequence, introduced and established the idea of a more permanent property in the soil than had hitherto been received and adopted. It was clear that the earth would not produce her fruits in sufficient quantities, without the assistance of tillage; but who would be at the pains of tilling it if another might watch an opportunity to seize upon and enjoy the product of his industry, art, and labour? Had not therefore a separate property in lands, as well as movables, been vested in some individuals, the world must have continued a forest, and men have been mere animals of prey. Whereas, now so graciously has Providence interwoven our duty and our happiness together, the result of this very necessity has been the ennobling of the human species, by giving it opportunities of improving its *rational,* as well as of exerting its *natural* faculties. Necessity begat property; and, in order to insure that property, recourse was had to civil society, which brought along with it a long train. of inseparable concomitants; states, governments, laws, punishments, and the public exercise of religious duties. Thus connected together, it was found that a part only of society was sufficient to provide, by their manual labour, for the necessary subsistence of all; and leisure was given to others to cultivate the human mind, to invent useful arts, and to lay the foundations of science.

Property, both in lands and movables, being originally acquired by the first taker, it remains in him, by the principles of universal law, till such time as he does some other act which shows an intention to abandon it; for then it becomes, naturally speaking, *publici juris* once more, and is liable to be again appropriated by the next occupant. So, if one is possessed of a jewel, and casts it into the sea or a public highway, this is such an express dereliction, that a property will be vested in the first fortunate finder that will seize it to his own use; but if he hides it privately in the earth or other secret place, and it is discovered, the finder acquires no property therein; for the owner has not by this act declared any intention to abandon it, but rather the contrary; and if he loses or drops it by accident, it cannot be collected from thence that he designed to quit the possession; and therefore in such a case, the property still remains in the loser, who may claim it again of the finder. This, in fact, is the doctrine of the law of England with relation to *treasure trove.*[27]

But this method of one man's abandoning his property, and another seizing the vacant possession, however well founded in theory, could not long subsist in fact. It was calculated merely for the rudiments of civil society, and necessarily ceased among the complicated interests and artificial refinements of polite and established governments. In these it was found that what became inconvenient or useless to one man, was highly convenient and useful to another, who was ready to give in exchange for it some equivalent that was equally desirable to the former proprietor. Thus mutual convenience introduced commercial traffic, and the reciprocal transfer of property by sale, grant, or conveyance, which may be considered either as a continuance of the original possession that the first occupant had, or as an abandoning of the thing by the present owner, and an immediate successive occupancy of the same by the new proprietor. The voluntary relinquishment by the owner, and delivering the possession to another individual, amount to a transfer of the property; the proprietor declaring his intention no longer to occupy the thing himself, but that his own right of occupancy shall be vested in the new acquirer.

Considering men as absolute individuals, and unconnected with civil society, all property would necessarily cease at death, and the next immediate occupant would acquire a right in all that the deceased possessed; but as, under civilized governments, which are calculated for the peace of mankind, such a constitution would be productive of endless disturbances, the universal law of almost every nation, which is a kind of secondary law of nature,

---

[27] Money or coin found hidden la the earth or other private place, the owner a unknown, belongs to the Crown. Concealing treasure trove is punishable by fine and imprisonment

has either given the dying person a power of continuing his property, by disposing of his possessions by *will;* or, in case he neglects to dispose of it, the municipal law of the country then steps in, and declares who shall be the successor, representative, or heir of the deceased; that is, who alone shall have a right to enter upon this vacant possession, in order to avoid that confusion which its becoming again common would occasion. And farther, in case no *testament* be permitted by the law, or none be made, and no heir can be found so qualified as the law requires, still, to prevent the normal title of occupancy from again taking place, the doctrine of *escheats* is adopted in almost every country; whereby the sovereign of the state, and those who claim under his authority, are the ultimate heirs, and succeed to those inheritances to which no other title can be formed.

The right of inheritance, or descent to the children or relations of the deceased, was allowed much earlier than the right of devising by *will.* It has nature on its side, and has been established by long and inveterate custom. It is certainly a wise and effectual civil institution, for the transmission of one's possessions to posterity has an evident tendency to make a man a good citizen and a useful member of society; it sets the passions on the side of duty, and prompts a man to deserve well of the public, when he is sure that the reward of his services will not die with himself, but be transmitted to those with whom he is connected by the dearest and most tender affections.

Wills, therefore, and *testaments, rights of inheritance,* and *successions,* are all creatures of the civil or municipal laws, and accordingly are in all respects regulated by them; every distinct country having different ceremonies and requisites to make a will completely valid; neither does anything vary more than the right of inheritance under different national establishments. In England particularly, this diversity is carried to such a length, as if it hail been meant to point out the power of the laws in regulating the succession to property, and how futile every claim must be that has not its foundation in the positive rules of the State. In general only the eldest son, but in some places only the youngest; in others all the sons together, have a right to succeed to the inheritance. Males are preferred to females, and the eldest male will usually exclude the rest. In the division of personal estates, the females of equal degree are admitted together with the males, and no right of primogeniture is allowed. [28]

There are some few things which, notwithstanding the general introduction and continuance of property, must still unavoidably remain in common; being such wherein nothing but an usufructuary property is capable of being had; and therefore they still belong to the first occupant, during the time he holds possession of them, and no longer. Such, among others, are the elements of light, air, and water, which a man may enjoy by means of his windows, his gardens, his mills, and other conveniences; such also are the generality of those animals which are said to be *feræ naturæ,* or of a wild and untameable disposition, which any man may seize upon and keep for his own use or pleasure. All these, so long as they remain in possession, every man has a right to keep without disturbance; but if once they escape from his custody, or he voluntarily abandons the use of them, they return to the common stock, and any man else has, under divers regulations and restrictions, an equal right to seize and keep them afterwards.

---

[28] Attention has been directed to this variable law of succession, and It la expected that some legislative enactment will be passed to abolish primogeniture, and assimilate the inheritance of land to the succession to goods and chattels.

Again, there are other things in which a permanent property may subsist, not only as to the temporary use, but also the solid substance, which would be frequently found without an owner, had not the wisdom of the law provided a remedy to obviate this inconvenience. Such are forests and waste grounds which were omitted to be appropriated in the general distribution of lands. With regard to these and some others, as disturbances and quarrels would frequently arise among individuals contending about the acquisition of this species of property by first occupancy, the law has therefore wisely cut up the root of dissension by vesting the things themselves in the sovereign of the state; or else in his representatives, appointed and authorized by him, being usually the lords of the manors. Thus the legislature of England has universally promoted, the grand ends of civil society, the peace and security of individuals, by steadily pursuing that wise and orderly maxim of assigning to everything capable of ownership a legal and determinate owner.

CHAPTER II
OF REAL PROPERTY

Having considered the *Rights of Persons* and the *Rights of Property in* general, we shall now direct our attention to the subjects of "dominion or property," which, in the law of England, are *Things* as contradistinguished from *Persons.* Things are distributed into two kinds, *Things Real,* and *Things Personal. Things Real* (legally called "realty") are such as are permanent, fixed, and immovable, and the rights and profits annexed to or issuing out of them. *Things Personal* ("personalty") consist of goods, money, and all other moveables which may attend the owner's person, and such rights and profits as relate to moveables.

Treating then of *Things Real,* let us first consider their several sorts or kinds; secondly, the *Tenures* by which they may be holden; thirdly, the *Estates* which maybe had in them; and lastly, the *Title* to them, and the manner of acquiring and losing the Title.

Explain "Things Real," and enumerate their several kinds.

THING REAL consist of Lands, Tenements, or Hereditaments. *Land* comprehends all things of a permanent, substantial nature, in its legal signification it comprehends any ground, soil, or earth whatsoever; as arable land, meadows, pastures, woods, moors, land covered with water, marshes, furzes, and heath. It legally includes also all castles, houses, and other buildings; for if the land or ground be conveyed, the structures or buildings thereupon pass therewith. Land has also in its legal signification indefinite extent upwards as well as downwards. *Cujus est solum, ejus est usque ad cælum;* therefore no man may erect any building to overhang another's land: for the word *land* includes, not only the face of the earth, but everything under it or over it, and therefore if a man grants all his lands, he grants thereby all his mines of metal and other fossils, his woods, his lands covered with water, and his houses, as well as his fields and meadows. Mines, lying under a piece of land, may be excepted out of a conveyance of such land, and they will then remain the corporeal property of the grantor.

Tenement is a word often, used in ordinary language to signify houses and other buildings, yet in its original, proper, and legal sense, it signifies everything that may be *holden,* provided it be of a permanent nature.

Hereditament includes every kind of property that can be *inherited,* be it *corporeal* or *incorporeal, real, personal,* or *mixed.* Hereditaments are of two kinds, *corporeal* and *incorporeal. Corporeal hereditaments* consist of such as may be seen or handled — of substantial and permanent objects, which may be also comprehended under the general denomination of land. *Incorporeal hereditaments* are rights annexed to, or issuing out of, land. It is not the thing corporate itself, but something collateral thereto, as a *rent* issuing out of lands or houses. An *annuity,* for instance, is an incorporeal hereditament; for though the money, which is the fruit or product of this annuity, is doubtless of a corporeal nature, yet the annuity itself, which produces that money, is a thing invisible, has only a mental existence, and cannot be delivered over from hand to hand.

INCORPOREAL HEREDITAMENTS are principally of ten sorts: —

1. ADVOWSONS, a right of presentation to an ecclesiastical benefice, and is in the nature of a temporal property as well as a spiritual trust.[29]

Advowsons are either advowsons *appendant* or advowsons *in gross.* Lords of manors being originally the only founders, and of course the only patrons, of churches, the right of patronage or presentation, so long as it continues annexed to the possession of the manor, is called an advowson appendant, and it will pass or be conveyed together with the manor as incident and appendant thereto, by a grant of the manor only, without adding any other words; but where the property of the advowson has been once separated from the property of the manor by legal conveyance, it is called an advowson *in gross,* or at large,

---

[29] Consult "Mirehouse on Advowsons."

and never can be appended any more; but is for the future annexed to the person of its owner, and not to the manor or lands.

Advowsons are of three kinds — *presentative, collative,* or *donative.* An advowson *presentatlve* is where the patron has a right to present a clerk canonically qualified to the bishop, and to require that he be instituted and inducted into the church. — An advowson *collative* is where the bishop and patron are one and the same person, in which case the bishop cannot present to himself; but presentation and institution are in such a case replaced by the one act of collation. — An advowson *donative* is when the Sovereign or any subject by his licence doth found a church or chapel, and ordains that it shall be merely in the gift or disposal of the patron, subject to his visitation only, and not to that of the ordinary; and vested absolutely in the clerk by the patron's deed of donation, without presentation, institution, or induction.

2. TITHES were the tenth part of the increase yearly arising and renewing from the profits of land, the stock upon lands, and the personal industry of the inhabitants. These are now, since August, 1836, commuted into a rent-charge, the amount of which is annually adjusted by a Board of Commissioners, as now constituted by the Tithe Commutation Acts,[30] according to the average price of corn.

3. RIGHT or COMMON is a profit which a man has in the land of another person. Common of *pasture* is the right of feeding one's beasts on another's lands; common of

---

[30] As to the exchange of Advowsons, see 3 & 4 Vict, c. 113, s. 73, and 4 & 5 Vict., c. 39, s. 22; for sale of Advowsons held by or in trust for parishioners, 19 & 20 Vict., c. 50. By the Lord Chancellor's Augmentation Act, 26 & 27 Vict., c. 120, the Lord Chancellor is authorized to sell the numerous Advowsons specified in the schedule to that Act, the proceeds to be applied in the augmentation of benefices and otherwise.

piscary, a liberty of fishing in another's waters; common of *turbary,* a liberty to dig turf on the ground of another. There is also a common of *digging* for coals, minerals, stones, and the like; and common of *estovers,* the *right* of taking necessary wood for the rise or furniture of a house or farm off another's estate.

4. RIGHT or WAY, the right of going over another man's ground. This must be understood to refer to private ways, in which a particular man may have an interest and a right, though another is the owner of the soil.

5. OFFICES are a right to exercise a public or private employment, and to take the foes and emoluments thereunto belonging. For instance, *public,* as in the case of magistrates, or *private,* as of bailiffs, receivers, and the like, for a man may have an estate, either to him and his heirs, or for life, or for a term of years, or during pleasure only, save only that offices of public trust cannot be granted for a term of years, especially if they concern the administration of justice.

6. DIGNITIES bear a near relation to Offices, a species of incorporeal hereditaments in which a man may have a property or estate.

7. FRANCHISES are incorporeal hereditaments synonymous with a liberty, — a royal privilege, or branch of the Sovereign's prerogative subsisting in the hands of a subject, such as a county palatine, which is a function vested in a number of persons; or a royal forest, or a park enclosed; or a right to hold a fair and take tolls therein, and the like.

8. CORODY was a right of sustenance, to receive certain allotments of victuals and provisions for one's maintenance; in lion of which, especially when duo from eccle-

siastical persons, a pension or sum of money is now substituted.

9. ANNUITIES are of much the same nature as *corodies,* except that they arise from temporal persons; whilst corodies are always due from spiritual incorporations. An annuity is very distinct from a *rent-charge,* with which it is frequently confounded; a rent-charge being a burden imposed upon and issuing out of *lands,* whereas an annuity is a yearly sum chargeable only upon the *person* of the grantor. So if a man, by deed, grant to another the sum of £20 per annum, without expressing out of what lands it shall issue, no land shall be charged with it; but it is a mere personal annuity; and yet a man may have a real estate in it, though his security is merely personal. The only requisite which now exists to the validity of an annuity when granted by deed is a registration in the Court of Common Pleas at Westminster.[31]

10. RENTS are the last species of incorporeal hereditaments. The word rent or render, *reditus,* signifies a compensation or return; it being in the nature of an acknowledgment given for the possession of some corporeal inheritance; that is, a certain profit issuing yearly out of lands and tenements corporeal.

There are at common law three manners of rent,—rent-service, rent-charge, and rent-seck. *Rent-service* is so called because it has some corporeal service incident to it. A *rent-charge* is where the owner of the rent has no future interest, or reversion expectant in the land; as where a man by deed makes over to others his *whole* estate in fee simple, subject to a certain rent payable thereout, and adds to the deed a covenant, or clause of distress, that if the rent be in arrear, it shall be lawful to distrain for the same. In

[31] See 18 & 19 Vict, c. 15. By section 14, annuities granted by *will* are exempted from the provisions of the Act.

this case the land is liable to the distress, not of common right, but by virtue of the clause in. the deed; and therefore it is called a rent-*charge*, because in this manner the land is charged with a distress for the payment of it. — *Rent-seek, reditus siccus,* or barren rent, is in effect nothing more than a rent reserved by deed, but without any clause of distress.

Fee-farm rent is where an estate in fee is granted subject to a rent in fee of at least one-fourth of the value of the lands, at the time of its reservation. — *Rents of* assize are the certain, established rents of the freeholders and ancient copyholders of a manor, and which cannot be departed from. Those of the freeholders are frequently called *chief-rents.* — *Quit-rents* are so called because the tenant goes quit and free of all services. — *Rack-rent* is rent of the full, or nearly of the full, value of the tenement.

CHAPTER III
THE FEUDAL SYSTEM

Before proceeding to treat farther of *Corporeal Hereditaments* and the "tenures" by which they may be holden, it will he necessary to make a few inquiries respecting *Feuds,* the nature of the feudal law, and the lay tenures that existed among our ancestors, wherein we shall he able to trace the ground-work of many parts of our public polity, and also the origin of such of our own "tenures" as were either abolished in the seventeenth century or still remain in force.

Explain the Nature and Doctrine of Feuds.[32]

The constitution of feuds had its origin from the military policy of the Northern or Celtic nations, the Goths, the Huns, the Franks, the Vandals, and the Lombards, who all migrating from the same *officina gentium,* poured themselves in vast numbers into all the regions of Europe at the declension of the Roman Empire. It was brought by them from their own countries, and continued in their respective colonies as the most likely means to secure their new acquisitions; and, to that end, large districts or parcels of land were allotted by the conquering general to the superior officers of the army, and by them dealt out again in smaller parcels or allotments to the inferior officers and most deserving soldiers. These allotments were called *feoda,* fends, fiefs, or fees; which last appellation in the northern languages signifies a conditional stipend or reward. Rewards or stipends they evidently were; and the condition annexed to them was, that the possessor should do service faithfully, both at home and in the wars, to him by whom they were given; for which purpose he took the *juramentum fidelitatis,* or oath of fealty; and in case of the breach of this condition and oath, by not performing the stipulated service, or by deserting the lord in battle, the lands were again to revert to him who granted them.

---

[32] By some writers the feudal law has been distinguished into four ages. In its infancy, the lands given to the soldiers were held by the mere will and pleasure of their lord. — The second age began when some regard was bad to descent. Grants were made to a tenant and his sons. — In the third age, those possessions which, while they were granted only for life, began to be made indefinitely inheritable, and took the name *of feuds,* the succession to which was for some time strictly lineal. These three periods of feudal law are called its infancy childhood, and youth. — Then commenced its fourth age, or *maturity,* when the order of descent was settled, collateral relations were admitted to inheritance, the reciprocal obligations of lord and tenant were fully understood; and some princes, the first of whom was the Emperor Conrad II., had published edicts in writing for regulating feudal successions.

Feuds at first did not extend beyond the life of the first vassal, but in process of time they were extended to his song, or perhaps to such one of them as the lord should name. If a feud was given to a man and his sons, all his sons succeeded him in equal portions, and as they died off, their shares did not descend, but reverted to the lord. When a feud was given in general terms to a man and his heirs, then a more extended rule of succession took place; for when the feudatory died, his male descendants, *in infinitum,* were admitted to the succession. When any such descendant who thus had succeeded died, his male descendants were also admitted; and in defect of them, such of his male collateral kindred as were of the blood or lineage of the first feudatory, but no other. It was an unalterable maxim in feudal succession that no one was capable of inheriting a feud, but such as was of the blood of, that is, lineally descended from the first feudatory. The descent being confined to males, originally extended to all the males alike, all the sons succeeding to equal portions of the father's feud. But ultimately, dividing the services being found inconvenient and tending to weaken the strength of the feudal union; and, *honorary* fends or titles of nobility being now introduced, which were not of a divisible nature, but only inherited by the eldest son; in imitation of these, military feuds began in most countries to descend, according to the rule of primogeniture, to the eldest son, in exclusion of all the rest.

Allotments thus acquired, naturally engaged, such as accepted them to defend them; and, as they all sprang from the same right of conquest, no part could subsist independent of the whole; so givers as well as receivers were mutually bound to defend each other's possessions. Every receiver of lands, or feudatory, was bound, when called upon by his benefactor, or immediate lord of his feud or fee, to do all in his power to defend him; and such benefactor or lord was likewise subordinate to and under the command of his immediate benefactor or superior; the prince or general himself, and the several lords were also reciprocally bound, in their respective gradations, to protect the possessions they had given. Thus the feudal connection was established, a proper military subjection naturally introduced, and an army of feudatories was always enlisted, and mutually prepared to muster, not only in defence of each man's own several property, but also in defence of the whole, and of every part of this their newly-acquired country; the prudence of which constitution was soon sufficiently visible in the strength and spirit with which they maintained their conquests.

But this feudal polity, which was by degrees established over all the continent of Europe, seems not to have been received in this part of our island, at least not universally as a part of the national constitution, till the reign of William the Norman.

This introduction, however, of the feudal tenures into England by King William does not seem to have been effected immediately after the Conquest, nor by the mere arbitrary will and power of the Conqueror, but to have been gradually established by the Norman Barons, and others, on such forfeited lands as they received as a gift from the Conqueror, and afterwards consented to by the great Council of the nation long after his title was established. Indeed, from the prodigious slaughter of the English nobility at the battle of Hastings, and the fruitless insurrections of those who survived, such numerous forfeitures had accrued, that William was able to reward his Norman followers with very large and extensive possessions, which caused the monkish historians, and such as have implicitly followed them, to represent him as having by right of the sword seized on all the lands of England, and dealt them out again to his own favourites.

This feudal polity does not seem to have been *imposed* by the Conqueror, but voluntarily and freely adopted by the assembly of the whole realm, in. the same manner as other nations of Europe had before adopted it, upon the principle of self-security.

In consequence of this change, it became a fundamental maxim and necessary principle, but in reality a mere fiction of our English tenures, "that the King is the universal lord and original proprietor of all the lands in his kingdom; and that no man can or doth possess any part of it, but what has mediately or immediately been derived as a gift from him, to be held upon. feudal services." For, this being the real case in pure, original, proper feuds, our nation, which adopted this system, was obliged to act upon the same supposition, as a substructure and foundation of a new polity. By thus consenting to the introduction of feudal tenures, our English ancestors probably meant no more than to put the kingdom in a state of defence by establishing a military system, and to oblige themselves, in respect of their lands, to maintain the King's title and territories, with equal vigour and fealty, as if they had received their lands from his bounty upon these express conditions, as pure, proper, beneficiary feudatories. But whatever their meaning was, the Norman interpreters, skilled in all the niceties of the feudal constitutions, and well understanding the import and extent of the feudal terms, gave a very different construction to this proceeding, and subsequently introduced, besides fealty and homage, *Aids, Reliefs, Fines* in alienation, *Escheats,* and *Forfeitures,* and such hardships and services, as if the English had, in fact as well as theory, derived everything they possessed from the bounty of their sovereign lord.

Our ancestors, therefore, who had consented to this fiction of tenure from the Crown as the basis of a military discipline, looked with reason upon the obligations thus imposed as grievous impositions and arbitrary conclusions from principles that to them had no foundation in truth. However, William and his son Rufus kept up all the rigours of the feudal doctrines with a high hand; but their successor, Henry I., when he set up his pretensions to the Crown, found it expedient to promise a restitution of the laws of King Edward the Confessor or ancient Saxon system; and accordingly, in the first year of his reign he granted a charter, whereby he gave up the greater grievances, but still reserved the fiction of feudal tenure for the same military purposes which induced his father to introduce it. But this charter was gradually broken through, and the former grievances were revived and aggravated by himself and succeeding princes, till in the reign of King John they became so intolerable, that they occasioned his barons, or principal feudatories, to rise lip in arms against him, which at length produced the famous *Magna Charta,* at Runnymede, which, with some alterations, was confirmed by his son Henry III. Further concessions were afterwards made, and ultimately a restoration was brought about of the ancient constitution, of which our ancestors had been defrauded by the art and *finesse* of the Norman lawyers, rather than deprived by the force of the Norman arms.[33]

CHAPTER IV
ANCIENT AND MODERN ENGLISH TENURES

In this chapter we shall take a short view, first, of the Ancient Tenures as they stood in force till the middle of the last century, by which we shall perceive that all the

[33] For a succinct narrative of the origin of Fends, see Hallam's "History of the Middle Ages."

peculiarities and hardships that attended these ancient tenures were the fruits of, and deduced from, the feudal policy; and secondly, of the Modern English Tenures which succeeded them.

Explain, first, the Ancient English Tenures, and state how and by whom they were abolished.

Almost all the real property of the kingdom is, by the policy of our laws, *supposed* to be granted by, dependent upon, and holden of some superior lord, in consideration of certain services to be rendered to the lord by the tenant or possessor of the property. The thing holden is therefore styled a *tenement,* the possessors thereof *tenants,* and the manner of their possession a *tenure.* The king was considered the lord *paramount,* and such tenants as held under him were called his tenants *in capite,* or in chief; and when those tenants granted out portions of their land to inferior persons, they became also lords with respect to those inferior persons, and being still tenants of the king, were called *mesne,* or middle lords.

Amongst our ancestors there were four principal species of lay tenures, — tenant by *knight-service,* tenant by *grand serjeanty,* tenant by *carnage,* and tenant by *escuage,* the grand *criteria of* which were the *natures* of the several services or renders that were due to the lords from their tenants. The services in respect of their QUALITY were either *free* or *base* services, and their QUANTITY and the time of EXACTING them were either *certain* or *uncertain.*

Free services were such as were not unbecoming the character of a soldier or a freeman to perform, as to serve under his lord in the wars, to pay a *sum* of money, and the like. *Base* services were such as were fit only for peasants, or persons of a servile rank; as to plough the lord's land, to make his hedges, to carry out his dung, or other mean employments. The *certain* services, whether free or base, were such as to pay a stated annual rent, or to plough such a field for three days. The *uncertain* depended upon unknown contingencies; as to do military service in person, or pay an assessment in lieu of it, when called upon; or to wind a horn whenever the Scots invaded the realm, which were *free* services; or, to do whatever the lord should command, which was a *base* or *villein* service.

The tenure by *knight-service* was the most universal, and it drew after it these seven exactions, — AIDS, RELIEF, PRIMER SEISIN, WARDSHIP, MARRIAGE, FINES FOR ALIENATION, and ESCHEAT.

Aids were originally mere benevolences granted by the tenant to his lord in times of difficulty and distress, but afterwards made compulsory, to ransom the lord's person if taken prisoner; to make the lord's eldest son a knight; or to marry the lord's eldest daughter by giving her a suitable portion — *Beliefs* were fines payable to the lord on taking up the estate at the death of the last tenant — *Primer seisin,* the right of the king on the death of a tenant *in capita ut de coronâ,* and not to those who held of inferior or mesne lords, or even *in capite* when *ut de honore;* a right which the king had, when any of his tenants *in capite* died seised of a knight's fee, to receive of the heir one whole year's profits of the lands. This gave a handle to the Popes, who claimed to be feudal lords of the Church, to claim in like manner from every clergyman in England the first year's profits of his benefice by way of *primitiœ,* or first-fruits — *Wardship,* the right of the lord to have the custody or wardship of the heir till the age of twenty-one in males and sixteen in females — *Livery of ousterlemain,* that is, the delivery of lands out of the guardian's hands, when a fine of half a year's profits was inflicted — *Marriage,* the right of the lord to dispose of his infant wards in marriage, which if the infants refused they forfeited the value of the marriage, the amount of which was assessed by a jury; and if the infants married without the guardian's consent, they forfeited double the value; *duplicem valorem maritagii* — *Fines,* sums due to the lord on alienation by the tenant — *Escheats,* the reversion of the fee to the lord on the extinction or corruption of the blood of the tenant.

The families of our nobility and gentry groaned under the burthens of these military tenures, which were introduced and laid upon them by the subtlety and *finesse* of the Norman lawyers. Many heirs on the death of their ancestors, if of full age, were plundered of the first emoluments arising from their inheritances by way of *relief* and *primer seisin;* and if under age, of the whole of their inheritances during infancy. These with other exactions forced many to sell their patronages, but they were not allowed even that privilege without paying an exorbitant sum for a licence of *alienation.*

Remonstrances were made, and palliatives were from time to time applied by successive Acts of Parliament, which assuaged some temporary grievances, till at length the military tenures, with all their heavy appendages, were destroyed at one blow by stat. 12 Car. II., c. 24, which enacts "that the court of wards and liveries, and all wardships, liveries, primer seisins, and ousterlemains, values, and forfeitures of marriage, by reason of any tenure of the king or others, be totally taken away; and that all fines for alienations, tenures by homage, knight-service and escuage, and also aids for marrying the daughter or knighting the son, and all tenures of the king *in capite,* be likewise abolished; and that all sorts of tenures be turned into free and common socage, save only tenures in frankalmoign, copyhold, and grand serjeantry," — a statute which was a greater acquisition than even *Magna Carta* itself, which only pruned the luxuries that had grown out of the military tenures, but the statute of King Charles extirpated the whole, and demolished both root and branches.

Explain the Modern English Tenures, and the tenure of "pure villenage," from which sprang our present "Copyhold" Tenures.

The oppressive or military part of the feudal constitution being abolished, the tenures of socage and frankalmoign, the honorary services of grand serjeanty, and the tenures by court roll were reserved, and all others were reduced to one general species of tenure then subsisting, called *free* and *common socage,* which signified a free or privileged tenure, but better known by its modern name or equivalent, *freehold,* by which the bulk of *real* property is holden at the present day.

Socage tenures (tenures by any certain determinate service) seem to have been relics of Saxon liberty, retained by such persons as had neither forfeited them to the king, nor been obliged to exchange their tenure for the more honourable, as it was called, but more burthensome tenure of knight-service. This is peculiarly remarkable in the tenure which prevails in Kent, called *gavelkind,* which is acknowledged to be a species of socage tenure, the preservation of which from the innovations of the Norman conqueror is a fact universally known; and those who thus preserved their liberties were said to hold in *free* and *common socage.*

The grand distinguishing mark of this species of tenure is having its renders or services *ascertained;* and as such it includes all other methods of holding free lands by certain and invariable rents and duties; and in particular, *petit serjeanty,* tenure in *burgage,* and *gavelkind.*

Petit serjeanty, as defined by Littleton, "consists in holding lands of the king by the service of rendering to him annually some small implement of war, as a bow, a sword, a lance, an arrow, or the like." This, he adds, "is but socage in effect, for it is no personal service, but a certain rent;" and *Magna Charta* respected it in this light when it enacted that no wardships of the lands or body should be claimed by the king in virtue of a tenure by petit serjeanty.

Tenure in *burgage* is described by Glanvil, and is expressly said by Littleton to be but tenure in socage; and it is where the king or other person is lord of an ancient borough in which the tenements are held by a rent certain. The free socage in which these tenements are held seems to be plainly a remnant of Saxon liberty, which may also account for the great variety of customs affecting many of these lands, the principal and most remarkable of which is called borough English, so named in contradistinction, as it were, to the Norman customs, viz., that the *youngest* son, and not the *eldest,* succeeds to the burgage tenement on the death of his father.

There are other special customs in different burgage tenures; as that in some the wife shall be endowed of *all* her husband's tenements, and not of the *third* part only, as at the common law; and that in others a man might, as in the Saxon times, dispose of his lands and tenements by *will,* which in general was not permitted after the Conquest till the reign of Henry VIII., but did not receive its full development until after the Restoration of Charles II.

Gavelkind tenure (of which notice has already been taken under the head "Customs") affords another proof that these socage tenures were remnants of Saxon liberties. A portion of the county of Kent is still subject to this tenure, as the Kentish men, by their submission to the

Conqueror, stipulated for the retention of their Saxon customs. The distinguishing properties of this tenure are various; some of the principal are these: — 1. The tenant is of age sufficient to aliene his estate by feoffment at fifteen. — 2. The estate does not escheat in case of an attainder and execution for felony — 3. In most places the tenant had a power of devising lands by *will,* before the statute for that purpose was passed. — 4. The lands descend, not to the eldest, youngest, or any one son only, but to all the sons together, which was anciently the usual course of descent all over England, though in particular places particular customs prevailed.

Explain the Origin and Nature of Manors, and how Copyholds arose out of Manors.

A MANOR, *manerium* — so called because it was the usual residence of the owner — seems to have been a district of ground held by a lord or great personage, who kept so much of the lands in his own hands as was necessary for the use of his family, which lands were called *terræ dominicales,* or *demesne* lands, bring occupied by the lord, or *dominus manerii,* and his servants. The other, or *tenemental* lands, were distributed among the tenants, and from the different modes of tenure were distinguished, by two different names. First, *bock-land,* or charter-land, which was held by deed under certain rents and free-services, and in effect differed nothing from free-socage lands. From these have arisen most of the freehold tenants who hold. of particular manors, and owe suit and service to the lord. The other was called *folk-land,* which was not held by any assurance in writing, but distributed among the common folk or people at the pleasure of the lord, and resumed at his discretion; being, indeed, land held in *villenage.* The residue of the manor, being uncultivated, was termed the lord's waste, and served for public roads, and for *common* of *pasture* to the lord and his tenants.

These villenages or folk-lands were tenures neither strictly feudal, Norman, nor Saxon, but mixed and compounded of them all. The tenants or villeins, belonging principally to lords of manors, were either villeins *regardant;* that is, annexed to the manor or the land; or else, they were *in gross,* or at large; that is, annexed to the person of the lord, and transferable by deed from one owner to another. They could not leave their lord without his permission; and, if they ran away, or were purloined from him, might be claimed and recovered by action, like beasts or other chattels. They held, indeed, small portions of land by way of sustaining themselves and families; but it was at the mere will of the lord, who might dispossess them whenever he pleased; and it was held upon the performance of vile services, such as to carry out dung, to hedge and ditch the lord's demesnes, and any other mean office; and their services were not only base, but uncertain both as to their time and quantity. A villein could acquire no property either in lands or goods; but, if he purchased either, the lord might enter upon them, oust the occupier, and seise them to his own use.

Villeins might have been enfranchised by *manumission,* and in process of time gained considerable influence over their lords, and strengthened the tenure of their estates to that degree, that they came to have in them an interest in many places as good, in others better, than their lords; for the good-nature and benevolence of many lords of manors having, time out of mind, permitted their villeins and their children to enjoy their possessions without interruption in a regular course of descent, the common law, of which *custom* is the life, now gave them title to prescribe against their lords; and, on performance of the same services, to hold their lands, in spite of any determination of the lord's will. For, though in general they are still said to hold their estates at the will of the lord, yet it is such a will as is agreeable to the custom of the manor; which custom is preserved and evidenced by the rolls of the several courts-baron in which they are entered, or kept on foot by the constant immemorial usage of the several manors in which the lands lie. As such tenants had nothing to show for their estates but these customs and admissions in pursuance of them entered on those rolls, or the copies of such entries witnessed by the steward, they now began to be called *tenants by copy of court roll,* and their tenure itself a *copyhold.*

Thus copyhold tenures, as Sir Edward Coke observes, although very meanly descended, yet come of an ancient house; for it appears that copyholders are in truth no others but villeins, who, by a long series of immemorial encroachments on, or by permission of the lord, have at last established a customary right to those estates, which before were held absolutely at the lord's will. This affords a very substantial reason for the great variety of customs that prevail in different manors, with regard both to the descent of the estates and the privileges belonging to the tenants. And these encroachments grew to be so universal, that when tenure in villenage was virtually abolished, (though copyholds were reserved) by the statute of Charles II. there was hardly a pure villein left in the nation.[34]

To support a copyhold tenure, it is requisite that the lands be parcel of and within the manor, and that they have been immemorially demised or demisable by copy of court-roll.

So freehold can now be converted into copyhold, the essence of that tenure being immemorial custom; but a

[34] For further information, consult Watkins or Scriven on "Copyholds;" also Hallam's "Middle Ages."

copyhold may be converted into freehold either by the lord conveying to the copyholder the freehold of the estate, or by his releasing to him the seignorial rights. Such transmutation is called *enfranchisement.*

The rights of lords of manors to fines and heriots, rents, reliefs, and customary services were productive of considerable inconvenience to copyhold tenants, but stat. 4 & 5 Vict., c. 35, amended by subsequent Acts, facilitates the commutation of these rights and interests; and by 15 & 16 Vict., c. 51, the enfranchisement of copyhold lands is made *compulsory* at the instance either of lord or tenant; but such enfranchisement does not affect the estates or rights of either party in any mines or minerals within or under the lands so enfranchised. It may be made by a simple conveyance of the fee-simple from the lord to his tenant.

There is another species of tenure— *ancient demesne,* which exists in certain manors. It is a species of copyhold, differing, however, from common copyholds in certain privileges, yet must be conveyed by *surrender,* according to the custom of the manor.

Besides these *lay* tenures, there is a spiritual tenure that still exists, called *frankalmoign,* or free alms; and by that tenure almost all the ancient monasteries and religious houses held their lands, and the parochial clergy and many ecclesiastical and eleemosynary foundations hold them at this day by the like tenure.[35]

---

[35] The Law student who is desirous of obtaining a further knowledge of Ancient English Tenures, how the restrictions that fettered estates were gradually loosened and the expedients that were invented to strip them of their privileges, will find full information in "Blackstone," vol. ii., cc. 6 & 7.

CHAPTER V
ESTATES OF INHERITANCE

Having examined the Feudal System, with some of its peculiar incidents of tenure, let us next consider the *nature and properties of estates,* and such interest as the tenant has in them. First, with regard to the *quantity of interest* which the tenant has in the land or tenement; secondly, with regard to the *time* at which the quantity of that interest is to he enjoyed; and thirdly, with regard to the *number and connection of the tenants or possessors.*

Explain the Nature and Properties of Estates.

The *estate,* which a man has in lands, tenements, and hereditaments, signifies the *interest* which he has therein, and the power he has over such tenements. It is called in Latin *status,* indicating the position or circumstances in which the owner stands with regard to his property. An actual permanent interest is implied in the term; a mere possibility is not sufficient.

The *quantity of interest* which the tenant has in the tenement is measured, by its *duration* and *extent;* and this occasions the primary division of estates, into such as are *freehold,* and such as are *less than freehold.*

An *estate of freehold, liberum tenementum,* or frank-tenement, is defined by Britton to be the *possession of* the soil by a freeman; but a freehold estate may consist either in *land* or in some *tenement* other than land. Estates of freehold are either estates or *inheritance,* or estates *not of inheritance.* The former are again divided into inheritances *absolute,* or fee-simple; and inheritances *limited,* one species of which is called *fee-tail.*

An *estate in fee-simple (feudum simplex)* or freehold is the greatest estate or interest a man can possess in landed property; for a tenant in fee-simple is he that hath lands, tenements, or hereditaments, to hold to him and his heirs for ever; generally, absolutely, and simply, without mentioning *what* heirs, but leaving that to his own pleasure; or, if dying intestate, to the disposition of the law.

The fee-simple or inheritance of lands and tenements is generally vested and resides in some person, though divers inferior estates may be carved out of it. As if one grants a lease for twenty-one years, or for one or two lives, the fee-simple remains vested in the grantor and his heirs; and after the determination of those years or lives, the land reverts to the grantor or his heirs, who shall hold it again in fee. Yet sometimes the fee may be in *abeyance;* that is, in expectation, intendment, and consideration of the law, there being no person *in esse* in whom it can vest and abide; but the law considers it as always potentially existing and ready to vest whenever a proper owner appears. Thus, in a grant to John for life, and afterwards to the heirs of Richard, the inheritance is plainly neither granted to John nor Richard, nor can it vest in the heirs of Richard till his death; it remains therefore in waiting, or *abeyance,*[36] during the life of Richard.

Estates in fee-simple are divided into three sorts: — 1. Fee-*simple.* — 2. Fee *qualified.* — 3. Fee *conditional.*

A *fee-simple,* as stated, is the greatest estate a man can possess, being free from all qualifications.

A *qualified fee* is such a one as has a qualification subjoined thereto, and which must be determined when-

[36] The strict interpretation of this word as to freehold interests has perplexed eminent lawyers. The accepted opinion is, that the inheritance remains in the grantor, until some person arises answering the description given, and so capable of taking under the grant.

ever the qualification annexed to it is at an end; as, in the case of a grant to A. and his heirs, *tenants of the manor of Dale.* In this instance, whenever the heirs of A. cease to be tenants of that manor, the grant is entirely defeated.

A *conditional fee,* at the common law, was a fee restrained in its form of duration to some particular heirs, exclusive of others: as to the heirs *of a man's body,* by which only his lineal descendants were admitted, in exclusion of collateral heirs; or, to the heirs *male of his body,* in exclusion both of collaterals and lineal females also. It was called a conditional fee, by reason of the condition expressed or implied in the donation of it, that if the donee died without such particular heirs, the land should revert to the donor; but the donee, in order to subject the lands to the ordinary course of descent, took care to aliene as soon as the condition was performed — by having issue; and he afterwards repurchased the lands which gave him a fee-simple absolute, which would descend to his heirs general, according to the course of the common law.

The inconveniences and disputes that attended these limited and fettered inheritances gave rise to the statute of Westminster the Second, commonly called the Statute *De Donis Conditionalibus* upon the construction of which the judges determined that the donee had no longer a conditional fee-simple which became absolute the instant the issue was born; but they divided the estate into two parts, leaving in the donee a new kind of estate, which they denominated a *fee-tail,* and vesting in the donor the ultimate fee-simple of the land expectant on the failure of issue, which expectant estate is that which we now call *a reversion.*

What is an Estate in Fee-tail, and explain it?

An *estate-tail (feodum talliatum)* is an estate cut off from or out of the greater estate in fee-simple. Estates-tail are either *general* or *special.* Tail-general is where lands and tenements are given to one, and the *heirs of his body begotten,* which is called tail-general, because, how often soever such donee in tail be married, his issue in general by all and every such marriage is, in successive order, capable of inheriting the estate-tail, *per formam doni.* Tenant in *tail-special* is where the gift is restrained to certain heirs of the donee's body by a particular person, as where lands and tenements are given to a man and the *heirs of his body, on Mary his now wife to be begotten.* Here no issue can inherit but such special issue as is engendered between these two; not such as the husband may have by another wife; and therefore it is called special-tail. The words of inheritance "to him and his *heirs*" give him an estate in fee; but they being heirs *to be by him begotten,* this makes it a fee-tail; and the person being also limited on whom such heirs shall be begotten, viz., *Mary his present wife,* this makes it a fee-tail special.

Estates in *general* and *special tail* are farther diversified by the distinction of sexes in such entails; for both of them may either be in tail *male* or tail *female.* As if lands be given to a man, and his *heirs male of his body begotten,* this is an estate in tail male general; lint if to a man and the heirs *female of his body on his present wife begotten,* this is an estate in tail female special. And, in case of an entail male, the heirs female shall never inherit, nor any derived from them; nor conversely, the heirs male, in case of the gift in tail female. Thus, if the donee in tail male has a daughter, who dies leaving a son, such grandson in this case cannot inherit the estate-tail; for he cannot deduce his descent wholly by heirs male; and as the heir male must show his descent wholly by males, so must the heir female wholly by females.

By 3 &4Wm. IV., c. 74, the Fines and Recoveries Abolition Act, a tenant-in-tail can, by a common deed *duly enrolled.,* aliene in fee-simple absolute, or for any less estate the lands entailed; and by 1 & 2 Vict, c. 110; 17 & 18 Vict., c. 75; 20 & 21 Vict., c. 57; all estates-tail are rendered liable to be charged for debts, and are subject to be sold for debts contracted by a bankrupt; and a judgment entered up against the debtor in any of the superior courts at Westminster shall operate as a charge upon all lands, tenements, or hereditaments of which the debtor shall be seised or possessed.

The word "*heirs*" in a deed is necessary to create a fee; so the word "*body*" or some other words of procuration are necessary to make a *fee-tail,* and ascertain to what heirs in particular the fee is limited. A gift by deed to a man and his heirs male or female is an estate in *fee-simple* and not in *fee-tail,* for there are no words to ascertain "the body out of which they shall issue." In last *wills* and testaments, however, indulgences and irregular modes of expression are allowed; the desire being to carry out the *intention* of the testator.

A devise of any real estate, *without words of limitation,* now carries the fee-simple, or the whole interest, whatever it may be, of the testator, unless a contrary intention appears by the will.

In grants of lands to sole corporations and their successors, the word "successors" supplies the place of "heirs;" for, as heirs take from the ancestor, so does the successor from the predecessor.

CHAPTER VI
ESTATES FOR LIFE

The next Estates that come under our observation are such estates of Freehold as are not of "Inheritance," but for "Life" only; of these some are *conventional,* created by the acts of the parties; others *legal,* or created by construction and operation of law.

Explain Estates "not of Inheritance," and how they are Created.

Estates for *Life* expressly created by *deed* or *will* are, where an estate is limited to a man, to hold for the term of his own life, or for that of another person, or for more lives than one; in any of which cases he is styled tenant for life; but when he holds the estate for the life of another, he is usually called tenant *pur antre vie.* These estates for life, like inheritances of a feudal nature, were for some time the highest estate that any man could have in a feud, which was not in itself hereditary.

Estates for life may also be created by a general grant, without defining or limiting any specific estate. As, if one grants to A. B. the manor of Dale, this makes him tenant for his (the grantee's) life. For though, as there are no words of inheritance or *heirs* mentioned in the grant, it cannot be construed to be a grant in fee; it shall, however, be construed to be as large an estate as the words of the donation will bear, and therefore an estate for life.

Such estates or life will, generally speaking, endure as long as the life for which they are granted; but there are some estates for life which may determine upon future contingencies, before the life for which they are created expires. As, if an estate be granted to a woman during her widowhood, or to a man until he be promoted to a benefice; in these, and similar cases, whenever the contingency happens — when the widow marries, or when the grantee obtains a benefice — the respective estates are absolutely determined and gone. Yet, while they subsist, they are reckoned estates for life, because the time for which they will endure being uncertain, they may lay possibility last for life, if the contingencies upon which they are to determine do not sooner happen. And, moreover, in case an estate be granted to a man for his life generally, it may also determine by his *civil* death; as if he be attainted. It is, therefore, usual in conveyances to say "during the term of his *natural life.*"

The incidents to a tenancy for life are: —

1. Every tenant for life, unless restrained by covenant or agreement, may, of common right, take upon the land demised to him reasonable *estovers* or *botes;* that is, an allowance of wood for fuel, repairs, and the like; for he has a right to the full enjoyment and use of the land, and all its profits, during his estate therein; but he is not permitted to cut down timber or do other waste upon the premises, for such things are not the temporary profits of the tenement, nor is the destruction necessary for the tenant's complete enjoyment of his estate, but tends to the permanent and lasting loss of the person entitled to the inheritance.

2. A tenant for life, or his representatives, shall not be prejudiced by any sudden determination of his estate, because such a determination is contingent and uncertain; therefore if a tenant for his own life sows the lands and dies before harvest, his executors shall have the *emblements* or profits of the crop; for the estate was determined by the *act of God;* and it is a maxim in law that *actus Dei nemini facit injuriam.* But if an estate for life be determined by the tenant's *own act,* as, by forfeiture for waste

committed; or, if a female tenant holding during her widowhood thinks proper to marry; in these, and similar cases, the tenants, having thus determined the estate by their own acts, shall not be entitled to take the emblements. The doctrine of emblements extends not only to corn sown, but to roots planted, and other annual artificial profits; but it is otherwise of fruit trees, grass and the like, which are not planted annually at the expense and labour of the tenant, but are either a permanent, or natural, profit of the earth; for when a man plants a tree, he cannot be presumed to plant it in contemplation of any present profit, but merely with a prospect of its being useful to himself in future and to future successions of tenants.

3. A third incident to estates *for life* relates to the undertenants or lessees, who have the same, nay, greater indulgences than their lessors, the original tenants for life. As in the case of a woman who holds *durante viduitate;* her taking a husband is her own act, and therefore deprives her of the emblements; but if she leases her estate to an under-tenant, who sows the land, and she then marries, this act shall not deprive the tenant of his emblements, who is a stranger, and could not prevent her. As regards tenants at rack-rent (that is, tenants who pay full value for the land) holding under landlords entitled for life or other uncertain interest, it is enacted by stat. 14 & 15 Vict., c. 25, that in such cases when the lease or tenancy shall determine by the death or by cessor of the estate of any landlord, entitled for his life or any uncertain period, the tenant shall, instead of claims to emblements, continue to hold until the expiration of the then current year of his tenancy, and shall then, without being required to give or receive any notice, quit upon the terms of his lease or holding in the same manner as if his tenancy were determined by effluxion of time or other lawful means during the continuance of his landlord's estate. The Act also

contains provisions dealing with the rights and interests of succeeding owners.

By the Settled Estates' Acts, stat. 19 & 20 Vict., c. 120, amended by 21 & 22 Vict., c. 77, and 27 & 28 Vict., c. 45, a tenant for life may, when the instrument does not contain an express declaration to the contrary, demise the premises for any term not exceeding twenty-one years; but such demise must be made without impeachment of waste, and with other covenants prescribed by the Act. Also by stat. 8 & 9 Vict., c. 56, tenants for life are empowered to apply to the Court of Chancery, with consent of the occupier, to get leave to make permanent improvements on the lands; the money expended on such improvements to be charged upon the inheritance; and by a more recent Act, 9 & 10 Vict., c. 101, tenants for life, and other owners of land, may obtain advances from Government for works of drainage, such advances to be repaid by a rent-charge on the land.

The next estate *for life is of* the *legal* kind, as contradistinguished from *conventional,* viz., that of "*tenant in tail after possibility of issue extinct.*" This happens where one is tenant in *special tail,* and a person, from whose body the issue was to spring, dies without issue; or, having left issue, that issue becomes extinct. In either of these cases the surviving tenant in *special* tail becomes *tenant in tall after possibility of issue extinct.* The *possibility* of issue is always supposed to exist in law unless extinguished by the death of the parties, even though the donees be each of them a hundred years old. The Court of Chancery may, however, modify this rule of law according to the circumstances of the case.

An estate *pur autre vie* is a life estate, held not for the life of the tenant, but of some other person, and the person for whose life it is held is called *cestui quo vie.* Where an estate is granted to a man and his heirs during the life of *cestui quo vie* and the grantee die without alienation, and while the life for which he held continues, the heir will succeed, and is called a *special occupant.*

Explain Tenancy by the Curtesy of England, Tenancy in Dower, and Tenancy in Jointure.

Tenancy by the Curtesy of England, is where a man marries a woman seised of an estate of inheritance; that is, of lands and tenements in fee-simple or fee-tail, and has had by her, issue born alive, which was capable of inheriting her estate. In this case, he shall, on the death of his wife, hold the lands for his life, as tenant by the curtesy of England. For if a woman seised of lands has issue by her husband and dies, the husband is the natural guardian of the child, and as such is in reason entitled to the profits of the lands in order to maintain it; and this estate being once vested in him by the birth of the child, was not suffered to determine by the subsequent death of the infant.

There are four requisites necessary to make a tenancy by the Curtesy: — 1. *Marriage.* — 2. *Seisin* of the wife, which must be an actual seisin or possession of the land; not a bare right to possess, which is a seisin *in law;* but an actual possession, which is a seisin *in deed.* — 3. *Issue,* born alive. — 4. The *Death* of the *Wife,* as the estate is not consummate till her death.

If the lands be in *gavelkind,* his title attaches, whether he has issue or not; but he has only a moiety of the wife's lands, and he loses his estate if he marries again.

Tenancy in Dower is where the husband of a woman was solely seised of an estate of inheritance, and dies. In this case, the wife shall have the third part of all the lands and tenements whereof he was seised at any time during the marriage to hold to herself for the term of her natural life for her own sustenance and the nurture and education of her children. If in gavelkind, she has a moiety, conditionally that she remains chaste and unmarried; and of lands held by the tenure of borough-English, she takes the whole for her life.

The inconvenience arising out of the ancient law was that dower attached, though the husband had parted with the land before his death; but now by stat. 3 & 4 Wm. IV., c. 74, the husband may by *will* or by *deed* bar or defeat the wife's dower; and no widow coming within the Act; that is, who was married since January 1, 1834, can be endowed of any land which shall have been disposed of by her husband or by his *will,* so that she can only be endowed out of lands of which he died intestate, or concerning which he has made no declaration against her dower.

Jointure, strictly speaking, signifies a joint estate limited to both husband and wife; but in common acceptation it is a sole estate limited to the wife on her surviving her husband, and must be either expressed or averred to be in satisfaction of dower. It may be made either before or after marriage. If *after* marriage, she may waive it, and claim her dower, unless it be provided by Act of Parliament.

Settlements upon the wife have long been in use, so that few widows have been able to claim dower under their general right.

CHAPTER VII
ESTATES LESS THAN FREEHOLD

The Estates that now come under our consideration are termed "Estates less than Freehold," of which there are three sorts: — 1. *An Estate for Years,* which is an interest in the possession of lands or tenements for some determinate period. — 2. *An Estate at Will;* that is, where lands and tenements are let by one man to another, to hold at the will of the lessor or lessee. — 3. *An Estate by Sufferance,* which is when one comes into possession under a lawful demise, and afterwards wrongfully continues in possession.

Explain those three Estates that come under the head of "Estates less than Freehold."

1. An *Estate for years* is a contract for the possession of lands or tenements for some determinate period, and it takes place where a man lets them to another for the term of a certain number of years, agreed upon between the lessor and the lessee, and the lessee enters thereon. If the lease be but for half a year, or a quarter, or any less time, this lessee is considered a tenant for years, a year being the shortest term of which the law in this case takes notice.

Every such estate must expire at a period certain and prefixed, by whatever words created; and, therefore, this estate is frequently called a term, *terminus,* because its duration or continuance is bounded, limited, and determined; it must have a certain beginning, and a certain end; so if a man make a lease to another, for so many years as A. shall name, it is a good lease for years, for though it is at present uncertain, yet when A. has named the years, it is then reduced to a certainty; and, if no day of commencement is named in the creation, of this estate, it begins from the making or delivery of the lease. A lease for so many years as B. shall live is void from the beginning, for it is neither certain, nor can ever be reduced to a certainty, during the continuance of the lease; and the same doctrine holds, if a parson make a lease of his glebe for so many years as he shall continue parson of Dale, for this is still more uncertain. But a lease for twenty or more years, if B. shall so long live, or if he should so long continue parson, is good; for there a certain period fixed beyond which it cannot last, though it may determine sooner, on the death of B., or his ceasing to be parson there.

If a tenant for a term certain, under a lease, keep possession after the expiration of the term and pay rent, this will constitute a tenancy from year to year, subject to the conditions contained in the lease.

2. The *second* species of estates not freehold is an *estate at mill.* An estate at *will* is where lands and tenements are let by one man to another, to hold at the *will* of the lessor, and the tenant by force of this lease obtains possession. It may be constituted by written or verbal agreement, if followed by entry, and may in some cases arise by construction of law. Such tenant has no certain indefeasible estate, nothing that can be assigned by him to any other, because the lessor may determine his will, and put him out whenever he pleases. But every *estate at will* is at the will of both parties, landlord and tenant, so that either of them may determine his will, and quit his connections with the other at his own pleasure. This must be understood with some restriction; for, if the tenant at will sows his land, and the landlord before the corn is ripe, or before it is reaped, ejects him, the tenant shall have the emblements, and free ingress, egress, and regress, to cut and carry them away. The tenant could not possibly know when his landlord would determine his tenancy, and could make no provision against it; and having sown the land, the law will not suffer him to be a loser by it. But it is otherwise where the tenant himself determines the holding, for in this case the landlord shall have the profits of the land. Neither party can determine this estate at a time when it would be prejudicial to the other; and six months'

notice must be given before bringing an action of ejectment.

Tenancy from *year to year* has almost superseded, the old tenancy at *will.* Thus if a man demise land to another at a yearly rent, no length of time being expressed, the law will construe this as a demise from year to year. In this case a half-year's notice to quit must always be given, on either part, so that the tenancy shall expire at the same period of the year that it commenced.

3. An *Estate at Sufferance* is where one comes into possession under a lawful demise, but holds such possession after it is determined. As if a man takes a lease for a year, and after the year is expired continues to hold the premises without any fresh leave from the owner of the estate. Or, if a man makes a lease at will, and dies, the estate at will is thereby determined; but if the tenant continues possession, he is tenant at *sufferance.*

By 4 Geo. II., c. 28, a tenant wrongfully holding over shall pay double the yearly value; and by 11 Geo. II., c. 19, if the landlord gives notice to quit and the tenant then holds over, he shall pay double his former rent.

In order to give landlords a check and speedy remedy against the tenants holding over when the property is of small value, it is now provided by 1 & 2 Vict., c. 74, that the landlord may proceed, after written notice, to recover possession by a summary proceeding before any two justices who may issue their warrant for possession accordingly; and by 19 & 20 Vict., c. 108, where the value or rent shall not have exceeded £50 per annum, the landlord may enter a plaint in the county court of the district, and after judgment, obtain possession through the high bailiff of the court, on a warrant to be issued by the registrar.

CHAPTER VIII
ESTATES UPON CONDITION

Besides the several Estates as classified in respect of their duration and interest, there is another species, called *Estates upon Condition* (the condition being expressed or implied) importing that the estate may be created, enlarged, diminished, or defeated; or the beneficial interest therein suspended upon the happening or not happening of some uncertain event. These estates are of two sorts: — 1. Estates upon Condition Implied. — 2. Estates upon Condition Expressed, under which last may be included Estates held in Vadio, Gage, or Pledge; and Estates held by Elegit.

Explain these "Estates."

An estate upon *condition implied in law,* is where a grant of an estate has a condition annexed to it inseparable from its essence and constitution, although no condition be expressed in words. As if a grant be made to a man of an *office* generally, without adding other words, the law tacitly annexes hereto a condition that the grantee shall duly execute his office, on breach of which condition it is lawful for the grantor, or his heirs, to oust him, and grant it to another person; for an office either public or private, may be forfeited by *mis-user* or *non-user.* In public offices that concern the administration of justice or the commonwealth, *non-user* is of itself a direct and immediate cause of forfeiture; but *non-user* of a private office is no cause of forfeiture unless some special damage is proved to be occasioned thereby; for in the one case delay must necessarily be occasioned in the affairs of the public, which require a constant attention; but private offices, not requiring so regular and unremitted a service, the temporary neglect of them is not necessarily productive of mischief.

Franchises also, being regal privileges in the hands of a subject, are held to be granted on the same condition of making a proper use of them; and, therefore, they may be forfeited either by abuse or neglect.

Upon the same principle proceed, all the forfeitures which are given by law, of life estates and others, for acts done by the tenant himself that are incompatible with the estate which he holds.

An estate on *condition expressed* in the grant itself, is where an estate is granted, either in fee-simple or otherwise, with an express qualification annexed, whereby the estate granted shall either commence, be enlarged, or be defeated, upon performance or breach of such qualification or condition. These conditions are therefore either *precedent,* or *subsequent.* Precedent are such as must happen or be performed before the estate can vest or be enlarged; *subsequent* are such, by the failure or non-performance of which an estate already vested may be defeated. Thus, if an estate for life be limited to A. upon his marriage with B., the marriage is a *precedent condition,* and till that happens no estate is vested in A. But if a man grants an estate in fee-simple, reserving to himself and his heirs a certain rent; and that, if such runt be not paid at the times specified, it shall be lawful for him and his heirs to re-enter, and avoid the estate; in this case the grantee and his heirs have an estate upon condition *subsequent* which is *defeasible;* that is, annulled or abrogated, if the condition be not strictly performed. These express conditions, if they be *impossible* at the time of their creation, or afterwards become impossible by the act of God, or of the feoffor himself, or repugnant to the nature of the estate, are void.

Estates held *in Vadio, Gage,* or *Pledge* — are of two kinds *Vidium Vadium,* or living pledge; and *Mortuun Vudium,* dead pledge, or *Mortgage.*

Vidium Vadium, or living pledge, is when a man borrows a sum (suppose £200) of another, and grants him an estate, say, of £20 per annum, to hold till the rents and profits shall repay the sum so borrowed. This is an estate conditioned, to be void as soon as such sum is raised; and in this case the land or pledge is said to be living; it subsists and survives the debt, and immediately on the discharge of that, reverts to the borrower.

Mortuum Vadium, a dead pledge, or *mortgage* (which is much more common), is where a man borrows of another a specific sum, and conveys to him an estate in fee, or for a less period, on condition that if he, the borrower or mortgagor, as he is called, shall repay the mortgagee the said sum on a certain day mentioned in the deed, then the mortgagor may re-enter on the estate so conveyed in pledge; or, as is now the more usual way, the mortgagee reconveys the estate to the mortgagor. In the event of the mortgagor not paying the debt on the day fixed by the deed, the right to the land which is so put in pledge is, by the common law, vested in the mortgagee, who may, by legal process, enter on the lands. But this will not prevent the Court of Chancery, in its office of administering equity, from interfering; for it holds, that after the day fixed for payment has passed, the mortgagor has *still a right* to redeem his estate, on payment of the mortgage money, with interest and expenses, within a reasonable time. So, though the estate be thus forfeited, and absolutely vested in the mortgagee at the common law, the courts of equity will interpose, and no agreement with the creditor, however stringent, can deprive the debtor of his equitable right. This is called the mortgagor's *equity of redemption;* that is, an *equitable* estate in the land.

The mortgagee may eject the mortgagor by an action of ejectment in a court of law, but the Court of Chancery will compel him to keep a strict account of the rents and profits; and, when he has received the full amount of the money lent with interest and expenses, it will compel him to reconvey the estate to the mortgagor. The Court of Chancery, however, is so far indulgent to the mortgagee that it will not deprive him for ever of the money which is due to him. On a foreclosure suit being instituted, the Court of Chancery is empowered to direct a sale of the property at the request of either party, instead of a foreclosure. No sale is to be made until after six months' notice in writing; after which sale the mortgagee is at liberty to retain for himself his principal, interest, and costs; and the surplus, if any, must be paid over to the mortgagor.

It is now the custom in general practice to introduce a *power of sale* into the mortgage deed, which enables the mortgagee, in case of default of payment, to effect a sale of the mortgaged premises after six months' notice in writing.

The principles of Equity as to *equity of redemption* now apply equally to leasehold or copyhold estates as to the mortgage of freehold.

A deposit of *title-deeds,* generally accompanied by a note in writing, on the borrowing of money, is, in equity, a mortgage of the lands therein mentioned.

Estates by *Statute Merchant* and *Statute Staple,* which were originally made applicable as securities for money, have been superseded by various statutes passed for the benefit of creditors.

The other estate, created by operation of law, for security and satisfaction of debts, is called an estate by *elegit.* An *elegit* is a writ, founded on the statute of Westminster 2, by which, after a plaintiff had obtained judgment for his debt at law, the sheriff used to give him possession of a moiety of the defendant's lands and tenements, to be occupied and enjoyed until his debt and damages were fully paid; and, daring the time he so held them, he was called tenant by *elegit;* but now, by stat. 1 & 2 Vict., c. 110, the judgment creditor can seize by that writ the whole instead of a moiety of the judgment debtor's lands and tenements.

By stat. 27 & 28 Vict., c. 112, it is provided that decrees and orders in equity, lunacy, and bankruptcy, whereby any money shall be payable to any person, shall have the effect of judgments in the superior courts of common law, and the persons to whom such money is payable are consequently, as judgment creditors, entitled to issue out this writ, and to become *tenants by elegit.* These courts may also direct a sale of the lands or tenements so taken by force of the writ of *elegit.*[37]

CHAPTER IX
ESTATES IN POSSESSION, REMAINDER, AND REVERSION

Hitherto we have considered. *Estates* solely with regard to their *duration* or the *quantity of interest* which the owners have therein; let us now consider them with regard. to the *time of their enjoyment,* when the actual taking or receipt of the rents and profits and other advantages arising therefrom begin.

---

[37] An estate by *elegit* is not strictly a freehold, estate, but is considered as a chattel Interest, and passes to the personal representatives.

Explain Estates in Possession, Remainder, and Reversion.

An estate in *possession,* which, is also called an estate *executed,* is where a present *interest* passes to and resides in the tenant, not depending on any subsequent circumstance or contingency, as in the cases of estates *executory.* An estate in possession does not in law mean that the owner has the *actual* possession, but that he has the *legal* right of possession.

An estate in *remainder* is an estate *limited* to take effect and be enjoyed after another estate is determined. As it a man seised in fee-simple grants lands to A. for twenty years, and, after the determination of the said term, then to B. and his heirs; here A. is tenant for *years,* remainder to B. In *fee.* So if land be granted to A. for twenty years, and after the determination of the said term to B. for life, and after the determination of B.'s estate for life to be limited to C. and his heirs, this makes A. tenant for years, with *remainder* to B. *for life,* and *remainder* over to C. in *fee.* Here the estate of inheritance undergoes a division into three portions: there is first A.'s estate for years carved out of it; after that B.'s estate for life; and then the whole that remains is limited to C. and his heirs; that is, the fee-simple, being the highest and largest estate that a subject is capable of enjoying. Although there are three parts, there is only one estate of inheritance.

The *first ride* with respect to the creation of a *remainder* is, that there must necessarily be some particular estate *precedent* to the estate in remainder, as no *remainder* can be created without such a precedent particular estate.

The *second rule* is that the remainder must commence or pass out of the grantor at the time of the creation of the particular estate. As where there is an estate to A. for life, with remainder to B. in fee; here B.'s remainder in fee passes from the grantor at the same time that seisin is delivered to A. of his life estate in possession.

The *third rule* is that the remainder must vest in the grantee during the continuance of the particular estate. As, if A. be tenant for life, remainder to B. in tail; here B.'s remainder is vested in him, at the creation of the particular estate to A. for life. Or, if A. and B. be tenants for their joint lives, remainder to the survivor in fee; here, though during their joint lives the remainder is vested in neither, yet on the death of either of them the remainder vests instantly in the survivor; therefore both these are good remainders. But, if an estate be limited to A. for life, remainder to the eldest son of B. in tail, and A. dies before B. has any son; here the remainder will be void, for it did not vest in any one during the continuance, nor at the determination, of the particular estate; and, even supposing that B. should afterwards have a son, he shall not take by this remainder; for, as it did not vest at or before the end of the particular estate, it never can vest at all, but is gone for ever.

The *fourth rule* is that a remainder may not be limited to a child of an unborn person, as a limitation tending to a perpetuity is absolutely void, and a limitation of such a void remainder makes all subsequent remainders bad.

Remainders are either *vested* or *contingent.* A vested remainder is where the estate is invariably fixed to remain to a determinate person after the particular estate is spent; as if A. be tenant for twenty years, remainder to B. in fee. B.'s is a *vested* remainder, and it may be transferred, aliened, or charged with debts.

Contingent or *executory remainders* are where the estate in remainder is limited to take effect, either to an uncertain *person,* or upon an uncertain *event.* As if A. be tenant for life, with remainder to B.'s eldest son (then unborn) in tail; this is a contingent remainder, for it is uncertain whether B. will have a son or not; but the instant that a son is born, the remainder is no longer contingent, but vested; for if A. had died before the contingency happened; that is, before B.'s son was born, the remainder would have been absolutely gone; for the particular estate was determined before the remainder could vest.

The second kind, or those limited on an *uncertain event,* may be exemplified thus: — By a lease to A. for life, remainder to B. for life, and if B. should die before A., then the remainder to C. for life. B.'s dying before A. is an event that may not happen, and therefore the remainder to C, is *contingent.*

Contingent remainders could have been *defeated* by destroying or determining the particular estate upon which they depended before the contingency happened whereby they became vested. Thus, where their was a tenant for life, with divers remainders in contingency, the tenant for life might not only by his death, but by alienation, surrender, or otherwise destroy and determine his own life estate before any of those remainders vested, the consequence of which was that he utterly defeated them all; but now the law relating to the defeating of contingent remainders has undergone material alteration by the Act amending the law of real property,[38] which provides that contingent remainders "shall be, and if created before the passing of the Act, shall be deemed to be, capable of taking effect, notwithstanding the determination by forfeiture, surrender, or merger of any preceding estate of freehold, in the same manner in all respects as if such determination had not happened."[39]

---

[38] See 8 & 9 Vict., c. 106., s. 8, repealing stat. 7 & 8 Vict., c. 76, a. 8.
[39] See "Uses and Trusts," p. 173.

Merger is when a less estate and a greater, limited subsequent to it, coincide and meet it one and the same person without any intermediate estate; then the less estate is said to be *merger* in the greater. Thus it A. be tenant for years with remainder to B. for life, and A. assigns his term to B.; or the two estates coming together in any other way, the term is merged in the freehold estate.

An *executory devise is* a limitation, of a future estate, or interest, in lands, or chattels personal, as the law admits, in the case of a will. It is contrary to the rules of limitation in conveyances at common law; and is an indulgence allowed to a man's last will and testament. The difference between a contingent remainder and a devise is this, that the first may be barred, but an executory devise cannot be prevented or destroyed by any alteration whatsoever in the estates out of which or after which it is limited. An executory devise, within which the contingency must happen, is restricted to the period of a life or any number of lives in being, and twenty-one years afterwards. Church property is not embraced by the law of perpetuity.[40]

An estate in *reversion* is the residue of an estate left in the grantor, to commence in possession after the determination of some particular estate granted out by him. As, if there be a gift in tail, the reversion of the fee is, without any special reservation, vested in the donor by act of law; and so also the reversion, after an estate for life, years, or at will, continues in the lessor; for the fee-simple of all lands must abide somewhere; and if he, who was before possessed of the whole, carves out of it any smaller estate, and grants it away, whatever is not so granted remains in him. Thus a grant of an estate by the owner of the fee-

---

[40] See Perpetuating Testimony Act, 5 & 6 Vict., c. 69; also 21 & 22 Vict., c. 93.

simple to "A. for life" leaves in the grantor this reversion in fee-simple, which will commence in possession after the determination of the life-freehold. A reversion is never, therefore, created by deed or writing, but arises from construction of law. A reversion being a vested interest, may be aliened and charged, much in the same manner as estates in possession.[41]

CHAPTER X
ESTATES IN SEVERALTY, JOINT-TENANCY, COPARCENARY, AND COMMON

We come now to treat of Estates with respect to the number and connections of their owners, and the tenants who occupy and hold them. Considered, in this view, estates of any quantity or length of duration, and whether they he in actual possession or expectancy, may he held in four different ways, viz.: — 1. In *Severalty.* — 2. In *Joint-Tenancy* — 3. In *Coparcenary.* — 4. In *Common.*

Explain the Nature of these Estates; how created; next, their Properties and respective Incidents; and lastly, how they may be Severed or Destroyed.

He that holds lands or tenements in *severalty,* or is sole tenant thereof, is he that holds them in his own right only, without any other person being joined or connected with him in point of interest, during his estate therein.

[41] By 8 & 9 Vict., c. 106, it is provided that a feoffment made after the let October, 1845, shall not have any tortious operation; see also 20 & 21 Vict., c. 57, as to reversionary interests of married women; and 31 & 32 Vict., c. 4, as to the sale of reversions.

An estate in *joint-tenancy* is where an estate is acquired by two or more persons in the same land, by the same title; and, at the same time, whether to hold in fee-simple, fee-tail, for life, for years, or at will.

The *creation* of an estate in *joint-tenancy* depends on the wording of the deed or devise, by which the tenants claim title; for this estate can only arise by purchase or grant; that is, by the act of the parties, and never by the mere act of law. Thus if an estate be given to a plurality of persons, without adding any restrictive, exclusive, or explanatory words; as if an estate be granted to A. and B. and their heirs, this makes them immediately joint-tenants in fee of the lands; for the law interprets the grant so as to make all parts of it take effect, which can only be done by creating an equal estate in them both. As the grantor has thus united their names, the law gives them a thorough union in all other respects.

The *properties* of a joint estate are derived from its *unity,* which is fourfold; the unity of *interest,* the unity of *title,* the unity of *time,* and the unity of *possession;* or, in other words, joint-tenants have one and the same interest accruing by one and the same conveyance, commencing at one and the same time, and held by one and the same undivided possession. While they all live, each tenant is said to be seised *per my et per tout;* when any die, the survivor or survivors have the same estate: and the heir of the survivor is the person who alone will be entitled to inherit.

Joint-tenancy may be *severed* by destroying any of its unities; by partition, by alienation, and by an accession of interest; for each joint-tenant possesses an absolute power to dispose in *his life-time* of his own share of the lands, by any of the usual modes of alienation.

A joint-tenant may make a valid lease of his share, a dealing of this kind being a severance *pro tanto;* the Court of Chancery will, if satisfied with the application, compel a partition,[42] or order a sale and distribution of the proceeds.

A demise, however, of one's share by *will* is no severance of the jointure; for no testament takes effect till after the death of the testator, and by such death the right of the survivor is already vested.

An estate held in *coparcenary is* where lands of inheritance descend from the ancestor to two or more persons. It arises either by common law, or particular custom. By common law; as where a person seised in fee-simple or in fee-tail dies, and his next heirs are two or more females, his daughters, sisters, aunts, cousins, or their representatives. In this case they shall all inherit, and these co-heirs or co-heiresses are then called *coparceners;* or, for brevity, *parceners.* Parceners by particular custom are where lands descend, as in *gavelkind,* to all the males in equal degree, as sons, brothers, uncles, &c. And, in either of these cases, all the parceners put together make but one heir, and have but one estate among them.

An estate in *coparcenary* resembles that of *joint-tenancy* in unity of *interest, title,* and *possession;* but differs materially in many points: — *Parceners* claim by *descent,* whereas joint-tenants always claim by *purchase.* So if two sisters purchase lands, to hold to them and their heirs, they are not *coparceners,* but joint-tenants; and hence it likewise follows, that no lands can be held in coparcenary but estates of inheritance, which are of a *descendible* nature. There is no unity of *time* necessary to an estate in coparcenary; for if a man has two daughters, to whom his estate descends in coparcenary, and one dies before the other, the surviving daughter and the *heir* of the other are parceners; the estates vesting in each of them at

---

[42] See Jointure Acts, 27 Heu. VIII., c. 10; amended by 26 & 27 Vict., c. 125.

different times, though it be the same quantity of interest, and held by the same title.

Parceners, though they have an *unity,* have not an *entirety,* of interest. They are properly entitled each to the whole of a distinct share; and of course there is no *jus accrescendi,* or *survivor-ship* between them; for each part descends severally to their respective heirs, though the unity of possession continues; and as long as the lands continue in a course of descent, and united in possession, so long are the tenants therein, whether male or female, called parceners. Though persons related in equal degree to the ancestor are entitled in equal shares; yet, as their heirs will represent them or stand in their place, there is no equality of interest amongst the parceners. Thus, if a man dies, leaving four granddaughters, three of them the issue of an elder daughter, and one of a younger daughter; all four shall inherit, but the daughter of the younger shall take as much as all the other three; that is, her mother's share.

An estate in *coparcenary* may be destroyed. 1. By partition, which disunites the possession, converting the estate into two or more estates in severally. 2. By alienation, which disunites the title, and may disunite the interest, changing the estate into a tenancy-in-common. 3. By the whole at last descending to and vesting in one single person, which brings it to an estate in severalty.

Formerly parceners of a copyhold could not make partition without the consent of the lord, but such consent is no longer necessary.[43]

---

[43] See 4 & 5 Vict., c. 35, as to the partition of copyhold and customary estates. See 8 & 9 Vict.. c. 106, as to the amendment of the law of Real Property; and 31 & 32 Vict.. c. 40, as to the power of the court to order a sale and distribution of the proceeds, instead of a division of the property.

Tenants-in-common are such as hold by several and distinct titles, but by unity of possession; because no one knows his own severally, and therefore they all occupy promiscuously. This tenancy therefore happens where there is a unity of possession merely, but perhaps an entire disunion of interest, of title, and of time. If there be two tenants in common of lands, one may hold his part in fee-simple, the other in tail, or for life; so that there is no necessary *unity of interest.* One may hold by descent, the other by purchase; or the one by purchase from A., the other by purchase from B.; so that there is no *unity of title.* One's estate may have been vested fifty years, the other's but yesterday; so there is no *unity of time.* The only unity is that of possession.

Tenancy in common may be created, either by the destruction of estates in joint-tenancy and coparcenary, or by special limitation in a deed. Thus, if one of two joint-tenants in fee alienes his estate for the life of the alienee, the alienee and the other joint-tenant are tenants in common; for they then have several titles, the other joint-tenant by the original grant, the alienee by the new alienation; and they also have several interests, the former joint-tenant in fee-simple, the alienee for his own life only.

Another illustration of a tenancy in common is this: — Where lands are given to two persons in different capacities, *without words of division,* they will take as tenants in common. Thus, if the donees be one a corporation and the other a natural person, the tenancy is not joint, but common.

A tenancy in common may be dissolved by uniting all the titles and interests in one tenant by purchase or otherwise, which brings the whole to one *severally;* or by making partition between the several tenants in common, which gives them all respective *severalties.*

CHAPTER XI
TITLE TO THINGS REAL

Hitherto we have been principally engaged in defining the nature of *Things Real,* hi describing the Tenures by which they may be holden, and in distinguishing the several kinds of *Estate* or *Interest* that may be had therein; let us now consider the *Title* to Things Real, with the manner of *acquiring* and *losing* it.

Define a "Title," and explain the several stages or degrees requisite to form a complete Title to Lands and Tenements?

A title is thus defined by Sir Edward Coke, "*titulus est justa causa possidendi id quod nostrum est:*" in other words, it is the means whereby the owner of lands has the just possession of his property. A complete title involves two elements — the *fact of* possession and the *right to* the possession.

The lowest and most imperfect degree of title consists in the mere *naked* possession or actual occupation of the estate, without any apparent right, or any shadow or pretence of right to hold and continue such possession. This may happen when one man invades the possession of another, and by force or surprise turns him out of the occupation of his lands, which is termed a *disseisin,* being a deprivation of that actual seisin, or corporal freehold of the lands which the tenant before enjoyed. Or, it may happen that after the death of the ancestor, and before the entry of the heir; or, after the death of a particular tenant and before the entry of him in remainder or reversion, a stranger may contrive to get possession of the vacant land and hold out him that had a right to enter. In all such cases the wrongdoer has only a mere *naked possession,* which the rightful owner may put an end to; but the harden of proof of title is thrown upon any one who claims to oust him; for without such *actual possession,* no title can be completely good. An uninterrupted possession for twenty years is *primâ facie* evidence of a good title.

The next ingredient to a good and perfect title is the *right* of *possession,* which may reside in one man, while the *actual* possession is not in himself but in another, as in the case of mortgagee and mortgagor.

A further ingredient is the right of property, the *jus proprietatis,* without either possession, or even the right of possession. As, if a person disseised or turned out of possession of his estate neglects to pursue his remedy within the limited time prescribed by law, the disseisor or his heirs gain the actual right of possession; for if the owner of lands, having a complete title, neglects to bring an action or make an entry within twenty years after the right to bring an action has accrued, his right of doing so is extinguished.

As to claims for the recovery of real estate, a person buying, with an apparently good title, is not bound by claims of which he has no notice, and in respect of which no action or suit has been actually commenced; indeed, a suit already commenced will not bind him, unless it has been registered within five years from the date of the purchase in books kept for that purpose in the Common Pleas.

In the absence of any stipulation to the contrary, a vendor must show a title to the estate to be sold of sixty years' duration.[44]

---

44 The Lord Chancellor's Land Bill, now before the House of Lords, proposes the simplification of the title to and transfer of land. There is to be a registration for all owners who choose to ask for it; and a title registered without investigation or certificate will, it not attached within ten years, be made absolute. Lord Selborne proposes to substitute ten years as the period within which suits may be brought for the recovery of land or rent.

CHAPTER XII
MODES OF ACQUIRING AND LOSING A TITLE TO REAL PROPERTY

Having considered the several ingredients requisite to form a complete title to lands, tenements, and hereditaments, let us next consider the *several manners* in which a complete title may be reciprocally *acquired* and *lost,* whereby the dominion of "Things Real" is either continued or transferred from one man to another.

Explain the various methods of acquiring on the one hand, and of losing on the other, a Title to Estates in "Things Real."

The methods of *acquiring* on the one hand, and of *losing* on the other, a title to estates in THINGS REAL are, by our law, reduced into two main divisions: — 1. By *Descent,* where the title is vested in a man lay the operation of law. — 2. By *Purchase,* where the title is vested in him by his own act or in pursuance of some agreement, and not by descent from any of his ancestors or kindred. This latter mode, as will be seen hereafter, includes several subdivisions.

I. By Descent.

Descent depends materially on the nature of kindred and the several degrees of *consanguinity* of the kindred or alliance in blood.

Consanguinity, or kindred, is the connection or relation of persons descended from the same stock or common ancestor. This consanguinity is either *lineal,* or *collateral.*

Lineal consanguinity is that which subsists between persons of whom one is descended in a direct line from the other, as between John Jones and his son, grandson, great-grandson, and so downwards in the direct *descending* line; or, between John Jones and his father, grandfather, great-grandfather, and so upwards in the direct *ascending* line. Every generation, in this lineal direct consanguinity, constitutes a different degree, reckoning either upwards or downwards: the father of John Jones is related to him in the first degree, and so likewise is his son; his grandfather and grandson in the second; his great grandfather and great-grandson in the third.

Collateral kindred are such as lineally spring from one and the same ancestor, who is the *stirps,* or root — the *stipes,* trunk or common stock, whence these relations are branched out. As if John Jones hath two sons, who have each a numerous issue; both these issues are cousins and are collateral kinsmen to each other, because they are all descended from this common ancestor, and all have a portion of his blood in their veins, which denominates them *consanguincos.* The very being of collateral consanguinity consists in their descent from one and the same common ancestor.

Explain Title by Descent, and briefly state the substance of the Rules of Descent as prescribed by the Act of 1833.

Descent, or hereditary succession, is the title whereby a man on the death of his ancestor acquires his estate by right of representation as his heir-at-law, and by the Act, "the word *descent* shall mean the title to inherit land by reason of consanguinity, as well where the heir shall be an *ancestor* or collateral relation, as where he will be a child or other issue." In every case the descent is to be traced to the *purchaser.*

In the year 1833 an Act,[45] called the "Inheritance Act," was passed, materially altering the former rules of descent; and these alterations apply to every kind of hereditament, whether it be subject to the common law of England or to any peculiar custom, such as that of *gavelkind* or *borough-English;* but in those cases only to the extent of providing that, on failure of direct lineal descendants, the direct lineal *ancestor* inherits in preference to collateral relations. It does not alter the descent where there are direct lineal descendants. This Act does not extend to any descent on the decease of any person who may have died before January 1,1834.

The "Canons of Inheritance," according to the new law, grafted upon the old, are the following: —

1. That inheritances shall lineally descend in the first place to the issue of the last *purchaser* or person entitled, unless it be proved that he *inherited* the same, in which case "the person from whom he inherited the same shall be considered to have been the purchaser; and in like manner the last person from whom the land shall be proved to have been inherited shall in every case be considered to have been the purchaser, unless it shall be proved that he inherited the same." That when any land shall have been devised by any testator who shall die after December 1, 1833, to the heir, or to the person who shall be the heir of such testator, such heir shall be considered to have acquired the land as a devisee, and not by *descent.*

2. That the male issue shall be admitted before the female, and that where the issue are two or more males in equal degree, the eldest only shall inherit, but the *females all together.* Thus, if a man has two sons, John and James, and two daughters, Mary and Eliza, and dies, John, his eldest son, shall alone succeed to his estate, in exclusion

[45] 3 & 4 Wm. IV., c. 106, amended by 22 & 23 Vict., c. 36, ss. 19 & 20.

of James and the two daughters; but if both the sons die without issue before the father, the daughters shall both inherit the estate as co-heiresses.

3. That all the lineal descendants, *in infinitum,* shall represent the ancestor; that is, shall stand in the same place as the person himself would have done had he been living. Thus the child, grandchild, or great-grandchild, either male or female, of the eldest son, succeeds before the younger son, and those representatives shall take neither more nor less, but just as much as their principal would have done. As, if there be two sisters, Jane and Eliza, and Jane dies, leaving six daughters, and then John Jones, the father of the two sisters, dies without other issue, these six daughters shall take among them exactly the same as their mother Jane would have done; that is, a moiety of the lands of John Jones in coparcenary; so that upon partition made, if the land be divided into twelve parts, Eliza, the surviving sister, shall have six thereof, and her six nieces, the daughters of Jane, one apiece. This taking by representation is called succession *in stirpes,* according to the roots, since all the branches inherit the same share that their root whom they represent would have done.

4. That on failure of lineal descendants or issue of the purchaser, the *lineal ancestor* shall be heir to any of his issue, so that the father shall be admitted before a brother or sister; and a more remote lineal ancestor to any of his issue other than a nearer lineal ancestor or his issue.

5. That none of the *maternal* ancestors of the person from whom the descent is to be traced, nor any of the descendants, shall be capable of inheriting until all his paternal ancestors and their descendants shall have failed; and also that no female paternal ancestor of such person, nor any of her descendants, shall be capable of inheriting until all his male paternal ancestors and their descendants shall

have failed; and that no female maternal ancestor of such person, nor any of her descendants, shall be capable of inheriting until all his male maternal ancestors and their descendants shall have failed.

6. That the mother of the more remote male ancestor be admitted before the mother of the less remote male ancestor.

7. That a kinsman of the *half-blood* shall be capable of being-heir; and that such relation by the half-blood shall inherit next after a kinsman in the same degree of the whole blood and his issue where the common ancestor shall be a male, and next after the common ancestor where such common ancestor is a female; so that the brother of the half-blood on the part of the father shall inherit next after the sisters of the whole blood on the part of the father and their issue; and the brother of the half-blood on the part of the mother, shall inherit next after the mother.

8. Where there shall be a total failure of heirs of the purchaser, or where any land shall be descendible as if an ancestor had been the purchaser thereof, and there shall be a total failure of the heirs of such ancestor, then and in every such case the land shall descend, and the descent shall thenceforth be traced, from the person last entitled to the land as if he had been the purchaser thereof.[46]

II. Purchase.

Purchase, taken in its largest and moat extensive sense, is the possession of lands and tenements which a man has acquired otherwise than by *descent.* In this sense it includes *every other method* of coming to an estate but that of inheritance. It is not only such acquisitions of land as are obtained by way of bargain and sale for money or

---

[46] The accompanying diagram will illustrate the application of the rules.

some other valuable consideration; for if I give land freely to another, he is in the eyes of the law a *purchaser*; or a man who has his father's estate settled upon him in tail before he was born, is also a purchaser. What we call purchase *(perquisitio)* the feudalists called *conquœstu* or *conquisitio* (conquest); denoting any means of acquiring an estate out of the common course of inheritance.

Tile difference in effect between the acquisition of an estate by descent and by purchase consists principally in these two particulars: — 1. That by *purchase,* the estate acquires a new inheritable quality, and is descendible to the owner's blood in general, and not, to the blood only of some particular ancestor. — 2. An estate taken by *purchase* will not make the heir answerable for the acts of the ancestor, as an estate by *descend* will; for if the ancestor, by any deed, obligation, covenant, or the like, bindeth himself and his heirs and dieth, the deed, obligation, or covenant shall be binding upon the heir, so far as he had any estate of inheritance vested in him by descent from that ancestor, whether he remains in possession or hath aliened it.

This is the legal signification of the word *perquisitio,* or purchase, and in this sense it includes the five following methods of acquiring a title to estates: — 1. Escheat. — 2. Occupancy. — 3. Prescription. — 4. Forfeiture. — 5. Alienation.

I. Escheat.

Escheat denotes an obstruction of the course of descent, and a consequent determination of the tenure by some unforeseen contingency, in which case the land naturally reverts to the original grantor or lord of the fee. Escheat also arises from default of heirs, when the tenant dies without any lawful and natural-born relations on the part of those ancestors from whom the estate descended; or when the intestate tenant, having been a bastard, does not leave any lineal descendants, since he cannot have any collateral descendants.

It also arises upon attainder of the tenant, but that is now seldom called into action, for the Crown in modern times usually waives its prerogative by making a grant, in order to restore the estate to the family of the attainted person, or to effectuate any disposition of it which the former tenant may have contemplated.

Aliens possessing no inheritable blood cannot claim by descent; but all subjects, being natural-born subjects of the Queen, may inherit, and make their titles by descent from any of their ancestors, lineal or collateral.[47]

II. Occupancy.

Title by *Occupancy* is the taking possession of those things which had no owner. This right of *occupancy,* so far as it concerns *real* property, was extended only to a single instance, namely, where a man was tenant *pur autre vie,* or had an estate granted to himself for the *life of another,* and died daring the life of *cestui que vie;* that is, *him* by whose life it was holden. In this case, he that could first enter on the land might lawfully retain the possession so long as *cestui que vie* lived, by right of occupancy; but this title of common occupancy is now regulated by the Wills Act, 7 Wm. IV. & 1 Vict., c. 26, which provides that an estate *pur autre vie,* of whatever tenure, and whether it be a corporeal or incorporeal hereditament, may be devised by last will and testament; that if no disposition by will be made of an estate *pur autre via* of a freehold nature, it shall be chargeable in the hands of the heir, if it

---

[47] Sea Alien Acts 6 & 7 Wm. IV., c. 11; 7 & 8 Vict, c. 66; 10 & 11 Vict., c. 83; and 31 &. 32 Vict., c. 72.

come to him by reason of special occupancy as assets by descent, as in the case of freehold land in fee-simple; but in case there shall be no special occupant of an estate *pur autre vie* of whatever tenure, and whether a corporeal or incorporeal hereditament, it shall go to the executor or administrator of the party that had the estate thereof by virtue of the grant, and that in every case where it comes to the hands of such personal representative, whether by special occupancy or by virtue of the Wills Act, it shall be assets in his hands, to be applied and distributed in the same manner as personal estates.

III. Prescription.

Another method of acquiring real property is that by *Prescription,* as when a man can show no other title to what he claims than that he and those under whom he claims have immemorially used to enjoy it.

Title by prescription has been very much modified by the Prescription Act[48], which enacts that with respect to rights of common and all other profits or benefits to be taken and enjoyed from or upon any land, where there shall have been an enjoyment of them by any person claiming right thereto without interruption for thirty years next before the commencement of any suit upon the subject, the prescriptive claim shall no longer be defeated by showing only that the enjoyment commenced at a period subsequent to the era of legal memory. But any other mode of defeating the claim, before the passing of the Act, other than those specially provided for by the Act, are still available in opposing the claim, except that an uninterrupted enjoyment for sixty years is to confer an absolute and indefeasible title.

[48] Called Lord Tenterden's Act, 2 & 3 Wm. IV., c. 71. See also 3 & 4 Wm. IV., c. 42.

When the right claimed is a right of way or other easement, as a watercourse, or the use of any water to be enjoyed upon, over, or from any land or water, and the claim to the access and use of light for any dwelling-house, workshop, or other building, if actually enjoyed otherwise than by consent or agreement in writing, the periods constituting a *prescriptive* right in the case of ways and other easements and waters are twenty and forty years, in lieu of thirty and sixty years respectively; and an uninterrupted enjoyment of lights for twenty years constitutes in every case an absolute and indefeasible right to them — any local usage or custom notwithstanding — unless it shall appear that the same was enjoyed by some consent or agreement expressly made or given by deed or writing.

IV. Forfeiture.

Forfeiture is a punishment annexed by law to some illegal act or negligence in the owner of lands, tenements, or hereditaments, whereby he loses all his interest therein, which thereupon vests in the person suffering the injury, or in the Crown, or in some representative of public interest.

Lands, tenements, and hereditaments may be forfeited by various means:[49] —

1. These may be forfeited by alienation, or conveying them to another contrary to law.

2. By *lapse,* which is a species of forfeiture whereby the right of presentation to a benefice accrues to the ordinary by the neglect of the patron to present, and to the Crown by the neglect of the metropolitan.

---

[49] Forfeiture on conviction of felony was abolished by 33 & 34 Vict., c. 23, which made various provisions as to the property of convicted felons.

3. By *simony,* which is the corrupt presentation of any one to an ecclesiastical benefice for money, gift, or reward.

4. By *breach,* or non-performance of a *condition* annexed to the estate, whether expressed by deed at its original creation, or implied by law from a principle of common sense.

5. By *wilful waste,* which is a spoil or destruction in houses, gardens, trees, or other corporeal hereditaments, to the disherison of him that hath the remainder or reversion in fee-simple or fee-tail.

6. Another species of forfeiture is that of copyhold estates by breach of the *customs* of the manor.

7. The last method whereby lands and tenements may become forfeited is that of *bankruptcy.* All the lands and all the property of the bankrupt are made available for the payment of his debts, all the property of the debtor vesting in the appointed assignee or trustee, whose duty it is to sell the property and distribute the proceeds.[50]

V. Alienation.

The most usual and universal method of acquiring a Title to Real Estates is that of *Alienation or Conveyance;* under which may be comprised any method wherein estates are voluntarily resigned by one man and accepted by another, whether that be effected by sale, gift, marriage, settlement, devise, or other transmission of property by the mutual consent of the parties.

The legal evidences of this alienation of property are called *common assurances,* whereby any man's estate is assured to him. There are four kinds: — 1. By *deed.* — 2.

[50] See 32 &. 33 Vict., c. 83, and 32 & 33 Vict., c. 71. See also Court of Bankruptcy.

By *matter of record.* — 3. By *special custom.* — 4. By *devise.*

First, then, to explain a deed. A *Deed* is a writing, scaled by the parties and delivered, and the *requisites* are that there be persons able to contract and be contracted with, for the purposes intended by the deed; and also a thing or subject-matter to be contracted for; all which must be expressed by sufficient words. That is, in every grant there must be a grantor, a grantee, and a thing granted; and in every lease a lessor, a lessee, and a thing demised.

Secondly, the deed must be founded upon good and sufficient *consideration.* The consideration may be either a *good* or a *caluable* one. A *good* consideration is such as that of consanguinity; the gift of an estate to a near relation, being founded on motives of generosity, prudence, and natural affection. Deeds made upon these considerations are regarded only as merely voluntary, and are frequently set aside in favour of creditors and *bonâ fide* purchasers. A *villa-able* consideration is such as money, marriage, or the like, which the law esteems an equivalent given for the grant, and is therefore founded in motives of justice. The deed ought to show clearly on the face of it what the *consideration is,* not only in order that there should be no fraud upon the revenue in respect of the stamp, but also to obviate all questions of fraud as between the parties. The deed must be either written or printed, and it must be on paper or parchment duly stamped. The language employed should be intelligible and clear. In its execution it requires to be *signed, sealed,* and *delivered,* in the presence of, and to be attested by, one, two, or more witnesses. It is necessary that the deed be read before execution if either of the parties request it; or, in case either of the signatories should be unable to write, it is absolutely necessary that the deed be read over to the party or parties, who should make his or their *mark* thereto; and the fact of its having been read over and that the person or persons understood the nature of the deed should be stated in the attestation clause.

Can a Deed be "Avoided" or rendered of no effect?

Yes, if it wants any of the essential requisites mentioned. Deeds may also be avoided in consequence of erasure, interlining, or other alteration in any material part, unless a memorandum be made thereof at the time of the execution and attestation. — By breaking off or defacing the seal. — By delivering it up to be cancelled or defaced. — By the disagreement of such whose concurrence is necessary in order that the deed may stand; as of the husband, where a married woman is concerned; or of an infant, or of a person under duress. — By the judgment or decree of a court of judicature, when it appears that the deed was obtained by fraud or other foul practice.

Alienation by Matter of Record.

Assurances by *matter of record* are such as do not entirely depend on the act or consent of the parties themselves; but the sanction of a Court of Record is called in to substantiate, preserve, and be a perpetual testimony of the transfer of property from one man to another, or of its establishment when already transferred. Of this nature are: — 1. Private Acts of Parliament. — 2. The King's Grants. — 3. Orders made by the Court of Chancery under certain Acts.

Private Acts of Parliament are not an uncommon mode of assurance; for it may sometimes happen that, by the ingenuity of some and the blunders of others, an estate is most grievously entangled by a multitude of contingent remainders, resulting trusts, springing uses, and other artificial contrivances, so that it is out of the power of the courts of law or equity to relieve the owner; and it is necessary to resort to the supreme power of Parliament to determine the title, and arrange the future management of the estate.[51]

Grants from the Crown are also matters of public record. Royal grants by letters patent apply now only to a few incorporeal hereditaments, such as dignities, offices, and the like.

Alienation by Special Custom.

This is a very narrow title, confined, to copyhold lands, and such *customary* estates as are holden in ancient demesne or in manors of a similar nature; which, being of a very peculiar kind, and originally only tenancies in pure or privileged villenage, were never alienable by deed; for as that might have tended to defeat the lord of his seigniory, it would have been a forfeiture of title.

The principal things personal, or chattel interests, that by custom vest in some particular persons, either by the local usage of some particular place, or by the almost universal usage of the kingdom, are. — 1. *Heriots,* where a lord of a manor, or other chief lord, is entitled, by custom, to the best live beast or other chattel of which a tenant dies possessed; or, as is now more usual, a payment of money in lieu of the chattel. — 2. *Mortuaries,* a sort of ecclesiastical heriot, being a customary gift claimed by and due to the minister in very many parishes on the death of his parishioners. — 3. *Heir-looms,* such goods and personal chattels as go by special custom to the heir along with the inheritance, and not to the executor of the last proprietor. Charters, deeds, court-rolls, and other evidences of the

[51] When a trustee refuses to convey the trust property when duly required to do so, and when a mortgagee has died without having entered into possession, and there is a difficulty in obtaining a conveyance of the legal estate, see Trustee Act, 13 & 14 Vict., c. 60; extended by 15 & 16 Vict., c, 55.

land, and monuments, &c., descend to the heir in the nature of heir-looms.

Alienation by Devise.

The last method of conveying property is by *devise* or disposition contained in a man's last *will* and *testament;* and the formalities necessary to a *will* are now made the same for all wills, whatever be the nature of the property with which they deal. The Wills Act, 7 Wm. IV. & 1 Vict., c. 26, prescribes the mode in which *wills* are to be made and executed, and the "Wills Act Amendment Act of 1852" declares that the signature of a testator shall be valid if it be placed at, or after, or following, or under, or beside, or opposite to the end of a *will,* so that it shall be apparent on the face of the *will* that the testator intended to give effect by such his signature to the writing signed as his *will;* and no such *will* is to be affected by circumstances which the statute expressly mentions.

Every *will* must be in writing, and signed at the foot or end of it by the testator, or by some other person, in his presence and by his direction; and the signature is to be made by the testator in the presence of two or more witnesses present at the same time, and such witnesses are to attest and subscribe the will in the presence of the testator and of each other; and if the testator cannot sign his name, he may depute another person to do so for him, or make his mark, and. then acknowledge the same; and the fact of its having been read over to, and *acknowledged* by the testator to be his *will* and *testament,* should appear in the attestation-clause.

Marriage in all cases revokes a *will,* except where it is made in exercise of a power of appointment over property which would not, if *unappointed,* pass to the testator's own representatives.

A *codicil* is a supplement to a will containing anything which the testator wishes to add, or any explanation or revocation of what the *will* contains, and it must also be executed and attested in the same manner as a *will.*

A will does not take effect until the decease of the testator. A will may be revoked by any writing, executed in the same manner as a will, or by a subsequent will or codicil executed as before.

Under the new Act, a will is not void on account of the incompetency of the witness to prove the execution, and if any person shall attest the execution of a will to whom, or to whose wife or husband, any beneficial interest whatsoever shall be given, the person attesting will be a good witness, but the gift of such beneficial interest will be void. A creditor, however, may attest the will without losing his rights; and executors are competent witnesses to a will.[52]

CHAPTER XIII
OF CONVEYANCES

Having explained the general Nature of *Deeds,* let us next consider *Conveyances,* their several species, together with their respective incidents, and the mode of operation used in the alienation of Real Estates.

Give a brief explanation of Conveyances.

Conveyances are of two kinds: — 1. Conveyances at common law. — 2. Conveyances by statute law. The conveyances at common law are the following: — 1. Feoffment. — 2. Gift. — 3. Grant. — 1. Lease. — 5. Exchange. — 6. Partition. — 7. Release. — 8. Confirma-

[52] As to proving a will see "Court of Probate."

tion. — 9. Surrender. — 10. Assignment. — 11. Defeazance.

1. A *Feoffment* is derived from the verb to enfeoff, *feoffare*, or *infeudare,* to give one a fend — the gift of one person of any corporeal hereditament to another. The giver is called the *feoffor,* and the person enfeoffed is denominated the *feoffee.* To perfect the feoffment, *livery* of *seisin* was necessary. This livery of seisin was the pure feudal investiture or delivery of corporeal possession of the land or tenement, which was held absolutely necessary to complete the donation; for, with our Saxon ancestors, the *delivery* of a turf was a necessary solemnity to establish the conveyance of lands; but by 8 & 9 Vict., c. 106, it is enacted that after the 1st October, 1845, all corporeal tenements and hereditaments shall, as regards the conveyance of the immediate freehold thereof, be deemed to lie in *grant* as Well as in *livery.*

2. The conveyance by gift, *donatio,* is properly applied to the creation of an estate *tail,* as feoffment is to that of an estate in *fee,* and *lease* to that of an estate for life or years. It differs in nothing from a feoffment, but in the nature of the estate passing by it; for the operative words of conveyance in this case are *do,* or *dedi.*

3. *Grants (concessiones)* are effected by mere deed. The operative words therein commonly used are *dedi et concessi,* — have given and granted. Conveyance by *grant* is now made applicable to all kinds of hereditaments.[53]

4. A *Lease* is properly a conveyance of any lands or tenements made for *life,* for *years,* or at *will;* but always for a less time than the lessor has in the premises; for if it be for the whole time, it is more an *assignment* than a

---

[53] See 8 & 9 Vict., c. 106, s. 1, which Act abolished the obsolete doctrines as to the effect of "give" and "grant." See also 8 & 9 Vict., c. 18, ss. 75, 77; and 31 & 32 Vict., c. 60, s. 20.

lease. It must be in writing, and the usual words of operation in it are: *demise, lease,* and *to farm let.*

5. An *Exchange* is a mutual grant of equal interests, the one in consideration of the other. The word *exchange* is so requisite and appropriated by law to this case, that it cannot be supplied by any other word or expressed by any circumlocution. The estates exchanged must be equal in *interest,* as fee-simple for fee-simple, a lease for years for a lease for years;[54] but it matters not whether the terms be equal in duration or not. *Entry* must be made on both sides; for if either party die before entry, the exchange is void. By the Statute of Frauds, writing is made essential to an exchange, and by 8 & 9 Vict., c. 106, s. 3, it must also be by deed in every case except that of an exchange of copyholds.

6. A *Partition* is where two or more joint-tenants, coparceners, or tenants in common agree to divide the lands so held among them, to be held thereafter in severally, each taking a distinct part. By stat. 8 & 9 Vict., c. 106, s. 3, partitions of all *hereditaments,* not being copyhold, shall be void at law unless made by deed.

7. A *Release* is a discharge or a conveyance of a man's right in lands and tenements to another, who has some former estate in possession. The words generally used therein are: — *remise, release,* and for ever *quitclaim;* but more usually *release* simply. These releases may enure: — 1. By way of *enlarging an estate;* as if there be tenant for life or years, remainder to another in fee, and he in remainder releases all his right to the particular tenant and his heirs, which gives him the estate in fee; but in this case the relessee must be in *possession* of

[54] Modern enactments have modified this strict rule, and the Court of Chancery will see justice carried out where there is any doubt as to the equality of the exchange.

some estate for the release to work upon; for if there be a lessee for years, and *before* he enters and is in possession, the lessor releases to him all his right in the reversion, such release is void for want of possession in the relessee. — 2. By way of *passing an estate,* as when one of two coparceners releases all right to the other, this passes the fee-simple of the whole. In both these cases there must be a privity of estate between the relessor and the relessee; that is, one of their estates must be so related to the other as to make but one and the same estate in law. — 3. By way of *passing a right,* as if a man be disseised, and releases to his disseisor all his right; hereby the disseisor acquires a new right which changes the quality of his estate, and renders that lawful which before was tortious or wrongful. — 4. By way of *extinguishment;* as if A., tenant for life, makes a lease to A. for life, remainder to B. and his heirs, and the holder of the fee-simple releases to A., this extinguishes his right to the reversion, which enures to the advantage of B.'s remainder, as well as of A.'s particular estate. — 5. By way of *entry* and *feoffment,* as if there be two joint disseisors of a tenant in fee-simple, and the disseisee releases to one of them, he shall be sole seised, and shall keep out his former companion; which is the same in effect as if the disseisee had entered, and thereby put an end to the disseisin, and afterwards had enfeoffed one of the disseisors in fee.

8. A *Confirmation* is of a nature nearly allied to a release. It is a conveyance of an estate or right *in esse.* For instance, if a tenant for life or in tail lease for forty years and die during that term, the lease for years is voidable by him in reversion; but if confirmed before the death of the tenant for life, it is no longer voidable, but sure.

9. A *Surrender,* or rendering-up, is of a nature directly opposite to a release; for, as a release operates by the greater estates descending upon the less, a surrender is the

falling of a less estate into the greater. It is defined as a yielding up of an estate for life or years to him that has the immediate reversion or remainder, wherein the particular estate may merge by mutual agreement between them. It is usually effected by the words, *surrender, grant,* and *yield up.*

10. An *Assignment* of land or real estate is properly a transfer or making-over to another of the right one has in any estate, but it is usually applied to express the transfer of an estate for life or years. It differs from a lease only in this: that by a lease one grants an interest less than his own, reserving to himself a reversion; but in assignments he parts with the whole property, and the assignee stands to all intents and purposes in the place of the assignor. The original lessee, however, is liable to the lessor or covenantor for the acts and defaults, not only of himself, but his assignee also, though entitled to an indemnity from the latter.[55]

11. A *Defeazance (defaire,* to make void) is a collateral deed, made at the same time with the conveyance, containing certain conditions, upon the performance of which the estate then created may be *defeated* or totally undone. Defeazances are of rare occurrence, the practice now being to include in the same deed both the conveyance of the land to the alienee and the conditions, if any, to which it is to be subject, and by which its effect may be defeated.

Conveyances by Force of the Statute of Uses:

Conveyances by the *Statute of Uses* depend much on the doctrine of *Uses* and *Trusts,* which are a confidence

[55] By 8 & 9 Vict., c. 106, s. 3, an assignment of a chattel interest, not being copyhold, made after October 1,1845, shall be void at law, unless made by deed.

reposed in the *terre*-tenant, or tenant of the land, that he shall permit the profits to be enjoyed according to the directions of the *cestui que use* or *cestui que trust;* that is, to him to whose *use* the estate is granted, and who is to take the profits.

Uses and *Trusts* are in their natures very similar to the *fidei commissum* of Roman law, which was a confidence reposed in another who was transferree of the things committed to him; that he should dispose of the land according to the intentions of *cestui que use.* As if a conveyance, called a feoffment, was made to A. and his heirs, to the *use* of (or in trust for) B. and his heirs; A., the *terre-tenant,* had the legal possession of the land, but B., the *ceslui que use,* was, in conscience and is equity, entitled to have the profits and disposal of it.

Though these conveyances to *uses* had a very equitable beginning, they introduced a great many unforeseen inconveniences, and subverted in many instances the institution and policy of the common law. First, estates passed, by way of *use,* from one to another, without any solemn ceremony or permanent record of the transaction, whereby a third person that had the right knew not against whom to bring his action. — Secondly, *Uses* passing by *will,* heirs were disinherited by the inadvertent words of dying persons. — Thirdly, lords lost their wardships, reliefs, marriages, and escheats; the trustees allowing the *cestui que use* to continue the possession, whereby the real tenants that held the lands could not be discovered. — Fourthly, the king lost the estates of aliens and criminals; for they made their friends trustees, who kept possession and secretly gave them the profits. — Fifthly, purchasers were insecure, for the alienation of *cestui que use* in possession was at common law a disseisin; and 1 Rich. III., c. 1, gave him power to aliene what he had, yet the feoffees might, nevertheless, enter to revest a remainder or contingent use, which was never published by any record or livery whereby the purchaser could know it. — Sixthly, the *use* was not subject to the payment of debts. — Seventhly, many lost their rights by perjury in averment of secret *uses*. — Eighthly, *uses* might be allowed in *mortmain*.

These grievances led the way to the STATUTE OF USES,[56] which exerts an important influence over the conveyance of real property. By this statute it is enacted, that where any person or persons *stand* or be *seised* of any lands or other hereditaments to the *use, confidence,* or *trust* of any other person or persons, the persons that have any such *use* shall be beneficially entitled. It, in fact, enacts that what is given to A., shall, under certain circumstances, not be given to A., but to somebody else. For instance, if a feoffment be made to A. and his heirs, *to the use* of B. and his heirs; A. takes no permanent estate, but is made by the statute to be merely a kind of trustee for conveying the estate to B.; A., the *terre-tenant,* having the legal property and possession of the land, but B. the *cestui que use, he* for whom the benefit of the gift is made, is to have the profits. The statute thug *executes the use,* as lawyers term it; that is, it conveys the possession to the use, and transfers the use into possession, thereby making the *cestui que use* complete owner of the lands and tenements, as well at law as in equity.

A *use* upon a *use is* invalid. Suppose a conveyance had been made to A. and his heirs, to the *use* of B. and his heirs, to the *use* of C. and his heirs, C. takes no estate in law, for the *use* to him is a *use upon* a *use.*

The duration of trusts cannot be extended beyond the bounds of legal limitation, viz., a life or lives in being and 21 years afterwards. If the trust exceeds this boundary, it

---

[56] 27 Henry VIII., c. 10. Its title on the Parliament Roil is "An Act concerning Uses and Wills."

is void *in toto,* and cannot be cut down to the legitimate extent.[57]

Trust estates, besides being subject to voluntary alienation, are also liable, like estates at law, to involuntary alienation for the payment of the owner's debts.

In the event of a trustee becoming bankrupt, the legal estate in the premises of which he is trustee remains vested in him, and does not pass to his assignees. If a trustee becomes a lunatic, the Lord Chancellor or the person or persons intrusted by authority of the Queen's sign-manual, may make an order for the appointment of a new trustee or new trustees.[58]

CHAPTER XIV
OF THINGS PERSONAL

We have now to discuss another species of property, which at present has a more extensive signification than it formerly had; for Courts now regard, a man's *personal property* or personalty almost with equal importance as his *realty.* Let us therefore inquire into the nature of the several species of personal property; then, into the interests which may be had in them; and lastly, as to the title by which they may be acquired and lost.

---

[57] See 39 & 40 Geo. III., c. 98, called the "Thellusson's Act," passed in consequence of the will of Mr. Thellusson, a London merchant, which directed the income of landed estates to be accumulated during the lives of all his children, grandchildren, and great-grandchildren who were living at the time of his death, for the benefit of some future descendants who should be living at the death of the survivor. The accumulated fund was computed at above £19,000,000 sterling.

[58] See Trustee Acts, 13 & 14 Vict., c. 60; 15 & 16 Vict., c. 55; 18 & 19 Vict., c. 91; 19 & 20 Vict., c. 120; also 30 & 31 Vict., c. 132, an Act to remove doubts as to the power of trustees, executors, and administrators to invest trust funds in certain securities, and to declare and amend the law relating to such investments.

Explain the Meaning of "Things Personal" as contra-distinguished from "Things Real"

Under the name of things *personal* are included all goods and chattels — terms equally applicable to interests in lands which are less than freehold — money, and other movables, and the rights and profits issuing out of them. Besides all movables, shares in canals and railways, and other similar interests, are made personal property by various Acts of Parliament; and so is funded property. The owner of an estate for a term of years possesses in law merely a chattel interest; and his leasehold estate, however long the term of years, is only part of his personal property.

Personal property in many instances is of an intangible or incorporeal nature, such as copyright, or patent right, or trade mark, as everyone has a right to enjoy, within the limits imposed by the several Copyright and other Acts, exclusive profit on the results of his intelligence and industry, or his power of invention.

By 5 & 6 Vict., c. 45,[59] the sole and exclusive liberty of printing or otherwise multiplying copies of any book is reserved for the author and his representatives for the term of his natural life and seven years afterwards; or for the term of forty-two years, whichever is the longer period. A copy must be presented, within one month after publication, to the British Museum; also within twelve months a copy must be sent to the Bodleian Library, Oxford; to the Cambridge University Library; to the Advocates' Library, Edinburgh; and to that of Trinity College, Dublin. The proprietorship must also be registered at Stationers' Hall. By that Act the same term is granted to musical composers and dramatic authors.

---

[59] As to International Copyright, see 7 & 8 Vict., c. 12; 15 & 16 Vict., c. 13: 25 & 26 Vict., c. 68; and for Colonial Copyright, 10 & 11 Vict., c. 95.

Patents for invention stand upon somewhat similar grounds as copyrights, and the rights of patentees are now regulated by 15 & 16 Vict., c. 83.

Sculptures[60] and casts are protected from being copied; as also are paintings, engravings, and photographs, &c.[61] Trade marks are protected by law,[62] as also are patterns or designs for manufactures.[63]

A qualified property may subsist in animals *ferœ naturœ per industriam hominis,* by a man's reclaiming and making them tame by art and industry, or by confining them within his own immediate power, that they cannot escape and use their natural liberty: such as deer in a park, pheasants or partridges in a cover, hares or rabbits in an enclosed warren, doves in a dovehouse, hawks that are fed by their owner, and fish in a private pond. These are no longer the property of a man than while they continue in his keeping or actual possession; but if at any time they regain their *natural* liberty, his property instantly ceases, unless they have *animum revertendi* (which is only to be known by their usual custom of returning), or unless instantly pursued by the owner.

A man may also have a qualified property in animals *ferœ naturœ propter privilegium;* that is, he may have some special privilege of hunting, taking, and killing them in exclusion of other persons. Here he has a transient property in these animals, usually called *game,* so long as they continue within his liberty, and may restrain any

[60] See Sculpture Copyright Acts, 54 Geo. III., c. 56; 13 & 14 Vict., c. 104; and 21 & 22 Vict, c. 70.
[61] Paintings Copyright Act, 25 & 26 Vict., c. 68.
[62] Trade Marks Act, 25 & 26 Vict., c. 88.
[63] Designs Act, 24 & 2S Vict., c. 73.

stranger from taking them therein; but the instant they depart into another liberty, this qualified property ceases.[64]

TITLES to *things personal* are, with few exceptions, now acquired and lost in much the same manner as the *title to realty.* As to *descent,* the feudal role still exists; that is, when the owner dies intestate, the whole of the *real estate goes* to the heir, while *things personal* are distributed amongst the next of kin.[65]

Previous to the passing of the Married. Women's Property Act (33 & 34 Vict., c. 93), personal property which belonged to a woman, was on marriage vested by act of law in the husband; but now earnings, money, or property acquired or gamed by her after the passing of this Act shall be held and settled to the wife's separate use; and personal property not exceeding £200 coming to a married woman after the passing of this Act shall belong to the wife for her separate use, and her receipts alone

---

[64] Several Acts have been passed with reference to the property in *game,* particularly 1 & 2 Win. IV., c. 32; 23 & 24 Vict., c. 90; and 24 & 25 Vict., c. 91.

[65] See Statute of Distributions, 22 & 23 Car. II., c. 10, explained by 29 Car. II., c. 3, which enacts that the surplusage of intestates' *personal* estate (except of *femes covert,* whose estates, by the principle of the common law, belong to their husbands), shall, after the expiration of one full year from the death of the intestate, be distributed in the following manner: — One-third goes to the widow of the intestate, and the residue in equal proportions to his children; or, if dead, to their representatives; that is, the lineal descendants. If there are no children or legal representatives subsisting, then a moiety shall go to the widow, and a moiety to the next of kindred, in equal degree, and their representatives; if no widow, the whole shall go to the children; if neither widow nor children, the whole shall be distributed among the next of kin, in equal degree, and their representatives; but no representatives are admitted among collaterals farther than the children of the intestate's brothers and sisters. On the failure of children, the father and mother succeed to the effects of their children who die intestate, and without wife or issue. Then if the nearest of kin of the intestate are great-uncles or aunts, first cousins and great-nephews or nieces, these being all related to the intestate in the fourth degree, will all be admitted to an equal distributive share of this estate.

shall be a good discharge for the same. Also the rents and profits of any freehold, copyhold, or customary-hold property coming to a woman married after the passing of the Act shall belong to such wife for her separate use. A married woman may now effect a policy of insurance upon her own life, or the life of her husband, for her separate use, and any married woman or woman about to be married may have any sum forming part of the public stocks and funds, not being less than £20, to which she is entitled, transferred to her own name, and the same shall be deemed to be the separate property of such woman, and the dividends paid as if she were un-married. She may also hold shares or debenture stock in a joint-stock company, or of any industrial and provident society, and the dividends and profits shall be paid to her as if she were an unmarried woman; but such investments must not be by means of moneys of her husband without his consent.

By the Married Women's Property Act, 1870, the husband shall not, by reason of any marriage which shall take place after this Act, be liable for the debts of his wife contracted before marriage, but the wife shall be liable to be sued for; and any property belonging to her for her separate use shall be liable to satisfy such debts as if she had continued unmarried.

A married woman, having separate property, is now liable to the parish for the support of her husband; also for the maintenance of her children.

A wife may acquire a property in some of her husband's goods, which shall remain to her after his death, and not go to the executors. These are called her paraphernalia, and by our law signify the apparel and ornaments of the wife, and a necessary bed suitable to her rank and degree. Jewels usually worn by her have been held to be paraphernalia, nor can the husband devise them by his *will,* though, during his lifetime, he may sell them or give them away.

Necessary apparel is protected against the claim of creditors.

Title to things personal may be also acquired by *bill of sale,* which is a grant or assignment of chattels personal. Unless a *bonâ fide* change of possession takes place, the assignment is void, not only as against the trustee of a subsequent bankruptcy of the assignor, but even against the sheriff seizing the property in execution. Statute 17 & 18 Vict., c. 36, passed to prevent fraud upon creditors by secret bills of sale of personal chattels, provides that every bill of sale must be filed in the Court of Queen's Bench, and the registry so made must be renewed every five years during the subsistence of the security.[66]

CHAPTER XV
OF CONTRACTS

We have now to inquire into the very important subject of Contracts, which may be considered as one of the species of title to things personal. In its widest and most general sense the word *contract* signifies an engagement, obligation, or compact; it may be *express* or *implied, executory* or *executed;* and there must be two or more contracting parties of sufficient ability to make a contract.

[66] See also 29 & 30 Vict., c. 96, by which the registration of bills of sale must be renewed every five years.

Define a Contract, and explain the "three" points to be contemplated in all contracts.

A *contract is* an *agreement,* or undertaking, upon *sufficient consideration,* to do, or *not to do,* a particular thing.[67]

First, then, it is an *agreement,* a mutual bargain, or convention, and therefore there must be at least *two* contracting parties of *sufficient ability* to make a contract, as where A. contracts with B. to pay him £100. A. thereby transfers a property in. such sum. to B., which property, however, is not in possession, but in action merely, and recoverable by suit at law.

A contract or agreement may be either *express* or *implied. Express* contracts are where the terms of the agreement are openly uttered and avowed at the time of the making, as to deliver an ox or ten loads of timber, or to pay a stated price for certain goods. *Implied* contracts are such as reason and justice dictate, which, therefore, the law *presumes* that every man undertakes to perform. As, if I employ a person to do any business for me, or perform any work, the law *implies* that I undertook, or contracted to pay him as much as his labour deserves; and if I do not make him amends, he has a remedy by bringing his action upon such implied promise, undertaking, or *assumpsit.* Or where a person buys an article without stipulating for the price, he is presumed to have undertaken to pay its market value or its worth.

A contract may be either *executory* or *executed.* An *executory* contract is one in which a party binds himself *to do* or *not to do* a particular thing; a contract *executed is* one in. which the *object of contract* is performed. As if A. agrees to change horses with B. and they do it immedi-

---

[67] For injuries affecting *rights* founded on contract.

ately, in which case the possession and the right are transferred, together. This is an *executed* contract; but if A. and B. agree to exchange horses next week, here the right only vests, and their reciprocal property in each other's horse is not in possession, but in action. A contract *executed* conveys a *chose in, possession;* a contract *executory* conveys only a *chose in action* — a thing in course of transmutation.

Secondly; a *sufficient consideration* is necessary to the validity of a contract.[68] A *nudum pactum (bare promise),* or agreement to do or pay anything on one side without *any* consideration on the other is totally void in law, and a man cannot be compelled to perform it: as if one man promises to give another £100; here there is nothing contracted for or given on the one side, and therefore there is nothing binding on the other. Any degree of reciprocity, however, which is held in law to be a sufficient consideration will prevent the contract from being void.

Thirdly; the *thing* agreed to be *done* or *omitted.* A contract is an agreement upon *sufficient consideration* to "*do* or *not* to do a particular thing."

These specific kinds of contracts are: — 1. By *Sale* or *Exchange.* — 2. *Bailment.* — 3. *Hiring* and *Borrowing.*

Sale or *exchange is* a transmutation of property from one man to another, in *consideration* of some price or recompense in value; for there is no sale without a recompense; there must be *quid pro quo.* If it be a commutation of goods for goods, it is an *exchange;* but if it be a transferring of goods for money, it is called a *sale.*

If a man agrees with another for goods at a certain price, he may not carry them away before he has paid for them; for it is no sale without payment, unless the contrary

[68] The *lex loci* sometimes governs contracts.

be expressly stipulated; and therefore if the vendor says the price of a beast is four pounds, and the vendee says he will give four pounds, the bargain is struck, and neither of them is at liberty to be off the bargain, provided immediate possession be tendered; but if neither the money be paid, nor the goods delivered, nor tender made, nor any subsequent agreement be entered into, it is no contract, and the owner may dispose of the goods as he pleases. If any part of the price is paid down, if it be but a penny; or any portion of the goods delivered by way of deposit, the property in the goods absolutely passes, and the vendee may recover the goods by action, as well as the vendor may the price of them.

If there be a sale of goods which are to be sent by a carrier to the purchaser, and the goods perish or sustain damage whilst *in transitu,* in the absence of *special* circumstances the rule of law applies; that is, delivery to the carrier is delivery to the consignee, who will, therefore, have to bear the loss. But if the parties agree that the vendor shall not merely deliver the goods to the carrier, but that they shall actually be delivered at their destination, and express such intention; in such a case, if the goods perish in the hands of the carrier, the vendor is not only liable for the loss, but for whatever damages may have been sustained by the purchaser in consequence of the breach of contract to deliver at the place of destination.

General rules may be modified by the *expressed* intentions of the parties. Where an offer to sell goods is made, and a letter accepting such offer, *without qualification,* is put into the post, the bargain is complete.

Where an unpaid vendor of goods has put them into the hands of a carrier to be by him conveyed and delivered to the vendee; and the vendee, or consignee, before actual delivery to him, becomes bankrupt or insolvent, the vendor, or consignor, has a right to resume possession of the goods by stopping them *in transitu;* but if, after their arrival at their place of destination, they are warehoused with the carrier, whose store the vendee uses as his own; or even if they are warehoused with the vendor himself, and rent is paid to him for them, that puts an end to the right to stop *in transitu.*[69]

Fraud destroys a contract *ab initio;* so that a fraudulent seller is precluded from insisting upon the completion of the contract, and a fraudulent purchaser gets no title.

Wilful misrepresentation to induce another to contract or to part with goods under the belief that such representation was true is not tolerated bylaw, and such misrepresentation may be alleged with a view to annulling the contract, and to compelling restitution of property transferred or money paid in pursuance of it. But where a contract for sale has intervened, preference will sometimes he given to the title of an honest purchaser over that of a vendor who has been defrauded of his goods. Also, a *bonâ fide* purchase in market overt, as a general rule, vests the property sold in the purchaser, even though stolen from the owner, unless such owner shall prosecute the thief to conviction, and obtain an order of restitution. If goods are stolen or wrongfully taken from the owner and sold *out* of market overt, his property is not altered, and he may take the goods wherever he finds them.

This deviation in favour of the contract of sale is to give security to titles honestly resting upon it, as it tends to the expansion of trade, which most flourishes when confidence is best assured.

Market overt in the country is only held on the special days for particular towns by charter or prescription; but in

---

[69] See Houston on the Law of "Stoppage In Transitu."

London every shop in which goods are exposed publicly for sale is market overt for such things as the owner professes to trade in.

But there is one species of personal chattels in which the property is not easily altered by sale without the express consent of the owner, viz., horses; for a purchaser gains no property in a horse that has been stolen, unless it be bought in a *fair* or *open* market; that is, between ten in the morning and sunset, in the public place used for such sales; and unless other requisites mentioned in the statute be duly observed. "Nor shall such sale take away the property of the owner, for if within six months after the horse is stolen he puts in his claim before some magistrate where the horse shall be found, and within forty days more proves such his property by the oath of two witnesses, he can reclaim his horse by tendering to the person in possession such price as he *bonâ fide* paid for him in market overt."

Any person suspecting his goods to have been unlawfully pawned, and satisfying a justice of the peace that there is probable ground for that suspicion, may obtain a warrant for searching the house of the person supposed to have taken them in pawn, and if on search they shall be found, and the property of the claimant proved, he shall be entitled to have them restored.[70]

Is a Warranty annexed to every Sale?

By the civil law an *implied* warranty was annexed to every sale in respect to the title of the vendor; and so, too,

[70] See 39 & 40 Geo. III., c. 99, amended by 22 & 23 Vict., c. 14; and 23 Vict., c. 21 By 35 & 36 Vict., c. 93, an Act for consolidating, with amendments, the Acts relating to Pawnbrokers in Great Britain, a discretionary power is given to the Court to allow the amount of the loan as the case may be, or any part thereof. See also Turner on the "Contract of Pawn."

in our law, a purchaser of goods and chattels may have a satisfaction from the vendor if he sells them as his own and the title proves deficient, without any express warranty for that purpose. But, with regard to the goodness of the wares so purchased, the vendor is not bound to answer, unless he expressly warrants them to be sound and good; or, unless it is proved that he knew them to be otherwise, and hath used art to disguise them; or, unless they turn out different from what he represented them to the buyer. Thus, if a man sells a horse, and espressos by warranty that it is sound, the contract is void if the horse is proved to be otherwise.

Where goods may be inspected by the buyer, and there is no fraud on the part of the seller, the maxim "*caveat emptor*" applies; the purchaser takes them at his risk, even though the defect which exists in them is latent, and not discoverable on examination.

Where goods are bought by sample, the law implies that the goods shall *reasonably* answer the specified description. If the bulk does not *reasonably* answer the description in. a commercial point of view, the seller is liable *for* the amount paid for the goods.

A *Guarantee* is a mercantile instrument, which is usually evidenced by writing, not under seal, whereby one man contracts on behalf of another an obligation to which he is made as liable as the proper and primary party. The fourth section of the Statute of Frauds enacts "that no action shall be brought whereby to charge the defendant upon any special promise to answer for the debt, default, or miscarriages of another, unless the agreement upon which action is brought, or some memorandum or note thereof, be in writing, signed by the party to be charged therewith, or some person thereunto by him lawfully authorized; if *verbal* only, no action shall be brought whereby to charge the defendant thereupon."

Bailment, from the French *bailler,* to deliver, is a delivery of goods in trust, upon a contract expressed or implied, that the trust shall be faithfully executed on the part of the baillee; as if cloth be delivered, or, legally speaking, bailed to a tailor to make a suit of clothes, he has it upon an implied contract to render it again when made up, and that in a workmanlike manner. Or, if money or goods be delivered to a carrier to be conveyed from Oxford to London, he is under a contract in law to pay, or carry them to the person appointed. Or if a debtor bail or *pawn* his goods to his creditor, the pawnee has them on the condition of restoring them on the debt being discharged. Again, if a friend deliver anything to his friend to keep for him, the receiver is bound to restore it on demand.

Bailees[71] have in certain, instances that right which is technically called a *lien* in respect of the goods committed to their charge; that is, the right of retaining the possession of a chattel from the owner until all legal claims upon it be satisfied. The rule of law is, that every person to whom a chattel has been delivered for the purpose of bestowing his labour upon it has a lien thereon, and may withhold it from the owner (in the absence, at least, of any special agreement to the contrary) until the price of the labour is paid.

The *bailment* of goods to a common *carrier* is another class. A common carrier is one who conveys the goods of applicants from place to place. If a man professes to be a carrier, the law creates for him a duty to receive goods brought to him for carriage, and he is bound to deliver them safely, and within a *reasonable* time, "except when prevented by the act of God or of the King's enemies." A

---

[71] For Larceny by bailee, see chapter on "Larceny."

carrier is not liable for damage arising from any inherent defect in goods delivered to him for conveyance by improper packing; nor is he liable for leakage. He must, however, exercise due skill and care.

The Railway and Canal Traffic Act[72] enacts, that every company shall be liable for the loss of, or injury done, to goods or chattels occasioned by the neglect or default of its servants.

Hiring and *borrowing* are also contracts by which a qualified property may be transferred to the hirer or borrower. They are both contracts whereby the possession and a transient property is transferred for a particular time or use, on condition to restore the goods so hired or borrowed as soon as the time is expired or use performed. The hirer or borrower gains a temporary property in the thing, with an implied condition "to use it and not abuse it," and the owner or lender retains a reversionary interest is the game, and acquires a new property in the price or reward.

The subject of *debt* is closely connected with that of *contract;* a debt being a legal relation which frequently arises out of a contract.

A debt by simple contract is where the contract upon which the obligation arises is neither ascertained by matter of record nor by deed or special instrument.

A debt by *specially* is where a sum of money becomes due by deed or instrument under seal; that is, by covenant, by deed of sale, or by bond or obligation.

A debt of *record* is a sum of money duo by the evidence of a court of record, when any specific sum is ad-

[72] See 17 & 16 Vict., c. 31: and 31 & 32 Vict., c. 119.

judged to be due from the defendant to the plaintiff in an action or suit at law.

Explain the Class of Written Contracts commonly used in Mercantile Transactions.

These are *Bonds* — *Bills of Exchange* — *Cheques* — *Promissory Notes* — *Bank Notes* — and certain *Contracts* of *Loans* and *Insurances.*

A *Bond* is a deed or instrument under seal, where the party from whom a security is intended to be taken declares himself bound to pay a certain sum of money to another on the day specified; but there is a condition added, that if the obligor does some particular act the obligation shall be void.

A *Bill of Exchange* is a negotiable instrument or security used among merchants and others for the more easy remittance of money from one country to another. It is in the form of an open letter of request from A. to B., desiring B. to pay a sum named therein to a third person on A's account, by which means a man at the most distant part of the world may have money remitted to him from any trading country. Thus, if A. lives in Jamaica, and owes B., who lives in England, £1,000; if C. be going from England to Jamaica, he may pay B. this £1,000, and take a bill of exchange, drawn. by B. in England upon A. in Jamaica, and receive it when he comes thither. Thus, B. receives his debt at any distance of place, by transferring it to C., who carries over his money in paper credit, without danger of robbery or loss. The person who makes the bill of exchange is called the drawer; he to whom it is written the drawee, and after acceptance by the person on whom it is drawn, the acceptor; and the third person, to whom it is payable, is called the payee; and the payee may endorse it to any other person, who becomes the payee; and thus it may be transferred to twenty persons or more before it arrives, as it is called, at *maturity*.

When a bill of exchange has been drawn, accepted, and indorsed, the person who accepted the bill is primarily and absolutely liable to pay it; the person who drew it is liable only upon the contingencies of default being made by the acceptor, and of the holder, to whom it may have been indorsed, performing certain conditions precedent to his right of suit being complete, viz., presenting the bill, and giving due notice to the drawer of the failure of the acceptor to pay it upon presentment.

Payment of the bill when refused must be demanded of the drawer without loss of time, as the holder must give the drawer notice thereof; and, if the bill has passed through many hands and been endorsed by them, the last holder, by giving notice of dishonour without *loss of time* to the endorsers, is at liberty to call on *any* or all of them to make him satisfaction, for each indorser is in the nature of a new drawer, and is a warrantor for the payment of the bill.[73]

A *Cheque* is a sort of an inland bill of exchange, drawn upon a banker, and made payable to the bearer or order. The banker is the depositary of the customer's money, which he, in compliance with usage, undertakes to pay out from time to time to the customer's order, evidenced by his cheque. The *crossing* the cheque indicates that it must be paid through a banker's house. The holder of the cheque is bound to present it for payment on the day after that on which he received it; or, if the cheque be on a banker in a distant town, the holder is bound to send it for

[73] See Common Law Procedure Act (17 & 18 Vict., c, 125). which enacts, *inter alia,* that in case of a bill of exchange or other negotiable instrument being lost, it shall be lawful for the court or judge to order that the loss of such instrument shall not be set up, provided a satisfactory indemnity be given against the claims of any other person upon such instrument.

presentment the following day. A party holding the cheque over the time specified loses all claim against the drawer, in the event of the failure of the bank.

If a banker cash a forged cheque, he, in the absence of gross negligence by his customer, must bear the loss.

A *Promissory Note,* or note of hand, is a plain and direct engagement in writing to pay a sum specified at the time therein mentioned to a person therein named, or to his order or to bearer. There are but two parties to such instrument, the maker (drawer), and the payee. Like bills of exchange in case of nonpayment by the maker, the last holder has the same remedy upon the several endorsees, observing the rules of notice as stated in respect of bills of exchange.

An ordinary *Bank-note* is a promissory note, payable to bearer on demand, passes from hand to hand by delivery, passes in currency like cash, and cannot be impugned upon proof that the note had, before coining for value into his hands, been stolen from its rightful owner.

A *Policy* of *Insurance*[74] is a contract between A. and B., that when A. pays a premium equivalent to the hazard to be incurred, B. will indemnify or insure him against a particular event then expressed. These insurances are either Life Policies, Insurances against Fire, or Marine Insurances against loss or damage by sea. As to Life Policies, by 14 Geo. III., c. 48, amended by 30 & 31 Vict., c. 144, it is enacted that no insurance shall be made on lives or any other event wherein the party insured hath no interest; and that in all policies the name of such interested party shall be inserted. Life insurances are also made available for effecting various useful objects, such as

[74] Introduced by the Lombards who settled in London in the 13th century.

making a settlement upon marriage or afterwards insuring a provision for wife and children.[75]

Bottomry is in the nature of a mortgage on a ship, when the owner or commander borrows money to enable him to carry on his voyage. This security is called a *bottomry bond.* Such bonds are allowed as valid in all trading nations, for the benefit of commerce, and as a *pretium periculi* for the extraordinary hazard run. *Respondentia,* money borrowed, not upon the vessel, but upon the goods and merchandise contained in it, which must necessarily be sold or exchanged in the course of the voyage, in which case the borrower personally is bound to answer the contract.

[75] See Government Life Annuities Acts, 10 Geo. IV., c. 24; 2 & 3 Wm. IV., c. 59. See also 27 and 28 Vict., c. 46; and 35 & 36 Vict., c. 41, an Act to amend the Life Assurance Companies Acts, 1870 & 1871.

BOOK III
PRIVATE WRONGS

CHAPTER I
REDRESS OF PRIVATE WRONGS

At the opening of the First Book, *Municipal Law* was defined as — "A rule of civil conduct, prescribed by the supreme power in a State, *commanding* what is *right* and *prohibiting* what is *wrong*." The primary objects, therefore, of the law are the *establishment* of *Rights* and the *prohibition* of *Wrongs*. Having considered the *Rights* that were *defined* and *established,* we shall now consider the *Wrongs* that are *forbidden* and *redressed* by the laws of England.

What is a Wrong, and how are "Wrongs" Divided?

All *wrongs* are a *privation* of *rights,* and they are divisible into two sorts or species, — *Private Wrongs* and *Public Wrongs*. Private wrongs, as formerly stated, are the infringement or privation of the private or civil rights belonging to individuals, and are therefore termed "*civil injuries.*" *Public Wrongs* are the breach and violation of public rights and duties which affect the whole community, and are distinguished by the harsher appellations of *crimes* and *misdemeanors.*

The more effectually to accomplish the REDRESS of *private injuries* courts of justice are instituted in every civilized country in order to protect the weak from the insults of the stronger, by expounding and enforcing those laws by which RIGHTS are *defined* and WRONGS *prohibited.*

The *Redress* of *Private* "Wrongs is distributed into three several species: — 1. That which is obtained by the *mere act* of the *parties themselves.* — 2. That which is effected by the *mere act* and *operation* of *law.* — 3. That redress which arises from *suit* or *action* in courts, which consists in a conjunction of the other two, the *act* of the parties *co-operating with the act of law.*

Of the first sort, or that which arises from the sole act of the injured party, is the DEFENCE OF ONESELF; or the mutual and *reciprocal defence* of such as stand in the relations of HUSBAND and WIFE, PARENT and CHILD, MASTER and SERVANT. In these cases, if the party himself, or any of these relations be forcibly attacked in person or property, it is lawful for him to repel force by force, and the *breach* of the peace which happens is chargeable upon him who began the affray; care must, however, be taken that resistance does not exceed the bounds of mere *defence* and *prevention,* otherwise the defender himself would become an aggressor. Self-defence is the "primary law of nature," and therefore it is not taken away by the law of society.

II. RECAPTION or *reprisal* is another species of remedy by the *mere act of the party* injured. This happens when any one has deprived another of his property in goods or chattels personal, or wrongfully detains one's wife, child, or servant; in which case the owner of the goods, the husband, parent, or master may lawfully claim and retake them wherever found, so it be not in a riotous manner, or attended with a breach of the peace. If, for instance, my horse is taken away, and I find him on a common, at a fair, or in a public inn, I may lawfully seize him to my own use; but I am not justified in breaking open a private stable, or entering on the grounds of a third person to take him; but must have recourse to an action at law. If feloniously stolen, a warrant may be obtained from a magistrate for its restitution.

As *recaption* is a remedy given to the party himself for an *injury* to his *personal* property, so a remedy of the same kind for injuries to *real* property is permitted by *entry* on lands and tenements where another person, without any right, has taken possession thereof. This depends in some measure on like reasons with the former; and like that, too, the entry must be made peaceably and without force.

III. ABATEMENT, or *removal* of a *nuisance,* is another species of remedy by the act of the party injured. Whatsoever unlawfully annoys or does damage to another is a *nuisance,* and such nuisance may be *abated;* that is, taken away or removed by the party aggrieved thereby, so that he commits no riot in doing it. The reason why the law allows this summary method of doing oneself justice is, because injuries of this kind require an immediate remedy, and cannot wait for the slow process of the ordinary forms of justice; but it is seldom advisable to pursue this course. The proper form of remedy is by *action on the case;* or an application to a court of equity for an *injunction* to restrain the wrong-doer from committing a nuisance, if one is threatened; or, to abate and remove it if committed.

IV. DISTRAINING *(districtio)* is another case in which the law allows a man to be his own avenger; that is, taking a personal chattel out of the possession of the wrong-doer into the custody of the party injured, to procure a satisfaction for the wrong committed. The usual injury for which a distress may now be taken is that of non-payment of any kind of rent in arrear. Formerly, as a general rule, all chattels *personal* were liable to be distrained for rent; but *now,* by the "Lodgers' Goods Protection Act,"[76] if any superior landlord shall levy a distress on any furniture, goods, or chattels of any lodger for arrears of rent due to such superior landlord, such lodger may apply to a justice of the peace for an order for the restoration of such goods. A horse standing in a smith's shop to be shod, or in a common inn; cloth at a tailor's house to be made up; workmen's tools; and corn sent to a mill or a market are protected and privileged for the benefit of trade, and are supposed, in common presumption, not to belong to the owner of the house, but to his customers.

With regard to the stranger's beasts which are found on the tenant's lands, the following distinctions are, however, taken: — If they are put in by consent of the owner of the beasts they are distrainable immediately afterwards for rent in arrear by the landlord. So, also, if the stranger's cattle break the fences and commit a trespass by coming on the land, they are distrainable immediately by the lessor, as a punishment to the owner of the beasts for the wrong committed through his negligence; but if the lands were not sufficiently fenced so as to keep out cattle, the landlord cannot distrain them till they have been *levant et couchant (levantes et cubantes* — rising up and lying down) on the land, which in general is held to be one night at least; and then the law presumes that the owner may have noticed whether his cattle have strayed, and it is his own negligence not to have taken them away. If the lessor or his tenant were bound to repair the fences and did not, and thereby the cattle escaped into their grounds without the negligence or default of the owner, in this case, though the cattle may have been *levant* and *couchant,* yet they are not distrainable for rent till actual notice is given to the owner that they are there, and he neglects to remove them;

---

[76] See 34 & 35 Vict., c. 79, an Act to protect the goods of lodgers against distresses for rent due to the superior landlord.

for the law will not suffer the landlord to take advantage of his own or his tenant's wrong.

A *distress* cannot be made ill the night; that is, after sunset and before sunrise, except in the case of cattle damage *feasant,* otherwise they might escape.

Distresses must be proportioned to the things distrained; for if a man takes an unreasonable distress for rent in arrear, he shall be heavily amerced for the same. The remedy for excessive distresses is by a *special action.*

By 2 & 3 Vict., c. 47, s. 67, any constable may stop and detain all carts employed in removing furniture between the hours of eight in the evening and six in the morning, or whenever the constable has good grounds for suspecting a removal for the evasion of the payment of rent.

When the distress is taken, the next consideration is the disposal of it, for which purpose the things distrained must, in the first place, be carried to some pound and there impounded by the taker. In cases of distress for rent, to prevent inconvenience to the tenant by the removal of the things distrained, a person is usually put into possession of them on the premises, who is paid by the tenant according to a recognized scale. In either case they are then considered to be in the custody of the law.

Under the recent statutes,[77] horses, cattle, and sheep distrained must be supplied with food by the distrainor; or, if confined without sufficient food and water for more than twelve hours, may be supplied therewith by any person at the cost of the owner, and the thing distrained may even be sold for reimbursement of the expenses thus incurred.

---

[77] See 12 ft 18 Vict., c. 67, amended by 17 & 18 Vict., c. 60.

In all cases of distress for rent, if the tenant or owner do not, within five days after the distress is taken, and notice of the cause thereof given him, replevy the same with sufficient security, the distrainor shall cause the same to be appraised by appraisers, and sell the same towards satisfaction of the rent and charges, paying the overplus, if any, to the owner himself.

V. REPLEVIN *(replegiare;* that is, to take back the pledge) is when a person distrained upon applies to have the distress returned into his own possession upon giving good security, by a replevin bond, to try the right of taking it in a suit at law; and, if that be determined against him, to return the cattle or goods once more into the hands of the distrainor. This policy is still recognized; but recent statutes[78] have altered the practice. Any *action of replevin* may now be brought in the county court or in a superior court, and the registrar of the county court of the district is empowered to approve of replevin bonds, to grant replevins, and to issue all necessary process in relation thereto. An action of replevin commenced in the county court may be removed by the defendant into a superior court by *certiorari,* security not exceeding £150 being given that the defendant will defend the action.

The seizure of *heriots,* when due on the death of a tenant of copyhold land, is also another species of self-remedy, not unlike the remedy by distress for rent. Thus a heriot being, according to the custom of the manor, the *render of* the best beast or other chattel to the lord of the manor on the death of the tenant, the lord may seize upon that chattel at the death of the tenant; the thing claimed being frequently of such a nature as might be out of the reach of the law before any action could be brought.

---

[78] See 19 & 20 Vict., c. 108, s. 120; and 23 & 24 Vict., c. 126, s. 22.

Explain the "Redress" of Injuries by the Joint Act of all the Parties.

They are confined to two, viz., *Accord* and *Arbitration.*

ACCORD is a satisfaction agreed upon between the party injuring and the party injured, which, when performed, is a bar of all actions upon this account. As, if a man contract to build a house or deliver a horse, and fail in it; this is an injury for which the sufferer may have his remedy by action; but if the party injured accepts a sum of money or other thing as a satisfaction, this is a redress of that injury, and entirely takes away the right of action.

ARBITRATION is where the parties, injuring and injured, submit all matters in dispute, concerning any personal chattels or personal wrong, to the judgment of two or more *arbitrators,* who are to decide the controversy; and if they do not agree, it is usual to add, that another person be called in as *umpire, to* whose sole judgment it is then referred; or frequently, there is only one arbitrator originally appointed. The decision in any of these cases — after a full investigation of all the facts and circumstances of the case, and examination of witnesses on oath if necessary — must be in writing, and is then called an *award;* and the question is thereby as fully determined, and the right transferred or settled, as it could have been by the agreement of the parties or the judgment of a court of law. The right to real property could not formerly pass by a mere award; but an arbitrator may now award a conveyance or a release of land: and it will be a breach of the arbitration bond to refuse compliance. For, though originally the submission to arbitration used to be by word or by deed, yet both of these being revocable in their nature, it is now become the practice to enter into mutual bonds, with condition to abide by the award or arbitration of the arbitrators or umpire therein named, or in default thereof to pay a certain penalty; and which submission, if in writing, is now usually made a *rule* of a court of a competent jurisdiction, which will enforce compliance with the award if necessary. Experience having shown the great use of these peaceable and domestic tribunals, especially in settling matters of account and other mercantile transactions which are difficult and almost impossible to be adjusted on a trial at law, the Legislature has now established the use of them, as well in controversies where causes are depending, as in those where no action is brought.[79]

What are the Remedies for Injuries by the mere Operation of Law?

The remedies for *Private Wrongs* which are effected by the mere operation of the law are principally these: — 1. *Retainer.* — 2. *Set-off.* — 3. *Remitter.*

First, then, as to RETAINER: — If a person indebted to another makes a creditor his executor; or, if such creditor obtains letters of administration to his debtor, in these cases the law gives him a remedy for his debt, by allowing him to *retain* so much as will pay himself before any other creditors whose debts are of *equal degree* with his own. This is a remedy by mere act of law and grounded upon this reason; that the executor cannot, without an apparent absurdity, commence an action against himself as representative of the deceased to recover that which is due to him in his own private capacity; but, having the whole personal estate in his hands, so much as is sufficient to answer his own demand is, by operation of law, applied to

---

[79] See Arbitration Acts, 9 & 10 Wm. III., c. 15; 3 & 4 Win. IV., c. 42; 14 & 15 Vict., c. 99, s. 16; 17 & 18 Vict., c. 125, ss. 3-17, also as to Joint-Stock Companies, 25 & 26 Vict., c. 96, ss. 72-73; as to Masters and Workmen, 5 Geo. IV., c. 96; 30 & 31 Vict., c. 105; as to Railway Companies, 22 & 23 Vict., c. 59.

that particular purpose. The doctrine of *retainer* is therefore the necessary consequence of that other doctrine of the law, the priority of such creditor who first commences his action: but the executor shall not retain his own debt, in prejudice to those of a higher degree; for the law only puts him in the same situation as if he had sued himself as executor and recovered his debt, which he never could be supposed to have done while debts of a higher nature subsisted. Neither shall one executor be allowed to retain his own debt in prejudice to that of his co-executor in equal degree, but both shall be discharged in proportion.

2. SET-OFF is a defence created by stat. 2 Geo. II., c. 22, previously to which relief was only obtainable by resorting to a court of equity, and is a right which exists where there are cross-demands between two persons. It can only be pleaded where there are mutual debts between plaintiff and defendant due in the same right. A set-off cannot be maintained in respect of a debt barred by the Statute of Limitations, which limits the time to recover a simple debt to a period of six years.[80]

3. REMITTER is where he who has the true property, or *jus proprietatis* in lands, but is out of possession thereof, and afterwards obtains possession by a defective title. In this case he is remitted, or sent back, by operation of law to his ancient and more certain title. The right of entry which he has gained by a bad title shall be annexed to his own inherent good one, and his defeasible estate shall be utterly defeated and annulled by the instantaneous act of law without his participation or consent. As, if A. disseises B.; that is, turns him out of possession, and dies leaving a son C.; hereby the estate descends to C., the son of A., and B. is barred from entering thereon till he proves his right in an action. If afterwards C., the heir of the disseisor,

[80] See 21 Jac. I., c. 16.

makes a lease for life to D., with remainder to B., and D. dies; hereby the remainder accrues to B., the disseissee, who, thus gaining a new freehold by virtue of the remainder, which is a bad title, is by act of law *remitted in* or of his former and surer estate; for he hath hereby gained a new right of possession, to which the law immediately annexes his ancient right of property. To every remitter there are regularly these incidents — an ancient right and a new defeasible estate of freehold uniting in one and the same person, which defeasible estate must be *cast upon* the tenant, not gained by his own act or negligence.

CHAPTER II
COURTS IN GENERAL[81]

The next and principal object of our inquiries is — *Redress by Action or Suit in Court,* wherein the act of the parties and the act of law co-operate; the act of the parties being necessary to set the law in motion, and the process of the law being in general the only instrument by which the parties are enabled to procure certain and adequate redress. Before treating of such remedy let us first consider the nature of Courts in general, and afterwards inquire as to the several species of Courts, the jurisdiction of each, and the method of obtaining the redress which they respectively afford.

---

[81] Lord Selborne's Judicature Bill, now before Parliament, proposes to merge in one law of England the divided and often antagonistic doctrines of Common Law and Equity. This will alter the present mode of procedure in the Courts. The object of the Bill is to enable a suitor to obtain his remedy in one court, instead of being left in doubt, as at present, whether to seek his relief in a Court of Common Law, the Court of Chancery, or in the Court of Admiralty.

Define a Court, and explain the difference between a Court of Record, and a Court "not" of Record.

A *Court* is defined to be a place wherein justice is judicially administered; either in *civil* cases, between individuals; or in *criminal* offences, between the Sovereign representing the State and the people.

A Court of *Record* is that where the acts and judicial proceedings are enrolled for a perpetual memorial and testimony. Courts of Record are the Queen's courts in right of her Crown and royal dignity. Courts *not of Record* are courts of inferior jurisdictions, such as the Court Baron, incident to a manor, where the proceedings are not formally recorded. Every Court of Record has authority to fine and imprison for contempt of its authority; but courts *not* of record have not this power, unless given by express Act of Parliament.

In every court there must be at least three constituent parts — the *actor, reus* and *judex.* The *actor* or *plaintiff,* who complains of an injury done; the *reus* or *defendant,* who is called upon to make satisfaction for it; and *the judex* or judicial power, which is to examine the truth of the fact, to determine the law arising upon that fact; and if any injury appears to have been done, to ascertain, and by its officers to apply the remedy. It is also usual in the superior courts to have attorneys and advocates, or counsel, as assistants. Any man, however, may prosecute or defend his own suit or action.

An attorney-at-law; or, as he is called in the courts of equity, a solicitor, is one put in the place or stead of another to manage his matters of law or equity, as the case may be. The duty of an attorney or solicitor towards his client flows from his *retainer;* and, if gross negligence is proved against him in conducting the case, he is responsible for the same.

Of advocates or counsel there are two species or degrees — barristers[82] and serjeants-at-law. From time to time members of the outer bar are selected to be her Majesty's Counsel, the two principal of whom are called her Attorney-General and her Solicitor-General.

A barrister is incapacitated from making a contract with his client, but takes upon himself an office or duty, in which not merely his client, but the court and the public at large have an interest. He is not answerable for any matter spoken by him relative to the cause in hand and suggested in his client's instructions; but if he states an untruth of his own invention, or even upon his instructions, if it be irrelevant to the case, he is liable to an action at the suit of the party injured.

Counsel are instructed by attorneys-at-law or solicitors, it being considered not in accordance with the etiquette of the English Bar for counsel to communicate with the parties themselves except in the presence of an attorney or solicitor.

CHAPTER III
PUBLIC COURTS OF COMMON LAW AND EQUITY

Let us now investigate the several species and distinctions of Courts of Justice of public and general jurisdiction throughout the country, constituted for the *redress* of civil injuries — the jurisdiction of each respectively,

[82] See recent stat., 35 & 36 Vict.. c. 94, an Act to amend the law relating to the appointment of Revising Barristers.

and the procedure appropriated therein for the redress of *civil* injuries.[83]

Explain (beginning with the lowest, and gradually ascending to the highest) the several species of "public" Courts by which justice is "civilly" administered in this country.

I. Court of Piepoudre.

The lowest, and at the same time the most expeditious court of justice known to the law of England, is the Court of PIEPOUDRE. It is a court of record, incident to every fair and market, where the market is included in the fair, of which the steward of him who owns or has the toll of the fair or market is the judge; and its jurisdiction extends to administer justice for all commercial injuries done in that very fair or market, and not in any preceding one; so that the injury must be done, complained of, heard, and determined within the compass of one and the same day, unless the fair continues longer. The court hath cognizance of all matters of contract that can possibly arise within the precinct of that fair, and the plaintiff must make oath that the cause of action arose there.

This court has now all but fallen into disuse.

II. The Court-Baron.

The COURT-BARON is a court incident to every manor in the kingdom, and is holden by the steward. This court is of two natures; the one is a customary court, appertaining entirely to the copyholders, in which their copyhold estates are transferred by surrender and admittance, and other matters transacted relative to their tenures only; the

[83] Those of a *criminal* jurisdiction we shall reserve for the Fourth Book, when treating of *criminal* law.

other is a court of common law, and it is the court of the barons, by which name the freehold tenants were sometimes called, who owe suit and service to the manor, the steward being rather the registrar than the judge. This latter court has now fallen into almost entire disuse.

III. A Hundred Court.

A HUNDRED Court is only a larger court-baron, being held for all the inhabitants of a particular hundred, instead of a manor. The free suitors are here also the judges and the steward the registrar, as in the case of a court-baron. Tills court has also fallen into disuse.

IV. The County Court.

The COUNTY COURT is a tribunal incident to the jurisdiction of a sheriff, and still exists; but from its dilatory and expensive proceedings, the *judicial* business has been transferred to the new County Courts, established by 9 & 10 Vict., c. 95, and by statutes subsequently passed. The alterations made by the County Court Extension Act of 1867 (30 & 31 Vict.)[84] are important both as relates to common law and equity jurisprudence, and as to costs.

The jurisdiction of these new county courts includes all personal actions or contracts, or otherwise where the *debt, damage* or *demand* does not exceed £50, whether on a balance or otherwise or after an admitted set-off. They may accordingly take cognizance of an action upon a bill of exchange or promissory note or for the recovery of goods *in specie* within the value of £50; but not of an action upon a judgment recovered in a superior court, nor where the claim is for beer consumed on the premises where sold or supplied, or money lent for obtaining the same.

---

[84] See also 32 Vict., c. 71.

A plaintiff cannot divide his cause of action for the purpose of bringing two or more suits in a county court, but he may abandon the excess, and recover to an amount not exceeding £50.

The court may now entertain actions of ejectment where neither the value of the lands, tenements, or hereditaments claimed, nor the rent payable in respect thereof, exceeds the sum of £20 yearly; and may also try cases where the title comes in question when neither the value of the land nor the rent of property exceeds £20 yearly.

The defendant, in actions brought in a superior court for malicious prosecution, illegal arrest, illegal distress, assault, false imprisonment, libel, slander, seduction, or other actions of tort, may, under certain circumstances, such as inability to pay costs, obtain an order remitting the cause to be tried in a county court, where the costs are much less.

An appeal in actions of ejectment and in actions of title is now *allowed,* if the judge shall think it reasonable and proper that such appeal should be permitted.

If in any action commenced after the passing of this Act in any of her Majesty's superior courts of record, the plaintiff shall recover a sum not exceeding £20 if the action is founded on contract, or £10 if founded on tort, whether by verdict, judgment by default, or on demurrer, or otherwise, he shall not be entitled to any costs of suit unless the judge certify on the record that there was sufficient reason for bringing such action in such superior court, or unless the court or a judge at chambers shall, by rule or order, allow such costs.

Where any action or suit is brought in any other court than the superior courts of law, which could have been brought in a county court, and the verdict recovered is for a less sum than £10, the plaintiff shall not recover from the defendant a greater amount of costs than he would have been allowed if the action or suit had been brought in such county court, unless the judge shall certify that the action or suit was a fit one to be brought in such other court.[85]

The *equitable* jurisdiction of the county court at present extends to suits by creditors, legatees, whether specific or residuary; devisees in trust or otherwise; heirs at law or next of kin, in which, the personal or real, or personal and real estate, against or for an account or administration of which the demand may be made does not exceed in amount or value £500. — Suits for the execution of trusts in which the trust estate does not exceed in amount or value £500. — Suits for foreclosure or redemption, or for enforcing any charge or lien, where the mortgage, charge, or lien does not exceed in amount the like sum. — Suits for specific performance of, or for the reforming, delivering up, or cancelling any agreement for the sale, purchase, or lease of any property where, in the case of a sale or purchase, the purchase money, or in case of a lease, the value of the property does not exceed £500. — Proceedings under any of the Trustees' Belief or Trustee Acts, in which the trust estate or fund to which the proceeding relates does not exceed in amount or value £500. — Proceedings relating to the maintenance or advancement of infants in which the property of the infant does not exceed in amount or value £500. — Any suit for the dissolution or winding-up of a partnership in which the whole property, stock, and credits of such partnership does not exceed in amount or value £500. — Proceedings for orders in the nature of injunctions, where the same are requisite for granting relief in any matter in which jurisdiction is given by 28 & 29 Vict., c. 99, to the county court, or for stay of

---

[85] See County Courts Acts Amendment, 30 & 31 Vict., c. 142, s. 23.

proceedings at law to recover any debt provable under a decree for the administration of an estate made by the court to which the application for the order to stay proceedings is made.

In all these suits and matters the judges and officers of county courts have respectively the general powers and authorities of the Court of Chancery.

The practice in equity of the county court is regulated by certain rules and orders in pursuance of the Act.[86]

The suit is commenced by filing a plaint in Equity, whereupon a summons is issued to the defendant to appear and submit to judgment.

Proceedings are generally instituted in the county court within the district of which the defendants, or any, or either of them may reside or carry on business.

The mode of removing a cause from the jurisdiction of the county court to that of a superior court is by writ of *certiorari.* By 9 & 10 Vict., c. 95, a cause may be thus removed when the debt or damage claimed exceeds £5, by leave of a judge of one of the superior courts, but upon such terms as he shall deem fit to impose; and even if the sum does not exceed £5, by 19 & 20 Vict., c. 108, the cause may be removed to a superior court, the required security being given as the judge in the exercise of his discretion may impose. This occurs when difficult questions of law may arise in the action or suit.

The judges, who have been barristers of not less than seven years' standing, are appointed by the Lord Chancellor, and are removable by him for inability.

These courts are usually held once or twice a month in the several districts and counties for which they have

[86] See 30 & 31 Vict., c. 142.

been appointed, and each court is considered a court of record.

SUPERIOR COURTS OF COMMON LAW.

The Court of Queen's Bench.

The COURT OF QUEEN'S BENCH, so called because the Sovereign used formerly to sit there in person, is the supreme court of common law in the kingdom, consisting of a chief justice and five puisne judges, who are by their office the sovereign conservators of the peace, and supreme coroners of the land. This court is the remnant of the *Aula Regia,* a court which in the middle ages accompanied the King wherever he went. The actual jurisdiction of the Queen's Bench is supreme. It keeps all inferior jurisdictions within their due bounds, and may either remove their proceedings to be determined by itself, or prohibit their progress below by a *writ* of *prohibition.* It superintends all civil corporations in the kingdom; it commands magistrates and others to do what their duty requires, in every case where there is no other specific remedy; it protects the liberty of the subject by speedy and summary interposition by writ of *mandamus;* it takes notice both of criminal and civil causes, the former in what is termed the crown side or crown office, the latter in the plea side of the court. An appeal from this court lies by *writ* of *error,* or *appeal,* to the Court of Exchequer Chamber.

Court of Common Pleas.

The COURT OF COMMON PLEAS or Common Bench is a court of record, and is presided over by a chief justice and five puisne judges. Its jurisdiction is altogether confined to civil matters, having no cognizance in criminal cases, and is concurrent with that of the Queen's Bench and Exchequer in personal actions and ejectments. By 31 & 32 Vict., c. 125 — the Parliamentary Elections' Act,

1868 — petitions against elections or returns are to be presented to the Court of Common Pleas. It is also the court of appeal from the decisions of revising barristers under 6 & 7 Vict., c. 18. An appeal from a judgment in this court lies by *writ* of *error,* or *appeal,* to the Court of Exchequer Chamber.

The Court of Exchequer.

The COURT OF EXCHEQUER consists of two departments; the first being the office of the receipt of the Exchequer, for collection of the royal revenue; and the second, the plea or common-law side, which administers redress in all personal actions between subject and subject, as in the Courts of Common Pleas and Queen's Bench; and in matters of revenue at the suit of the law officers of the Crown. It is a court of record, and is presided over by a lord chief baron and five puisne barons.

The Court of Exchequer formerly exercised an extensive equity jurisdiction, but by stat. 5 Vict., c. 5, its equity jurisdiction was transferred to the Court of Chancery. Proceedings in error, or on appeal, may be taken from this court into the Court of Exchequer Chamber.

The Court of Exchequer Chamber.

The COURT OF EXCHEQUER CHAMBER is a court of appeal to correct the errors of other jurisdictions. The present constitution, altered from its ancient one, was formed in 1828 by 11 Geo. IV., and I Wm. IV., c. 70. In it the judgments of the superior courts of common law, in all suits whatever, are — upon proceedings in error of law, or on appeal, being instituted — subject to revision by the judges of the other two courts sitting collectively as a court of error for that purpose. From the decision of this court proceedings in error may be taken to the House of Lords.

Court of Chancery.

The COURT OF CHANCERY consists of a court of common law as well as a court of equity. As a court of common law it is a court of *record,* but now seldom resorted to. Its equity jurisdiction in matters of civil property is by much the most important of any of the superior and original courts of justice. It has its name of Chancery, *cancellaria;* from the judge who presides. The Lord Chancellor, *cancellarius,* is so termed a *cancellando,* from having the power to cancel the Queen's letters patent when granted contrary to law, which is the highest point of his jurisdiction. He is appointed by the mere delivery of the Great Seal by the Sovereign into his custody, without writ or patent, and is superior in point of precedency to every temporal lord.

The Lord Chancellor is the highest judicial officer in the kingdom. He appoints all justices of the peace, is a Privy Councillor by his office, and prolocutor of the House of Lords by prescription. He is visitor in right of the Crown of all hospitals and colleges of royal foundation, and patron of all the Queen's livings under the value of twenty marks per annum in the Queen's books; he is the guardian of infants, idiots, and lunatics, and has the general superintendence of all charitable uses in the kingdom.

The equitable jurisdiction of the Court of Chancery particularly relates to *fraud, trust, accident,* or *mistake,* and matters of account. Equity takes care that a right shall be actually enjoyed, and with this view will interfere to prevent a violation of the true right, which is usually effected by injunction. The court will at all times restrain the infringement of a patent of invention, the counterfeiting of a trade-mark, and the piracy of a copyright. The Court of Chancery also rectifies the defects of the common law, by extending relief to those rights of property which the law does not recognize, and by giving more ample and distributive redress than the ordinary tribunals afford.

As component parts of the equity jurisdiction in Chancery there are, in addition to the Lord Chancellor's Court, other tribunals, presided over by separate judges: —

1. The *Lords Justices'* Court, which is a court of appeal. It is composed of two judges, sometimes sitting with the Lord Chancellor when a full court of appeal is necessary. From a decision of the Lords Justices an appeal lies to the House of Lords.

2. The *Master of the Rolls,* an ancient officer appointed originally only for the superintendence of all *writs* and records appertaining to the common-law department; but who sat as a subordinate judge of the Court of Chancery on its equity side in a separate court. He is now, by statute 1 & 2 Vict., c. 94, invested with the custody and superintendence of all the public records of the kingdom which are in process of being collected together. The Master of the Rolls and the *three Vice-Chancellors* are the judges before whom all suits in the Court of Chancery are commenced, and from their decisions appeals are taken to the Lord Chancellor or Lords Justices. An appeal from a decree or order of the Court of Chancery, if *duly enrolled,* lies to the House of Lords.

The Judicial Committee of the Privy Council.

This tribunal has of late years been constituted what is now, and is still more likely to be, a most important and efficient court of justice. It consists of the Lord President of the Council, the Lord Chancellor, such members of the Council as shall from time to time hold certain judicial offices enumerated in the Act, and other paid members.[87] This court entertains appeals from our colonies and dependencies, and when it has decided upon any case it reports its opinion to the Sovereign for approval and confirmation.

The House of Lords.

The HOUSE OF LORDS, consisting of the Peers of the realm, which is the supreme court of judicature in the kingdom, has no original jurisdiction over causes, but jurisdiction only upon appeals and writs of error, to rectify any injustice or mistake of the law committed by the courts in the United Kingdom. To such authority this august tribunal succeeded upon the dissolution of the *Aula Regia;* for as the Barons of Parliament were constituent members of that court, it followed that the right of receiving appeals and superintending all other jurisdictions still remained in the residue of that assembly, from which every other great court was derived. Hence the House of Lords, as a general rule, is a tribunal of appeal in all causes of common law or equity commenced in any court in the United Kingdom; and from whose judgment no further appeal is permitted.

In appeals from the common law courts all the judges of the Courts of Queen's Bench, Common Pleas, and Exchequer are sometimes summoned to attend, and advise their lordships upon points of law.

Courts of Assize and Nisi Prius.

The COURTS of ASSIZE and NISI PRIUS act as collateral auxiliaries to the Courts of Queen's Bench, Common Pleas, and Exchequer. They are composed of two or more

---

[87] See 5 & 6 Vict., c. 45; 7 & 8 Vict., c. 12; and 34 & 35 Vict., c. 91, a recent Act to make further provision for the despatch of business by the Judicial Committee of the Privy Council.

commissioners, who are twice or oftener in every year sent by a special commission of the Crown into several counties of England and Wales (except London and Middlesex, where courts of *Nisi Prius* are holden in and after every term), to administer justice in the several counties, by trying by a jury matters of fact which are then under dispute.

The judges usually make their circuits in the respective vacations after Hilary and Trinity Terms, and sit by virtue of four several commissions, issued by the clerks of the Assize: — 1. The Commission of the Peace. — 2. *Oyer* and *Terminer*. — 3. General Gaol Delivery. — 4. *Nisi Prius,* which empowers the judges to try all questions of fact issuing out of the courts of Westminster that are then ripe for trial by jury.

There are in all Eight Circuits, viz. — Northern Circuit; Home Circuit; Western Circuit; Oxford Circuit; Midland Circuit; Norfolk Circuit; North Wales Circuit; South Wales Circuit.

The judges preside simultaneously in the civil and criminal courts; but the judge who takes the civil side in one county takes the criminal side in the next, and so on alternately throughout the circuit.

Explain the Three other Courts of general jurisdiction recently established, viz., the "Court of Bankruptcy;" the "Court of Probate;" the "Court of Divorce and Matrimonial Causes."

I. The Court of Bankruptcy.

The courts and tribunals by which the laws relating to bankruptcy in England have been administered from the time of the first Bankruptcy Act in the reign of James I., have been multitudinous. Different legislative provisions were enacted from time to time, with more or less severity. They were all, however, consolidated by Act 1 & 2 Wm. IV., c. 56; and subsequently by 5 & 6 Vict., c. 122.

The recent Bankruptcy Act, 82 & 33 Vict., c. 71, cited as "The Bankruptcy Act, 1869," now governs the proceedings in bankruptcy.[88]

The Act, *inter alia,* provides for the equal division of the property of the debtor amongst his creditors without delay. This division is conducted and managed by the creditors themselves, either under the immediate supervision of the Court of Bankruptcy, or by process of *liquidation,* which does not entail upon the creditors such extended resort to the court.

The new Act constitutes two distinct jurisdictions: —

1. THE LONDON DISTRICT.

2. THE COUNTRY DISTRICT.

The *London Bankruptcy District* comprises the City of London and its liberties, and all places situated within the Metropolitan county court districts. The *Country* or *Local* Bankruptcy Courts are now the county courts of the district in which the bankrupt resides or carries on his business.

The *London Bankruptcy Court* consists of a judge, called the Chief Judge in Bankruptcy, now one of the vice-chancellors, and the officers of the court, consisting of not more than four registrars, clerks, ushers, and other subordinate officers.

---

[88] See 32 & 33 Vict., c. 83, an Act to provide for the winding up of the business of the late Court for the relief of insolvent debtors in England, and to repeal enactments relating to insolvency, bankruptcy, imprisonment for debt, and matters connected therewith — 33 & 34 Vict., c. 76, an Act to facilitate the arrest of absconding debtors — 34 & 35 Vict., c. 50, an Act for disqualifying Bankrupts from sitting or voting in the House of Lords.

The London Court of Bankruptcy is now a court of law and equity and a court of record, and the chief judge has all the powers, jurisdiction, and privileges of the judges of the superior courts of common law, or a judge of the Court of Chancery. He is also empowered to alter, reverse, or confirm any order of a local bankruptcy court on appeal, in respect of a matter of fact or law.

All persons, traders and non-traders, and members of Parliament of either House, may now be adjudged bankrupts whose debt, or joint debts, amount to a *liquidated* sum of £50 and upwards; but before a petition can be presented, the debtor must have committed one of the acts or defaults which are constituted *acts of bankruptcy:* — 1. Making a conveyance or assignment of all his property for the benefit of his creditors generally. — 2. Making a fraudulent conveyance, gift, delivery, or transfer of his property, or any part of it.[89] — 3. Doing an act with intent to defeat or delay his creditors. — 4. Filing, in a manner prescribed by the court, a declaration that he is unable to pay his debts. — 5. Having execution levied by seizure and sale of his goods for payment of a debt of £50 or upwards. — 6. Having neglected to pay or compound the petitioner's debt.

The Act also contains provisions for liquidating the affairs of a debtor by arrangement, otherwise than in bankruptcy.

When so adjudged by the court, upon the petition of a creditor or creditors, all the property of the bankrupt, whether real or personal, vests in the trustee or trustees appointed by the creditor or creditors with the important powers of — Receiving and deciding upon proof of

---

[89] For protection of creditors from sales of a secret and fraudulent character, see 17 & 18 Vict., c. 86, called "The Bills of Sale Act, 1854"; also 29 & 30 Vict., c. 96, explained at p. 178,

debts — Carrying on the business of the bankrupt for the beneficial winding-up of the same — Bringing or defending actions, suits, or other legal proceedings relating to the property — Selling all the property of the bankrupt by public auction or private sale — Giving receipts for money received, which receipts shall effectually discharge the person from all responsibility in respect of the application of such moneys.

When the bankruptcy is closed or during its continuance the bankrupt may, with the assent of the creditors, apply to the court for an *order* of *discharge;* but the order of discharge will not be granted unless it is proved to the court that a dividend of not less than 10s. in the pound has been paid out of the property, or might have been paid, except through the negligence or fraud of the trustee, or under such circumstances for which the bankrupt cannot justly be held responsible.

In case the bankrupt does not obtain his *discharge,* no portion of a debt provable under a bankruptcy shall be enforced against his property until after three years from the close of the bankruptcy. And if, during that time the bankrupt pay to his creditors such additional sum as, with the dividend paid out of his property, amounts to 10s. in the pound, he will be entitled to his discharge. If at the expiration of that period he has not obtained his discharge, any balance remaining unpaid of any debt proved in the bankruptcy will be deemed a *subsisting judgment debt,* capable of being enforced against the debtor's property, but subject to the rights of persons becoming creditors after the close of the bankruptcy.

By the Debtors' Act, 1869, no person can, after the first of January, 1870, be arrested or imprisoned for making default in payment of a sum of money, with certain exceptions, thus specified: —

1. Default in payment of a penalty.

2. Any sum recoverable summarily before a justice of the peace.

3. Default of a trustee ordered by a court of equity to pay any sum in his possession or under his control.

4. Default by an attorney or solicitor in payment of costs when ordered to pay the same; or for misconduct.

5. Default in payment for the benefit of creditors of salary or other income ordered to be paid by a court of bankruptcy.

6. Default in payment of sums ordered.

All persons may be committed to prison in pursuance of any order or judgment of the court. The imprisonment will not discharge any debt or cause of action.

II. Court of Probate.

The law relating to *Last Wills* and *Testaments* has been very materially altered by the late Act, 20 & 21 Vict., c. 77,[90] called "The Court of Probate Act," by which all the jurisdiction and authority of the Ecclesiastical Courts in respect of the granting and revocation of probates of wills and letters of administration have been taken from such courts, and now centres in the Court of Probate.

The court is presided over by a judge, who ranks with the judges next after the Lord Chief Baron of the Court of Exchequer. He is also the Judge Ordinary of the Divorce Court, which has also recently been called into operation.

The Court of Probate now exercises jurisdiction over the granting of probates and letters of administration, and determines all questions relating to matters in testamen-

[90] See also 25 & 26 Vict., c. 22; 27 & 28 Vict., c. 56, 31 & 32 Vict., c. 124.

tary cases; and its business consists in pronouncing upon the validity of wills and codicils, and deciding in cases of intestacy upon the person to whom the administration of the deceased's estate shall be given. Public Registries, under the control of the Court of Probate, called District Registries, are established in various parts of the kingdom, the district registrars having similar powers within their districts as to granting probate and letters of administration as the Probate Court itself.

The judge has also power to appoint an administrator *pendente lite,* to deal with the personalty, and a receiver to deal with the real estates, and the court has the same power to enforce its various decrees and orders as is now possessed by the Court of Chancery.

Where the personal property of the deceased is under £200, and where the real property is under £300, the judge of the county court of the district where the deceased had his fixed place of abode has the same power to determine the suit as the Court of Probate.

The rules and principles of evidence observed in the superior courts of common law and equity at Westminster are applicable to all trials of questions of fact in the Court of Probate.

New trials and rehearings may be granted, and any party dissatisfied with the judgment of the court may appeal to the House of Lords as of right from a final decree, and by leave of the judge from interlocutory decrees or orders.

III. Court for Divorce and Matrimonial Causes.

The cumbrous and protracted machinery of the old Ecclesiastical Courts, so far as related to Divorce and Matrimonial Causes, has been superseded by a new jurisdiction, created under the title of the "Court for Divorce and Matrimonial Causes."[91]

It is a court of record, and the judge of the Court of Probate is the ordinary judge. It is hold at Westminster, and all the judges of the Courts of Queen's Bench, Common Pleas, and Exchequer are component parts of the court; but the Judge Ordinary is enabled either alone, or with one or more of the other judges, to hear and determine all matters arising therein.

The Court for *Divorce and Matrimonial Causes* is invested with very important and distinctive powers. It exercises exclusive authority in respect *of divorces* and *judicial separation;* suits of nullity of marriage; suits of jactitation of marriage, now almost obsolete; suits for restitution of conjugal rights; and in all causes, suits, and matters matrimonial, except in respect of marriage licences.

The court may pronounce decrees for the restitution of *conjugal rights* in cases of desertion. It may grant a decree of *judicial separation* on the ground of adultery, or cruelty, or desertion for two years and upwards — Of *dissolution* of marriage in cases of adultery at the suit of the husband; and at the suit of the wife in cases of adultery aggravated by cruelty, or some other unlawful offence — Of *nullify of marriage* where it is proved to have been invalid either by some informality in the celebration or by reason of incapacity, either legal or physical, in either of the contracting parties.[92]

Application for restitution of conjugal rights, or for judicial separation or divorce on anyone of these grounds, may be made by either husband or wife by petition to the

---

[91] See 20 & 21 Vict., c. 85; 22 & 33 Vict. c. 61; 23 & 24 Vict., c. 144.

[92] By 32 & 33 Vict., c. 68, s. 3, the parties to any proceeding instituted in consequence of adultery, and the husbands and wives of such parties, are now competent to give evidence in such proceeding.

court; and the court may decree restitution of conjugal rights, or judicial separation; and where the application is by the wife, may make any order for alimony which is just.

In all cases in which the court makes a decree or order for alimony, it may direct the same to be paid either to the wife herself or to any trustee on her behalf, and may impose any terms or restrictions which it deems expedient.

The court is also empowered to make such orders with respect to the custody of the children of the marriage as it may deem just and proper, and may, if it thinks fit, direct proceedings to be taken for placing the children under the protection of the Court of Chancery.

The court has also the power of granting an order — as is the case with some of the inferior magisterial jurisdictions — protecting a wife's earnings from her husband and his creditors in cases where the wife has been deserted; and in every case of a judicial separation the wife shall be considered as a *feme sole* with respect to property of every description which she may acquire, or which may come to, or devolve upon her.

A novel provision of the Act is that it allows the alleged adulterer to be made a co-respondent to the petition for a divorce; and the Court has the power to make such an order upon him as to the whole or part of the costs of the proceedings as it may deem fit; and the Court has also power, in the case of a wife's petition, to make the woman with whom the husband is alleged to have committed adultery, a party to the suit, with a view to the costs.

By this Act no action in future will be maintainable in England for *criminal conversation;* but the husband may, in a petition for dissolution of marriage or for judicial separation, claim damages from the adulterer, and the suit will be heard and tried on the same principles as actions for *crim. con.* were formerly tried.

The court, in cases of dissolution of marriage, has the power to inquire into the terms of any marriage settlement which has been executed, and to make orders for the application of the whole or part of the fund, either for the benefit of the innocent party and of the children of the marriage, as it may think fit; or either or any of them.[93]

An appeal from the judgment of the court for a decree *absolute,* in a case of dissolution of marriage, may be made to the House of Lords. If no appeal be lodged within the prescribed time, either or both the parties may marry again as if the prior marriage had been dissolved by death.

CHAPTER IV
COURTS ECCLESIASTIGAL, MILITARY, AND MARITIME

Besides the several Courts which have been treated of, in which all injuries are redressed that fall under the cognizance of the common law of England, or that spirit of equity which ought to be its constant attendant, there still remain other Courts of a jurisdiction equally public and general that require consideration.

What are these Courts, and explain them?

I. Courts Ecclesiastical.

The *Ecclesiastical Courts* at one time exercised a very extended jurisdiction; but the business of these courts, of which the principal are the Consistory Courts of the bishop of each diocese and the Court of Arches, are *now*

[93] See 20 & 21 Vict., c. 85, s. 45; 23 & 24 Vict., c. 44, s. 6.

mainly confined to inquiring into charges of heresy, of improperly conducting the services of the Church, and of immoral and scandalous conduct on the part of clergymen.[94]

These courts also entertain suits of a *quasi*-criminal nature against laymen for damaging the church, or the churchyard, or for not repairing the chancel, or aisle, when it is incumbent on them to do so; also against churchwardens for neglect of duty, and against any person for defacing, or removing the monuments, or pews, or otherwise interfering with the church or churchyard, without a power previously granted by the Ordinary.[95]

The COURT of ARCHES referred to is the court of appeal belonging to the Archbishop of Canterbury; whereof the judge is called the *Dean of the Arches.* His proper jurisdiction is only over the thirteen peculiar parishes belonging to the Archbishop in London; but the office of Dean of the Arches having been for a long time united with that of the archbishop's principal official, he now, in right of the last-mentioned office, receives and determines appeals from the sentences of all inferior ecclesiastical courts within the province, and from him the appeal now lies to the Judicial Committee of the Privy Council.

II. Courts-Martial.

A jurisdiction similar to that exercised over clergymen by the Ecclesiastical Courts is exercised over soldiers by courts-martial. Their proceedings are regulated by the provisions of the Annual Mutiny Act and the Articles of War founded upon that Act, signed by the Sovereign and promulgated annually, which is re-enacted with slight modification in each session of Parliament. Courts-martial

---

[94] For former Jurisdictions of the Ecclesiastical Courts, see Blackstone, vol. iii.

[95] See 21 & 22 Vict., c. 77; 18 &19 Vict., c. 41; 23 & 24 Vict., c. 32: also 32 & 33 Vict.. c. 85.

are empowered to punish any officer or soldier who shall excite or join any mutiny, or knowing of it shall not give notice to the commanding officer; who deserts or enlists in any other regiment, or sleeps on his post, or leaves it before he is relieved, or holds correspondence with a rebel or enemy, or strikes or uses violence to his superior officer, and other similar offences. For such offences the offender suffers such punishment as a court-martial shall inflict, including judgment of death, provided for by the Articles of War.

This military code is administered by courts-martial with different degrees of authority, and in all of them the members are sworn to determine according to the evidence and to the best of their understanding.[96]

III. The High Court of Admiralty.

This court now exercises a jurisdiction, equitable as well as legal, and has a power of enforcing its decrees and orders similar to that possessed by courts of common law. By 24 Vict., c. 10, the High Court of Admiralty is constituted a court of record for all intents and purposes, and has power either to proceed *in rein,* or *in personam; in personam,* by calling upon the masters or owners of vessels to show cause why they should not appear and defend the suits instituted against them; and *in rem,* by arrest of the ship itself, which is only released, upon bail being given to the fall amount of the claim and the costs likely to be incurred in the suit.

The usual suits entertained by the court relate to bottomry or *respondentia* bonds; salvage; wages due to the crew; towage or pilotage services; and to cases of collision, damages, and breaches of contract in maritime affairs.[97]

---

[96] See 29 & 30 Vict., c. 100.
[97] See 3 & 4 Vict., c. 65.

The court also entertains questions of prize-money and booty of war, but it exercises this jurisdiction by virtue of a warrant, giving it special powers in that behalf.

Many of the powers exercised by the High Court of Admiralty have recently been conferred on certain county courts, to entertain maritime questions of a limited amount; and in cases of difficulty, the County Court may, at the request of either party, be assisted by two mercantile assessors.[98]

An appeal from the County Court in these cases maybe made to the High Court of Admiralty, subject to security for costs; and an appeal from the High Court of Admiralty lies to the Judicial Committee of the Privy Council.

CHAPTER V
COURTS OF SPECIAL JURISDICTION

Having considered the several Courts whose jurisdiction is public and general, and in which redress for every possible injury is administered, let us now discuss those Courts whose jurisdiction is private and special, confined, to particular spots, or instituted, only to redress particular injuries.

Explain those Courts, and state their particular jurisdictions.

I. Forest Courts.

The *Forest Courts* were originally instituted, for the government of the King's forests in different parts of the kingdom, and for the preservation of, and punishment of

---

[98] See 31 & 32 Vict., c 71; and 32 & 33 Vict., c. 51.

injuries done to, the King's deer; or to the vert or greensward, and to the covert in which such deer were lodged. The forest laws gradually fell much into disuse. They are, however, administered in a mitigated form, but within very restricted limits. There are now only three Royal forests existing in England, viz., the New Forest in Hampshire, Dean Forest, and that of Waltham, called Epping Forest, in Middlesex. All the other Crown forests have been disafforested.

II. The Stannary Courts.

The *Stannary Courts* in Devonshire and Cornwall, for the administration of justice among the miners therein, are courts of record, but of a private and exclusive nature. They are held before the Lord Warden of the Stannaries or his deputy the vice-warden, in virtue of a privilege granted to the workers in the tin mines to sue and be sued only in their own courts, that they may not be drawn from their business by attending their law-suits in other courts. An appeal lies to the lord warden, and every judgment of the lord warden is subject to an appeal to the House of Lords.

III. The Palatine Courts of Chester, Lancaster, and Durham.

These courts are of a limited local jurisdiction, but have an exclusive cognizance of pleas in matters both of law and equity. When the privileges of counties palatine and franchises were abridged by stat. 27 Henry VIII., c. 24, it was also enacted that all writs and processes should be made in the King's name, but should be witnessed in the name of the owner of the franchise. Therefore all writs whereon actions are founded and which have concurrent authority must be under the seal of the respective franchises, the two former of which are now united to the Crown. By 15 & 16 Vict., c. 76 (1852), writs issuing out of the superior courts of the common law at Westminster to be executed in the counties palatine are directed and delivered to the sheriff and executed and returned by him, and all records to the superior courts are brought to trial and entered and disposed of in the counties palatine in the same manner as in other counties.

The Court of the Duchy Chamber of Lancaster is a jurisdiction concerning all matters of equity relating to lands holden of the Crown in right of the Duchy distinct from the Court of the County Palatine of Lancaster. The court is held before the Chancellor of the Duchy or his deputy. The proceedings are the same as in the Court of Chancery, which has a concurrent jurisdiction with the Duchy Court.

IV. Courts of Commissioners of Sewers.

A COURT OF COMMISSIONERS OF SEWERS is a temporary tribunal instituted by virtue of a commission under the Great Seal. The jurisdiction is to overlook the repairs of sea banks and sea walls, and the cleansing of rivers, public streams, ditches, and other conduits whereby waters are carried off.

Stat. 3 & 4 Wm. IV., c. 22, amended by subsequent enactments, contains provisions as to the levying of rates, making new works, levying fines and penalties, and other matters.[99]

V. Courts of the University of Oxford and Cambridge.

The Chancellor's Courts of the Universities of Oxford and Cambridge formerly exercised peculiar privileges. These two learned bodies enjoyed the sole jurisdiction, in exclusion of the Queen's courts, over all civil actions and

---

[99] See 4 & 6 Vict., C. 45: 12 & 13 Vict., c. 50; 18 & 19 Vict., c. 32; 20 & 21 Vict., c. 1; and 24 & 25 Vict., c. 183; see also Metropolitan Board of Works (Loans) Act, 32 & 33 Vict., c. 102.

suits whatsoever, where a scholar or other privileged person is one of the parties; excepting in such cases where a right of freehold is concerned. And by the University Charters they were at liberty to try and determine offences and pecuniary demands in which any member or servant of the University is concerned, either according to the common law of the land, or according to their own local customs. These privileges were granted that the students might not be distracted from their studies by legal process from distant courts.

These privileges are still exercised at Oxford; but at Cambridge they have been taken away by a recent private statute.

The Chancellor has jurisdiction in almost all causes, whether civil, spiritual, or criminal; and the Vice-Chancellor is the presiding judge. In pursuance of 25 & 26 Vict., c. 26, s. 12, the form of procedure in civil causes very much resembles the forms in the new county courts.

The jurisdiction of this court is not affected by the County Court Acts.

Appeals lie to the House of Congregation; then to the House of Convocation; and finally to the Queen in Chancery.

VI. Courts of London.

The several courts within the City of London, and other cities, and boroughs, and corporations throughout the kingdom, held by prescription, charter, or act of Parliament, are also of the same private nature, and the jurisdictions limited to particular cases arising in those limited localities.[100] They arose originally from the favour of the Crown to those particular districts wherein we find them

[100] See 30 & 31 Vict., c. 142,s. 36.

instituted, upon the same principle that Hundred Courts, and the like, were established for the convenience of the inhabitants; that they might prosecute their suits, and receive justice at home. For the most part, the courts at Westminster Hall have a concurrent jurisdiction with these, or else a superintendency over them; and the proceedings in these local and special courts are to be according to the course of the common law, unless otherwise ordered by Parliament; for though the Sovereign may erect new courts, the Crown cannot alter the established course of law.

The customs of London are various, and are against the common law; but they have been made good by special usage, and confirmed by Act of Parliament. An action upon the custom of London can only be brought in the Lord Mayor's Court; but the custom may be pleaded in bar in a superior court. It may be used in a superior court by way of defence, and in such cases the superior court will take notice of the custom.[101]

CHAPTER VI

WRONGS AFFECTING THE PERSON — REPUTATION — LIBERTY — AND RELATIVE RIGHTS

Let us now discuss *Private Injuries;* that is, the several injuries between, subject and subject that are cognizable in the Courts of Common Law; as, in one or the other of these Courts, every possible injury that can be offered to a man's Person may meet redress.

---

[101] The customs of London as to the distribution of intestates' effects are abolished by 19 & 20 Vict., c. 91.

Explain the several Injuries cognizable in the Common-Law Courts.

All WRONGS being a *privation* of *right,* the plain natural remedy for every species of *wrong* is the being put in possession of that *right* whereof the party injured has been deprived. This may either be effected by the specific delivery or restoration of the subject-matter in dispute to the legal owner, as where lands or personal chattels are unjustly withheld or invaded; or, where that is not a possible, or at least not an adequate remedy, by making the sufferer a pecuniary satisfaction in damages; as in case of assault, or breach of contract, to which damages the party injured has acquired an incomplete or inchoate right the instant he receives the injury, though such right be not fully ascertained till they are assessed by the intervention of the law. The means whereby this remedy is obtained is in general by a *suit* or *action,* defined to be "*the lawful demand of one's right.*"

ACTIONS are subject, in the first place, to this principal division. They are distinguished into three kinds: — Actions *Personal, Real,* and *Mixed.*

Personal Actions are those whereby a man claims the specific recovery of a debt, or of a personal chattel, or damages for breach of contract; and likewise whereby a man claims a satisfaction in damages for some injury done to his person or property.

The forms of *personal actions* now in use are: — *Debt — Covenant — Assumpsit — Detinue — Trespass — Trespass on the Case — Replevin.*

Real actions, which formerly had regard to *real property* only, were such whereby the plaintiff claimed the specific recovery of lands, tenements, or hereditaments. Real actions, as such, are now altogether abolished by 3 &

4 Wm. IV., c. 27; see also 23 & 24 Vict., c. 126. The only mode now by which land is specifically recovered is by action of *Ejectment,* which will be afterwards explained.

Mixed Actions partake of the nature of the two, wherein some real property is demanded and personal damages for a wrong sustained; as, for instance, an *action* of *waste* to recover damages is brought by him who has the inheritance in remainder or reversion against the tenant for life who has committed waste therein, to recover not only the land wasted, which would have made it what was termed a *real* action; but also a *personal* recompense for a wrong sustained.

Under these three heads every action in a court of common law may now be maintained.

How are "Injuries" which affect the personal security of individuals divided? and explain them.

The absolute "*rights*" of each individual were defined to be the *right* of "PERSONAL SECURITY," the *right* of "PERSONAL LIBERTY," and the *right* of "PRIVATE PROPERTY," so that the *wrongs* affecting those "*rights*" must be of a corresponding nature.

I. Personal Security.

1. As to *injuries* which affect the personal security of individuals, they are either *injuries* against their lives,[102] their limbs, their bodies, their health, or their reputation.

The two next species of *injuries* affecting the limbs or bodies may be committed: —

---

[102] With regard to the first subdivision, or injuries affecting the life of man, being one of the most atrocious species of crimes, we reserve its consideration for the Fourth Book.

1. By *threats,* or menaces. A menace alone makes not the injury; but only, if any consequent inconvenience ensue.

2. By *assault,* which includes an attempt or offer to beat another without touching him; as if one lifts up his cane, or his fist, in a threatening manner at another; or strikes at him, but misses him; this is an assault and is described to be "an *unlawful setting-upon one's person.*" It is an inchoate violence, and though no actual suffering be proved, the party may have redress by *action of trespass,* wherein he may recover damages.

3. By *battery,* which is the beating of another. The least touching of another man's person wilfully, or in anger, is a battery; for the law cannot draw the line between different degrees of violence, and therefore totally prohibits the first and lowest stage of it — "every man's person being sacred, no other has a right to meddle with it, in the slightest manner."

4. By *wounding,* which consists in giving another some dangerous hurt. This is an aggravated species of battery.

5. By *mayhem,* which is an injury still more atrocious, and consists in violently depriving another of the use of a member proper for his defence or occupation.

For these three last offences an indictment, at the suit of the Crown, may be brought, as well as a *civil action* for damages.

To render these acts, however, either *actionable* or *indictable,* they must be committed unlawfully; for they are all in some cases justifiable. Thus assault and battery are justifiable in the case of a parent or master who *moderately* corrects his child, his scholar, or his apprentice. So also, on the principle of self-defence; for if one strikes me first, or even only assaults me, I may strike him in my own defence; and if sued for it, may plead son *assault demesne;* or that it was the plaintiff's own original assault that occasioned it. So likewise in defence of my goods or possessions. If a man endeavours to deprive me of my goods, I am justified in laying hands upon him to prevent him; and in case he persists with violence, I may proceed to beat him away. Thus, too, in the exercise of an office, as that of churchwarden or beadle, a man may lay hands upon another to turn him out of church and prevent the disturbance of the congregation; and if sued for this, or the like battery, he may set forth the whole case, and plead that he laid hands upon him gently — *molliter manus imposuit* — for this purpose.

II. INJURIES *affecting a man's health* may be constituted by selling him bad provisions or wine; by the exercise of an obnoxious trade, which infects the air in his neighbourhood; or by the neglect or unskilful management of his physician, surgeon, or apothecary. *Mala praxis* is a great misdemeanor and offence at common law, whether it be for curiosity and experiment, or by neglect; because it breaks the trust which the party had placed in the medical practitioner, and tends to the injury of the patient. These are wrongs or injuries unaccompanied by force, for which there is a remedy in damages by a special action of *trespass on the case.*

In cases of gross misconduct the party may also be indicted. This action, of *trespass* — or *trespass upon the case* — is a universal remedy, given for all personal wrongs and injuries without force; so called, because the plaintiff's whole case or cause of complaint was set forth at length in the original writ, and is so now raised by the pleadings.

III. INJURIES *affecting a mans reputation* or good name are, first, by malicious and defamatory *words*, tending to his damage and derogation. As if a man utter any slander or false tale of another, which may either endanger him in law, by impeaching him of some punishable crime, as to say that a man has poisoned another, or is perjured; or which may exclude him from society, as to charge him with having an infectious disease; or which may impair or hurt his trade or livelihood, as to call a tradesman a bankrupt, a physician a quack, or a lawyer a knave. But with regard to words that do not upon the face of them import such defamation as will be injurious, it is necessary that the plaintiff should aver some particular damage to have happened. Words of heat and passion, as to call a man rogue and rascal, if productive of no ill consequence, and not of the dangerous species before mentioned, are not actionable; neither are words spoken in a friendly manner, as by way of advice, admonition, or concern, without any ill-will; for, in both these cases, they are not *maliciously* spoken, which is part of the definition of slander. Neither are any disparaging words made use of in legal proceedings pertinent to the cause in hand, a sufficient cause of action for slander. Also if the defendant be able to justify and prove the words to be true, no action will lie; but the repeating of a rumour, which is false, is *not* justifiable. For this injury the remedy is by *trespass on the case.*

A SECOND way of *affecting a man's* reputation is by publishing a *libel* upon him, which may be by writing, print, pictures, signs, or the like, calculated to set him in an odious or ridiculous light, done with a *malicious intent* to affect his reputation.

The publication of a libel may be evidenced in various ways, — by reading it aloud; by selling it, or distributing it gratis; or by sending it through the post, or otherwise, to a third person. Such publication is presumed to have been *malicious.* By Lord Campbell's Libel Act, 6 & 7 Vict., c. 96, amended by 8 & 9 Vict., c. 75,[103] for amending the law respecting defamatory words and libels, it is provided that in pleading to any indictment or information for a defamatory libel, the defendant may, by way of defence, allege the truth of the matters charged; and further, that it was for the public benefit that the matters charged should be published, showing the particular fact or facts by reason whereof it was for the public benefit. The same Act contains provisions intended to relieve editors and proprietors of newspapers and other publications from hardships to which they were formerly subject. It is enacted that in an action for a libel in any public newspaper or other periodical publication, it shall be competent to the defendant to plead that such libel was inserted therein without *actual malice* and without *gross negligence;* and that before the commencement of the action, or at the earliest opportunity afterwards, he inserted in such newspaper, or other periodical publication, an apology for the said libel. The defendant is also at liberty to pay into court a sum of money by way of amends for the injury supposed to have been sustained by the publication of the libel complained of.

With regard to *libels* in general, there are, as in many other cases, two remedies; one by *indictment* or by *criminal information* in the Court of Queen's Bench, and another by *action;* the former for the public offence, for every libel has a tendency to cause a breach of the peace on the part of the person libelled; the latter, by *action,* to compensate such person in damages for the injuries sustained.

---

[103] See also 16 & 16 Vict., c. 76, an Act to amend the process, practice, and mode of pleading in the Superior Courts of Common Law.

A THIRD way of destroying or injuring a man's reputation is by preferring *malicious indictments* or *prosecutions* against him; which, under the mask of justice and public spirit, are sometimes made the engines of private spite and enmity. For this, however, the law has given a very adequate remedy in damages, either by an action for *conspiracy,* which cannot be brought but against two at the least; or, which is the only way now in practice, by a special *action on the case* for a false and malicious prosecution.

II. The Violation of the Right of Personal Liberty.

This may be constituted by *False Imprisonment* and by *Malicious Arrest.* For the injury of false imprisonment the law has not only decreed a punishment as a heinous public crime, but has also given a private reparation to the party, as well by removing the actual confinement; as, after it is over, by subjecting the wrong-doer to a civil action on account of the damage sustained by the loss of time and liberty.

To constitute the injury of false imprisonment there are two circumstances requisite: — 1. The detention of the person. 2. The unlawfulness of such detention.

Every confinement of the person is an imprisonment, whether it be in a common prison, or in a private house, or even by forcibly detaining one in the public street. Unlawful or false imprisonment consists in such confinement or detention without sufficient authority which may arise either from some process from the courts of justice, or from some warrant from an officer having power to commit, under his hand and seal, and expressing the cause of such commitment; or from some other special cause warranted by the necessity of the thing, such as the arresting of a felon by a private person without warrant. False imprisonment may arise by executing a lawful warrant or process at an unlawful time, as on a Sunday; for the statute declares that such service or process shall be void, except in cases of treason, felony, breach of the peace, or other indictable offences.

The remedy for false imprisonment is twofold; by an action of trespass, wherein the party will recover such damages for the injury he has received as a jury shall award; and by the writ of *Habeas Corpus*[104] *ad subjiciendum,* which is directed to the person detaining another, and commanding him to produce the body of the prisoner, with the day and cause of his capture and detention, to "do, submit to, and receive" whatsoever the judge or court awarding such writ shall consider right in that behalf. On the return of the writ, the court will discharge the prisoner out of custody, if his detention be unlawful.

This is a high prerogative writ issuing out of any of the superior courts of Westminster, including the Court of Chancery; not only in term time, but also during the vacation, and running into all parts of the Queen's dominions.

III. Rights of Private Property.

With regard to the third absolute right of individuals; that of holding private property; though the enjoyment of it when acquired is strictly a private right, yet as its nature and origin and the means of its acquisition and loss fall more directly under the general division of the "Rights of Things," and as the *wrongs* that affect these *rights* must be referred to in the corresponding division, it will be more convenient to consider together, rather than in a separate view, the *injuries* that may be offered to the *enjoyment,* as

[104] See Habeas Corpus Act, 31 Car. II., c. 2, amended by 56 Geo. III., c. 100, "An Act for the better securing the liberty of the subject, and for prevention of imprisonments beyond the seas." See also 16 & 17 Vict, c. 108; 30 & 31 Vict., c.36.

well as to the *rights* of property. This will be discussed in the following chapter.

IV. Relative Rights.

Injuries affecting the *rights* of individuals in their *private relations;* or such as are incident to persons considered as members of society, and connected with each other by various ties, are four in number, viz.: — 1. Husband and Wife — 2. Parent and Child — 3. Guardian and Ward — 4. Master and Servant.

Injuries that may be offered to a person considered as a husband are principally three: — 1. *Abduction,* or taking away a man's wife. — 2. *Adultery,* or criminal conversation with her. — 3. *Beating,* or otherwise abusing her.

Abduction may either be by fraud and persuasion, or open violence; though the law in both cases assumes force and constraint; the wife having no power to consent; it therefore gives a remedy by action of trespass, and the husband may also sue in an action on the *case* for damages against such persons as persuade and entice the wife to live separate from him without a sufficient cause.[105]

Adultery is a grievous civil injury, for which the law up to a recent period gave satisfaction to the husband by an action of *criminal conversation,* but this action is now abolished, and its place supplied by 20 & 21 Vict., c. 85, which provides, *inter alia,* that the husband may petition the new Court of Divorce, established by that statute, for damages from any person on the ground of his having committed adultery with the petitioner's wife; and that the claim of damages shall be heard and tried on the same principles and according to the same rules as formerly applied to an action of *criminal conversation,* and the dam-

[105] See 24 & 25 Vict., c. 100, ss. 53 & 55.

ages ascertained by the verdict of a jury. A new principle is, however, introduced— that of giving power to the court, after the verdict has been given, to decide in what manner the damages shall be paid or applied; and to direct that the whole or a part shall be settled for the benefit of the children, if any, of the marriage; or, as a provision for the maintenance of the wife.

Beating a man's wife, or otherwise ill-using her. The law gives a satisfaction to the husband for it by an action of trespass, which must be brought in the names of the husband and wife *jointly,* but if the beating or other maltreatment be very enormous, so that thereby the husband is deprived for any time of the company and assistance of his wife, the law then gives him a *separate* remedy by an action of trespass, in nature of an action upon the case, for this ill-usage *per quod consortium amisit;* in which he shall recover *satisfaction* in damages.

An action is maintainable at the suit of the parent for the seduction of his daughter, or for the abduction or battery of his child. This is rather in his character of master, and not as parent; for actual or constructive loss of service must be shown and proved.

Of a similar nature is the relation of *guardian* and *ward,* but the usual method of redressing all complaints relative to wards and guardians with respect to their persons and property, and generally as to their custody, education, &c., is by an application to the Court of Chancery, which is the supreme guardian, and has the superintendent jurisdiction of all the infants in the kingdom.

There are two species of *injuries* incident to the relation between master and *servant,* and the rights accruing therefrom. The one is, retaining another man's hired servant before his time is expired; the other is beating, confining, or disabling him in such a manner that he is not able to perform his work. As to the first, the retaining another person's servant during the time he has agreed to serve his present master is also an illegal act. For every master has, by his contract, purchased for a valuable consideration the service of his domestics for a certain time; the enticing away or hiring his servant, which induces a breach of this contract, is therefore an injury to the master; and for that injury the law has given him a remedy by a special action on *the case;* and he may also proceed against the servant for the non-performance of his agreement. But if the new master was not apprised of the former contract, no action lies against *him,* unless he refuses to allow the servant to leave. The other injury is that of beating, confining, or disabling a man's servant, which depends upon the same principle as the last, viz., the property which the master has by his contract acquired in the services of the servant. In this case, besides the remedy of an action of battery or imprisonment which the servant himself, as an individual, may have against the aggressor, the master also, as a recompense for *his* immediate loss, may maintain an action of trespass, in which he must allege and prove the *special damage* he has sustained by the beating of his servant, *per quod servitium amisit;* and then the jury will award him a proportionable pecuniary satisfaction.

Injuries may also be sustained by an individual in respect of his *public* rights. These are remedied by *indictment or* action on the *case* where any loss has been experienced by the party. An injury of this kind has been recently provided for by 31 & 32 Vict., c. 125, s. 48, which provides that if any returning officer shall wilfully delay, neglect, or refuse duly to return any person who ought to be returned to serve in Parliament for any county or borough, such person may sue the officer in any of her Majesty's courts of record at Westminster, and recover double the damages he shall have sustained, together with full costs of suit.

By Death by Accident Compensation Act, 9 & 10 Vict., c. 93,[106] an Act "for compensating the families of persons killed by accident," an injury to the relation of parent or child is actionable, and the damages shall be for the benefit of the wife, husband, parent, or child of the person whose death shall have been so caused. The action must be commenced within twelve calendar months, and damages may be recovered commensurate with the pecuniary loss caused by the defendant; such damages to be assessed by the jury.

CHAPTER VII
INJURIES TO PERSONAL PROPERTY

In the preceding chapter we considered the *Wrongs* or *Injuries* that affect the *rights* of persons, either considered as individuals or as related to each other; let us now discuss such *injuries* as affect the *rights* of *property* and the remedies which our law has given to repair or redress them. First, then, as to the *injuries* that may be offered to the rights of *personal* property, which, as before stated, consists of goods, money, and all other movable chattels, and things thereunto incident; and secondly, in accordance with the former division of property, the *wrongs* to *real* property, which consists of such things as are permanent, fixed, and immovable.

[106] See also 31 & 32 Vict., c. 119, s. 22, which, for the safety of passengers, enacts that every company shall provide and maintain in good order efficient means of communication between the passengers and the servants of the company in charge of the train. In default, the company shall be liable to a penalty of £10; and any passenger who makes use of the said communication without reasonable excuse, shall be liable for each offence to a penalty not exceeding £5.

Explain such Injuries as affect the Rights of "Personal" Property, with their respective Remedies.

The *rights* of PERSONAL PROPERTY in possession are liable to two species of injuries: The *Amotion,* or *Deprivation* of that possession; and the *Abuse* or *Damage* of the chattels, while in possession of the legal owner.[107]

The *deprivation* of possession is divisible into several branches: such as taking them away unlawfully; their unlawful detention; tortious acts which subject the owner to the loss of them; or, doing damage to them while in his possession.

The wrongful *taking* of goods being clearly an *injury,* the next consideration is, the *remedy* the law of England has given for it; and this is, by an *action of trespass,* wherein the plaintiff may recover, not the thing itself, but damages for the loss of it; or by the action of *replevin,* which means the delivery of the goods to the proper owner on his giving security to prosecute the necessary action to try the legality of the *taking.*

Detinue and *replevin* are the only actions in which the specific possession of the identical personal chattel is restored to the proper owner; for things personal are looked upon by the law as of a nature so transitory and perishable, that it is for the most part impossible to ascertain their identity, or to restore them in the same condition as when they came to the hands of the wrongful possessor. Our law, therefore, contents itself, not by restoring the thing itself, but by giving the party injured a satisfaction in damages.[108]

Deprivation, of possession may be by an unjust *detainer* of another's goods, though the original *taking* was

[107] See Malicious Injuries to Property Act, 24 & 25 Vict., c. 97.
[108] See 23 & 24 Vict., c. 126.

lawful. As if I distrain another's cattle *damage-feasant,* and before they are impounded, he tenders me sufficient amends; though the original taking was lawful, my subsequent detention of them after tender of amends is wrongful, and he shall have an action of *replevin* against me to recover them; in which he shall recover damages for the *detention,* and not for the *caption,* because the original taking was lawful. Or, if I lend a man a horse, and he afterwards refuses to restore it; this injury consists in the detaining, and not in the original taking, and the regular method for me to recover possession is by *action of detinue.* In this *action of detinue,* it is necessary to ascertain the thing detained, in such a manner so that it maybe specifically known and recovered. Therefore it cannot be brought for money, corn, or the like; for that cannot be known from other money or corn; unless it be in a bag or a sack, for then it may be distinguishably marked.

Trover or *Conversion* is a species of *trespass* on the *case,* and an action originally lay for recovery of damages against such person as had *found* another's goods and refused to deliver them on demand, but *converted* them to his own use; from which finding and converting it is now called an *action of trover and conversion.* The injury lies in the conversion; for any man may take the goods of another into possession, if he finds them; but no finder is allowed to acquire a property therein, which the law presumes him to do, if he refuses to restore them to the owner; for which reason such refusal alone is, *primâ facie,* sufficient evidence of a conversion. If the plaintiff proves that the goods are *his* property, and that the defendant had them in his possession, then in this action he shall recover damages equal to the value of the thing converted.

Injuries direct or consequential. These may occur in many ways, as a man may be deprived either of goods or money in consequence of false representation, as to the circumstances or character of another, and other similar acts. The remedy for such is by action *on the case.* Where there are representations as to character, ability, or dealings, by Lord Tenterden's Act, Geo. IV., c. 14, s. 6, the representation must have been made in writing.

Abusing and *damaging things personal* while in the possession of the owner — hunting a man's deer, shooting his dogs, or in any way injuring his chattels; the remedies given by law to redress these wrongs are by action of *trespass* or by action on *the case.* It is not material whether the damage be done by the defendant himself or by his servant, for the action will lie against the master as well as against the servant. If a man keeps a dog which does mischief, the owner must now answer for the consequences thereof, whether he *knows* of such evil habit or not; for, by 28 & 29 Vict., c. 60, s. 1, "it shall not be necessary for the party seeking such damages to show a previous mischievous propensity, or that the injury was attributable to neglect on the part of such owner."

Explain "Injuries" affecting rights founded on "Contract," both "Express" and "Implied," with their respective "Remedies."

A *Contract,* as formerly stated,[109] is "an agreement, upon sufficient consideration, *to do* or *not to do* a particular thing," and the violation or non-performance of such contract is an *injury,* for which the law provides a remedy.

Express contracts include three distinct species — *debts, covenants,* and *promises.*

Debt is a sum of money due by certain and express agreement; as, by a bond or other instrument under seal for a certain sum; a bill or note; a special bargain; or a rent

---

[109] See "Contracts."

reserved on a lease, where the amount is fixed and specific, and does not depend upon any subsequent valuation to settle it. The non-payment of these is an injury, for which the proper remedy is by *action of debt* or *covenant,* to compel the performance of the contract or recover the sum due.

A *Covenant* is an agreement, convention, or promise of two or more parties by *deed in writing,* signed, sealed, and delivered by the parties, who pledge themselves to *do* a direct act, or to *omit* one, the violation of which is a civil injury. The remedy for either party is by *action* of *covenant;* but in the case of a covenant or a lease to *pay rent,* the breach of it may be redressed either by *action* of *covenant* or of *debt.*

A *Promise* is in the nature of a verbal covenant, and wants nothing but the solemnity of writing and sealing to make it absolutely the same. If therefore it be to do any explicit act, it is an express contract, as much as any covenant; and the breach of it is an equal injury. The remedy indeed is not exactly the same; since, instead of an action of covenant, there only lies an action upon *the case,* for what is called the *assumpsit* (promise) or undertaking of the defendant; the failure of performing which is the wrong or injury done to the plaintiff, the amount of damage a jury is to estimate and settle.

Implied contracts, as formerly stated,[110] are such as reason and justice dictate, and which, therefore, the law presumes that every man has contracted to perform. Of this nature are the fundamental constitutions of government, to which every man is assumed to be a contracting party; and thus it is that every person is bound and hath virtually agreed to pay such particular sums of money as are legally charged on him, assessed by the interpretation

[110] See "Contracts."

of the law; for it is a part of the original contract entered into by all mankind who partake of the benefits of society to submit in all points to the municipal constitutions and local ordinances of the State. Whatever, therefore, the law orders any one to pay, that becomes instantly a debt, the payment of which the law enforces. Also, where a person has laid out and expended his own money for the use of another, at his request, the law implies a promise[111] of re-payment, and an action of debt will lie on this *assumpsit.*

CHAPTER VIII
"WRONGS" TO "REAL" PROPERTY

We shall now consider such *injuries* as affect that species of *Property* which the laws of England have denominated "*Real;*" being, as previously stated, of a more substantial and permanent nature than the more transitory *rights* of which *personal* chattels are the object.

What are the "Wrongs" that affect "Real Property," and explain those Wrongs?

The injuries affecting real property are principally: — 1. Ouster. — 2. Trespass. — 3. Nuisance. — 4. Waste. — 5. Subtraction. — 6. *Disturbance.*

1. *Ouster,* or dispossession, is a *wrong,* or *injury* in respect of hereditaments, either corporeal or incorporeal, that carries with it the *amotion* of possession; for thereby the wrong-doer gets into the actual occupation of the land or hereditament, and obliges him that has a right to seek his legal remedy, in order to gain possession of it, and damages for the injury sustained; as for instance, "where

---

[111] The promise of a debtor to pay a debt barred by the Statute of Limitations, or of an adult to pay a debt contracted during his nonage, is void, unless it be in writing and signed by the party

the tenant, though not entitled, had entered, without fraud or tort, into possession of land, by the deed or consent of one who himself either came into possession of such land unlawfully, or had but a particular or defeasible estate in it."

In the time of our Saxon ancestors, *possession* seems only to have been recoverable by *writ of entry,* which, after the Conquest, when all causes were drawn into the King's Courts, became much more dilatory than it had been before.[112] The law underwent many changes, but ultimately *real* actions for the recovery of land were abolished by stat. 3 & 4 Wm. IV., and now the only direct mode of procedure for trying the title to real property is by *action of ejectment.*[113]

I. EJECTMENT is now a very important action, and by it alone possession of land is recovered. The form of the action is totally remodelled, and the proceedings in it are minutely pointed out by the common Law Procedure Act of 1852.

A writ is issued out of any of the superior courts of common law, directed to the person or persons in possession, and to all persons alleged to be entitled to defend the possession of the premises therein described, and commanding those to whom it is directed to appear in the court out of which the writ issued within sixteen days of the service thereof, to defend the possession of the property, or such part of it as they shall see fit. It also contains a notice that in default of appearance the defendants will be turned out of possession. The writ is served by delivering it personally to the tenant in possession, on the land or elsewhere, or by delivering it personally on the prem-

---

[112] For the old law respecting *writs of assize, wits of entry,* &c., see Blackstone, vol. iii.

[113] See 15 & 16 Vict., c. 76; 23 & 24 Vict., c. 126; 30 & 31 Vict., c. 142.

ises to some member of the family or household; and in either case it should be read over, or its purport explained.

The trial of the issue joined then proceeds in the usual way, and a verdict is found. If it is for the plaintiff, judgment is entered up for the possession of premises with costs, and possession will be delivered to him by the sheriff.

Upon the judgment, after a special verdict, or a bill of exceptions, or by consent after a special case, *error* may be brought in the same manner as in other actions. To complete the remedy in an ordinary case, recourse is had to another supplementary action, viz., an ordinary action of trespass, *quare clausum fregit,* to recover the mesne profits which the defendant has received during the period of his wrongful possession.

In the case of what is called a *vacant possession,* where the premises are wholly deserted, the writ must be served by pasting a copy upon the door of the dwelling-house or other conspicuous part of the property sought to be recovered.

II. TRESPASS. — *Trespass,* in its largest and most extensive sense, signifies any transgression or offence against the law of nature, of society, or of the country in which we live, whether it relates to a man's person or his property; but, in its limited sense, in which it is here referred to, it signifies an entry on another man's land without lawful authority, and doing some damage, however inconsiderable, to his property; for the right of *meum* and *tuum,* or property in land, being once established, it follows, as a necessary consequence, that this right must be exclusive; and the law of England, Justly considering that much inconvenience may happen to the owner, treats every entry upon another's land [unless by the owner's leave, or in some very particular cases] as an injury or wrong, for satisfaction of which an *action of trespass* will lie to recover such damage as a jury may assess. This injury is called trespass — *quare clausum fregit* — (breaking a man's close) — for every man's land is, in the eye of the law, enclosed, either by visible and material fence, or an invisible boundary existing only in the contemplation of law, and set apart from that of his neighbours.

A man is answerable not only for his own trespass, but that of his cattle also; for if, by his negligent keeping, they stray upon the land of another, and they there tread down his neighbour's herbage, and spoil his corn or his trees, this is a trespass for which the owner must answer in damages. And the law gives the party injured a double remedy in this case, by permitting him to distrain[114] the cattle thus *damage-feasant,* or doing damage, till the owner shall make him satisfaction; or else leaving him to his common remedy by *action.*

In some cases *trespass* is justifiable; as, if a man enters to demand or pay money, or to execute in a legal manner the process of the law. Also, a man may justify entering into an inn or public-house; so a landlord may justify entering to distrain for rent, and a reversioner to see if any waste be committed on the estate; but in cases where a man misdemeans himself, or makes an ill use of the authority with which the law entrusts him, he shall in general be accounted a trespasser *ab initio.*

III. NUISANCE. — *Nuisance (nocumentum,* or annoyance), signifies anything that works *hurt, inconvenience,* or *damage.* Nuisances are of two kinds — *public* or *common* nuisances — which affect the public, and are an annoyance to all the Queen's subjects;[115] and *private* nuisances, which may be defined as anything done to the hurt

---

[114] See "Distraining."
[115] See "Prescription"; also "Abatement."

or annoyance of the lands, tenements, or hereditaments of another.

There are two kinds of Nuisances: — Such *nuisances* as may affect a man's *corporeal* hereditaments; and those that may damage such as are *incorporeal.* First, as to *corporeal* hereditaments. If a man builds a house so close to mine that his roof overhangs my roof and throws the water off his roof upon mine; this is a nuisance, for which an action will lie, even without proof of actual damage. Likewise, to erect a house or other building go near to mine that it obstructs my *ancient* lights and windows is a nuisance of a similar nature, for light and air are indispensable to every building. Also, if a person keeps his hogs, or other offensive animals so near the house of another, that the stench of them incommodes him and makes the air unwholesome. A like injury is, if one's neighbour sets up and exercises any offensive trade, as a tanner's, a tallow-chandler's, or the like; for, though these are lawful and necessary trades, yet they should be originated in remote places.

The rule is — *Sic utere tuo, ut alienum non laedas:* "Make use of your own property so that you injure not another's."

Not only a nuisance, but a *breach of duty* causing damage to real property, is actionable. If my neighbour, who ought to scour a ditch, does not, whereby my land is overflowed, this is an actionable nuisance.

As to *Incorporeal Hereditaments,* the law enforces similar principles of justice. It is a nuisance to stop or divert water that runs to another's meadow or mill; to corrupt or poison a water-course, by erecting a, dye-house or a lime-pit for the use of trade, in the upper part of the stream; or in short, to do any act therein that in its consequences must necessarily tend to the prejudice of one's neighbour. Also, if a person has a right of way over another's ground, by grant or prescription, and he is obstructed in the use of it, either by its being totally stopped, or by logs put across it, or by ploughing over it, by which, means he cannot enjoy his right of way; or, at least, enjoy it so commodiously as he ought to do, he may have his remedy by an action *on the case to* recover damages.

Again, if I am entitled to hold a fair or market, and another person sets up a fair or market so near mine that ho does me a prejudice, it is a nuisance to the freehold which I have in my market or fair. But in order to make this out to be a nuisance, it is necessary — 1. That my market or fair be the elder, otherwise the nuisance lies at my own door. — 2. That the market be erected within the third part of twenty miles from mine, so that if the new market be not within seven miles of the old one, it is no nuisance.

Likewise if a ferry is erected on a river, so near another ancient ferry as to draw away its custom, it is a nuisance to the owner of the old one; for where there is a ferry by prescription, the owner is bound to keep it always in repair and readiness, for the use of all the Queen's subjects; otherwise he may be amerced. It would be therefore extremely hard if the owner of a new ferry were suffered to share his profits, who does not also share his burthen. But where the reason ceases, the law also ceases with it; therefore it is no nuisance to erect a mill so near mine as to draw away the custom, unless the miller also intercepts the water. Neither is it a nuisance to set up any trade, or a school, in the neighbourhood or in rivalship with another; for by such competition the public are like to be gainers; and, if the new mill or school occasion any damage to the old one, it is *damnum absque injuria.*

The remedy at law in the case of a *public* nuisance is by *indictment* at the instance of the Attorney-General.

In the case of a *private* nuisance, the remedy at *law* is by action of *trespass on the case,* for damages; the remedy in equity is by *bill,*[116] praying for an *injunction* to remove the nuisance.

Where *a public* nuisance is also a *private* nuisance, the individual thus aggrieved may have his private remedy at law by *action on the case,* for damages; or in equity, by *bill* for an *injunction.*

An action for nuisance will not lie, nor a bill for an injunction be entertained, unless evidence be given of damage resulting from the nuisance.

IV. WASTE. — *Waste* is a spoil and destruction of an estate by the tenant either in houses, woods, or lands during the continuance of his particular estate therein, by demolishing, not the temporary profits only, but the very substance of the thing, thereby rendering it wild and desolate. The common law expresses this waste by the word *vastum;* and this *vastum,* or waste, is either voluntary, or permissive; the one by an actual designed demolition of the lands, woods, or houses; the other arising from mere negligence and want of sufficient care in reparations, fences, and the like.[117]

The persons who may be injured by *waste* are such as have some *interest* in the estate wasted; for if a man be the absolute tenant in fee-simple, without any incumbrance or charge on the premises, he may commit whatever waste his own discretion may prompt him to do, without being impeachable or accountable for it to any one. And though his heir is sure to be the sufferer, yet *nemo est hæres*

---

[116] See "Bill in Chancery."
[117] See 17 & 18 Vict., c. 125, s. 79.

viventes: no man is certain of succeeding him, as well on account of the uncertainty which shall die first, as also because he has it in his own power to constitute what heir he pleases, according to the civil law notion of a *hæres natus* and a *hæres factus;* or, in the more accurate phraseology of our English law, he may aliene or devise his estate to whomsoever he thinks proper, and by such alienation or devise may disinherit his heir-at-law.

One species of interest which may be injured by *waste, is* that of a person who has a right of *common* in the place wasted, especially if it be common of estovers, or a right of cutting and carrying away wood for house-bote, plough-bote, &c. Here, if the owner of the wood demolishes the whole wood, and thereby destroys all possibility of taking estovers, this is an injury to the commoner, for which he may have his remedy by an *action on the case.*

A mortgagee in possession will be restrained from cutting down timber, and so will a mortgagor in possession.

The most important interest that is hurt by this commission of *waste* is that of him who has the remainder or reversion after a particular estate for life or years; so if the tenant for life or years commit or suffer any waste, the law now gives an adequate remedy to him in remainder or reversion to whom the inheritance appertains in expectancy, by an action *on the case,* to recover such damage as a jury may award; or by *bill* in Chancery praying for an injunction to restrain the tenant from committing waste which may be threatened.

V. DISTURBANCE. — A *wrong* may be done to an incorporeal hereditament by hindering and disquieting the owner in his regular and lawful enjoyment of it. Such may be constituted by *disturbance:* — 1. Of a *Franchise.* — 2.

Of a Common. — 3. Of a *Way.* — 4. *Of Tenure.* — 5. *Of Patronage.*

1. Disturbance of a *franchise* happens when a man has the franchise of holding a court-leet, of keeping a fair or market, of free warren, of taking toll, of seizing waifs or estrays, or any other species of franchise, and he is disturbed in the lawful exercise thereof by which his property is damnified; he is entitled to sue for damages by a special *action on the case;* if for toll, the owner may take a *distress* if he pleases.

2. The *disturbance* of *common* occurs where an act is done by which the right of another to his common is incommoded or diminished, which may happen when a stranger who has no right of common, puts in cattle. Or by *surcharging* it; that is, putting more cattle therein than the pasture or herbage will reasonably sustain, or the party has a right to do. In all cases of *disturbance* the commoner may bring an *action on the case to* recover damages; and in cases of *surcharging* the common, by distraining or impounding so many of the beasts as are above the accustomed number.

3. The *disturbance* of *ways* happens when a person who has a right of way over another's grounds by grant or prescription is obstructed by enclosures or other obstacles; or, by ploughing across it, by which means he cannot enjoy his right of way; or, at least, not in so commodious a manner as he ought to do. The remedy for such disturbance is by an *action on the case* to recover damages; or by *bill* in Chancery for an *injunction.*

4. The *disturbance* of *tenure* occurs where a stranger, either by menaces or threats, or by unlawful distresses, or by fraud, contrives to drive a tenant away, or inveigle him to leave his tenancy. This the law justly construes to be a

wrong and an injury; the usual remedy for which is an *action on the case* to recover damages.

5. The *disturbance* of *patronage* is a hindrance or obstruction of a patron to present his clerk to a benefice. This happens when a stranger who has no right presents a clerk, who is thereupon admitted and instituted, by which usurpation the patron, by the common law, lost not only his turn of presenting *pro hâc vice,* but also the absolute and perpetual inheritance of the advowson, so that he could, not present again upon the next vacancy unless in the meantime he recovered his right by a *real* action.[118] The reason given for his losing the present turn and not being able to eject the usurper's clerk was, that the final intent of the law in creating this species of property being to have a fit person to celebrate divine service, it preferred the peace of the Church, provided a clerk were once admitted and instituted, to the right of any patron whatever. Usurpation now[119] gains no right to the usurper with regard to any future avoidance, but only to the present vacancy if not remedied within six months; and during those six months it is only a species of disturbance. The remedy is a writ of *quare impedit,* now the only action for the *disturbance* of patronage, in which the patron, not the clerk, is plaintiff. It is commenced by a writ of summons in the same manner and form as in an ordinary action.

After an adverse possession of one hundred years, the right to an advowson is extinguished.

[118] A writ of *right of advowson* is now abolished.
[119] See 6 & 7 Vict., c. 54; and 23 & 24 Vict., c. 126. s. 26.

CHAPTER IX
INJURIES PROCEEDING FROM OR AFFECTING THE CROWN

Having considered the *Injuries* or *Private Wrongs* that may be offered by one subject to another, and how they are remedied, let us now inquire into the mode of redressing those "Injuries" to which the Grown itself is a party, — injuries where the Crown is the *aggressor,* or the *sufferer,* and which are remedied by peculiar forms of process, appropriate to the Royal prerogative. In treating therefore of these, let us consider first the manner of redressing those wrongs or injuries which a subject may suffer from the Crown; and then of redressing those which the Crown may receive from a subject.

Explain the Redress of Wrongs inflicted by the Crown.

"That the Sovereign can do no wrong" is a necessary and fundamental principle of the English Constitution; meaning that, in the first place, whatever may be amiss in the conduct of public affairs is not chargeable personally on the Sovereign; and secondly, that the prerogative of the Crown extends not to do an injury; for, being created for the benefit of the people, it ought not to be exercised to their prejudice. Whenever, therefore, it happens that through misinformation or inadvertence the Crown has been induced to invade the private rights of any of its subjects, though no action or suit will lie against the Sovereign, yet the law has furnished the subject with a decent and respectful mode of removing that invasion by informing the Crown of the true state of the matter in dispute, by *petition of right,* which will then be put in a regular train for adjudication and adjustment.

Injuries to the rights of property can scarcely be committed by the Crown without the intervention of its officers; and for them the law in matters of right entertains no respect or delicacy, but furnishes various methods of detecting the errors or misconduct of those agents by whom the Sovereign has been deceived, and induced to do a temporary injustice.

The common-law methods of obtaining possession or restitution from the Crown of either "real" or "personal" property are: —

1. By *petition de droit,* or petition of right. — 2. By *monstrans de droit,* or manifestation or plea of right.

The former is of use when the Sovereign is in fall possession of any hereditaments or chattels, and the petitioner suggests such a right as controverts the title of the Crown grounded on facts disclosed in the petition itself; in which case he must be careful to state truly the title of the Crown, otherwise the petition shall abate; and then, upon this answer being endorsed or underwritten by the Sovereign — *soit droit fait al partie* (let right be done to the party), a commission will issue to inquire as to the truth of this suggestion; after the return of which the Attorney-General may plead in bar, and the merits will be determined upon issue or demurrer, as in suits between subject and subject.[120]

Monstrans de droit is where the right of the party as well as the right of the Crown appear upon record. In that case the party shall have *monstrans de droit,* which is putting in a claim of right grounded on facts already acknowledged and established, and praying the judgment of the court, whether upon those facts the Crown or the sub-

[120] See Petition of Right Act, 23 & 24 Vict., c. 34.

ject has the right. These proceedings are had in the Petty Bag Office in the Court of Chancery, and upon any of them being determined against the Crown, the judgment is — *quod manus domini regis amoveantur,* and by such judgment the Crown is instantly out of possession.

Explain the methods of Redressing such Injuries as the Crown may receive from the subject.

They are redressed — 1. By certain common-law actions such as *quare impedit or* trespass, which are deemed not inconsistent with the Royal prerogative and dignity of the Crown.

2. By *inquisition* or *inquest* of office, which is an inquiry made by the Sovereign's officer, or escheator, or by writ sent for that purpose; or by commissioners specially appointed, concerning any matter that entitles the Sovereign to the possession of land or tenements, goods or chattels. This is done by a jury of no determinate number, being either twelve, or less, or more.

3. By writ of *scire facias* in Chancery, where the Crown has unadvisedly granted any exclusive privilege by letters-patent, which ought not to have been granted; or, where the patentee has done an act that amounts to a forfeiture of the grant.

4. By *information* on behalf of the Crown, filed in the Exchequer by the Attorney-General — a method of suit for recovering money or other chattels, or for obtaining satisfaction in damages for any *personal wrong* committed on the lands or other possessions of the Crown.

5. By writ of *quo warranto*, which is in the nature of a writ of right for the Crown against him who has claimed or usurped any office, franchise, or liberty, to inquire by what authority he supports his claim, in order to determine

the right. The more modern method of prosecution now is by *information* filed in the Court of Queen's Bench by the Attorney-General, in the nature of a writ of *quo warranto,* which is properly a criminal method of prosecution, as well to punish the usurper by a fine for usurpation of the franchise, as to oust him, or seize it for the Crown. This proceeding is now applied to the decision of corporate disputes between party and party, by filing an information in the nature of *quo warranto,* against any person usurping or unlawfully holding any franchise or office in any city, borough, or town corporate.[121]

6. By the prerogative writ *of mandamus,* which issues out of the Court of Queen's Bench, and is directed to a person, corporation, or court, and in the Sovereign's name commands such person, body corporate, or tribunal to do a certain specified act, as matter of duty, agreeably to right and justice. It is a *remedial writ* of a very extensive nature, and is chiefly confined to cases where relief is required in respect of the infringement of some *public* right or duty, and where none can be obtained by an action at law.

Whenever the law requires a thing to be done, and the public at large are interested, a *mandamus* will issue to order it to be done by the person upon whom the obligation of doing it is imposed.

A party applying for a *mandamus* must make out a legal right and a legal obligation; and if he shows such right, it is sufficient. A legal obligation which is the proper foundation for a *mandamus* can only arise from. common law, from statute, or from contract; and if a writ of *mandamus* commands the defendant to do more than he is under a legal obligation to perform, the writ is invalid; and where a *mandamus* orders several things to be done and is

---

[121] See 7 Wm. IV. & 1 Vict., c. 78; and 6 & 7 Vict., c. 89.

bad in respect of one of the things commanded, it is bad *in toto.*[122]

CHAPTER X
PURSUIT OF REMEDIES BY ACTION

Having considered the *Injuries* cognizable by the Courts of Common Law, let us now investigate the *Remedies* by *Action,* and the manner in which those several remedies are pursued and applied, and the course of proceedings in the Courts of Common law.

Give briefly a general account of an "Action at Law," and explain the method of proceeding in, and prosecuting an action upon any of the "personal" writs before mentioned.

An Action at Law.

An *Action at Law* is the form prescribed by law for the recovery of one's due; or the lawful demand of one's right. Actions are *real, mixed, or personal.*

REAL ACTIONS were those brought for the recovery of *real* property only; but now, as before stated, by action of *ejectment; mixed,* for the recovery of *real* property and damages for its being wrongfully with holden; while *personal* actions extend to all claims for money due on contracts, or for damages for breach of contract, or injury to person or property, and also to the recovery of specific goods and chattels. *Personal actions,* therefore, embrace a conspicuous range of those civil differences that become the subject of litigation.

[122] The provisions of the Common Law Procedure Act,1852 apply to the proceeding and upon pleading a prerogative writ of *mandamus* issued by the Court of Queen's Bench.

The forms of the ordinary PERSONAL ACTIONS are *assumpsit, debt, covenant, trespass, case, trover, detinue,* and *replevin,* which have been already explained.

The ordinary and regular steps in an "Action at Law" are: —

I. The Process.

The first step to be taken in an action is, by issuing a summons for the party to appear, by himself or attorney, in the Court in which the action is intended to be carried on. This is effected by a *writ of summons,* which, if for the recovery of an ascertained amount, is indorsed with the statement of the grounds of claim or cause of action, and must be indorsed with the name and place of abode of the attorney actually suing it out; or, the address of the plaintiff, if it be sued out by him in person. It may be issued at the option of the plaintiff out of any one of the superior Courts of common law, viz., the Queen's Bench, the Common Pleas, or the Exchequer, except in cases within the exclusive jurisdiction of the county courts.

The service of the writ, whenever it is practicable, must be personal. If the defendant, after reasonable efforts have been made to effect personal service, fails to appear, a judge of the court in which the action is brought may direct that the plaintiff shall be at liberty to enter an appearance for the defendant, and proceed in the action as if personal service had been effected.[123]

---

[123] The Common Law Procedure Acts of 1852, 1854, and 1860 render actions in superior courts of Common Law much more simple and speedy than formerly. The remedial provisions of these Acts have practically removed any danger of an action being defeated on grounds purely technical, and they have swept away needles and fictitious averments altogether. See 15 & 16 Vict., C.76; 17 & 13 Vict., c. 128; 28 & 24 Vict., c. 126, amended by 30 & 31 Vict., c. 142, s. 43.

II. The Declaration.

When the defendant appears to the *writ,* or an appearance is entered for him, formal pleadings preparatory to the trial commence.

The successive steps are: —

The *Declaration,* which contains the cause of action for which the plaintiff sues. It must omit no allegation that is material to the cause of action, and must also state the *venue;* that is, the county in which it is intended that the action shall be tried. This is of two kinds: *transitory* or *local.* Transitory for injuries that might have happened anywhere, in which case the plaintiff may adopt any county he pleases as a *venue;* local when the cause of action has arisen in a particular place or county, and then the *venue* must be laid in that county; but the court may allow a suggestion to be entered on the record for the trial of the cause in another county.

When the plaintiff has stated his case in the *declaration,* it is Incumbent on the defendant, within the time prescribed, to make his *defence,* and plead to it.

III. The Subsequent Pleadings.

If the *declaration* contains matter insufficient in point of law to support the plaintiff's case, the defendant's course is to file a *demurrer,* which is argued before the court; if sufficient, he files a *plea,* which is the defendant's answer to the *declaration,* and is either a *plea* in *abatement* or a *plea in bar.*

A *plea in abatement does* not contain an answer to the cause of action, but shows some defect or informality, and makes prayer to that effect. This is argued and determined by the court.

A plea in *bar* is a peremptory and substantial answer to the action, which is either a plea in *traverse* or a plea in *confession* and *avoidance;* that is, denying or showing justification or excuse for the matter charged in the declaration. This raises an *issue of fact,* and is tried by a jury.

Pleas that totally deny the cause of complaint are either the *general issue* or a *special plea.* The general issue or general plea traverses and denies the whole declaration, and the litigants are then said to be at issue, and being thus apprised of the exact question in dispute, they can now prepare their proofs in support of their respective cases.

Pleadings must neither be *double,* nor *repugnant.* Duplicity occurs when the *narratio,* or declaration, alleges several causes of action in support of the same demand. *Repugnancy is* when the different allegations are inconsistent with each other. *Prolixity* must be avoided; also *verbosity, vagueness,* and *argumentativeness.*

The great attributes of pleading are *certainty, brevity,* and *precision.*

The *replication* follows the plea, containing the plaintiff's answer to the plea. A *rejoinder is* the defendant's answer to the replication; there then may be a *sur-rejoinder,* and a *rebutter.* At each of these steps the party replying, rejoining, or framing any other pleading, must either *traverse* or *confess and avoid;* that is, must either deny some material part of the adversary's last pleading, or must admit such pleading to be true, but allege some new matter, altering the legal effect of it, and showing that he himself is entitled to judgment.

In the course of pleading, if either party neglects to put in his declaration, plea, replication, rejoinder, and the like within the time allotted by statute, or the standing rules of the court in which the action is commenced, the plaintiff, if the omission be his, is said to be *nonsuited,* and shall lose the benefit of his action; or if the negligence be on the side of the defendant, judgment may be had against him by default.

IV. Issue and Demurrer.

ISSUE, *exitus,* is the conclusion of all the pleadings, which is either upon matter of *law,* or matter of *fact.*

Issues of fact are generally arrived at by the *replication* or the *rejoinder.* As to issues of law, these are raised by *demurrer,* to which *joinder in demurrer is* pleaded. This raises an issue of law, and is argued before the judges.

V. Trial.

The action being now ripe for trial, *notice of the time and place of trial* must be given to the defendant.

Before trial the important duty devolves upon the litigants of preparing evidence, which will be either documentary or oral.[124]

The cause being called on for trial, the jurors, twelve indifferent persons selected by lot from a greater number, attend, having been previously summoned for that purpose. Jurors may be "challenged" *propter affectum,* for suspicion of bias or partiality, or other good reasons, by either plaintiff or defendant, and if the "challenge" is allowed, they are put aside, and others take their places in the jury-box. They are then separately sworn to give a true

---

[124] A power to compel either party to allow the applicant an *inspection of* all documents in his custody or under his control relating to the action is now exercised by a court of law. See 14 & 15 Vict., c. 99; also the Common Law Procedure Act: 23 & 24 Vict., c. 126, amended by 30 & 31 Vict., c. 142.

verdict according to the evidence, and hence they are denominated the jury, *jurata,* and jurors, *juratores.*

After the jury are sworn, the junior counsel for the plaintiff generally *opens;* that is, states the pleadings, and the leading counsel then addresses the jury and states his case at length. After which he calls his evidence in support of his case.

All witnesses, of whatever religion or country, that have the use of their reason, are admissible, except such as are infamous, or such as are ignorant of the nature of an oath. Each witness after giving evidence may be cross-examined by the opposite party, which cross-examination being concluded, he may then be re-examined by the party who called him in reference to any matters suggested by the cross-examination.

In the event of the counsel for the defendant announcing, at the close of the evidence adduced by the plaintiff his intention not to call witnesses, the counsel for the plaintiff sums up the evidence. The counsel for the defendant, not having adduced evidence, thus reserves for himself that which is considered to be a very important point, the right of addressing the jury last. But if he adduces evidence, he loses this right, and the party beginning has the general reply.

The evidence and the speeches of counsel for the plaintiff and defendant being concluded, the judge states the nature of the issue, and sums up the whole of the evidence, observing wherein the main question and principal interest lie — stating what evidence has been given to support it, with such remarks as he thinks necessary for the direction of the jury concerning the law upon the subject.

The verdict must, by our law, be unanimous; but if the jury declare to the judge that there is no chance of their agreeing, the judge may discharge them, which involves a second trial, at a future time.

The jury, if they express a wish to withdraw, leave the court to consider their verdict. When unanimous, the jury then give their verdict for the plaintiff or defendant by their foreman; and judgment to that effect is entered on the Record.

VI. Judgment.

After judgment is entered, *execution* will immediately follow, unless the unsuccessful party thinks himself unjustly aggrieved by the verdict, or by something which has passed at the trial, and applies to the court, *in banc,* for a *new trial;* or, for *arrest of judgment;* or, for *judgment non obslante veredicto;* or, for a *repleader;* and if the court, on the allegations made by the counsel moving, are of opinion that the matter should be further investigated, a rule *nisi* is granted, which means that unless the opposite party displaces that opinion, a new trial will be allowed. A rule to show cause is usually called a rule *nisi;* and it becomes *absolute,* unless cause is shown.

VII. New Trial.

A motion for a *new trial* cannot be made after the expiration of the first four days of the next term after the day of trial, unless entered in a list of postponed motions by leave of the court.

The question as to a *new trial* comes on for argument before the *full court,* and after hearing counsel on *both* sides, the court either directs a *new trial* or refuses it; in other words, it grants a new trial by making the rule *nisi, absolute;* if otherwise, it discharges the rule *nisi.*

Grounds of moving for a *new trial,* besides that of a misdirection of the judge, or the improper admission or rejection of evidence, are: — That the verdict is *against* the weight of evidence; that the damages are *excessive;* misconduct of the jury; or that the plaintiff or defendant has been taken by *surprise.*

When the verdict is not disturbed, and judgment follows, the usual time at which execution may issue is fourteen days from the verdict, unless the court or a judge orders execution to issue at an earlier or later period, with or without terms.

VIII. Motions.

A motion for *arrest* of *judgment* may be made by a *defendant,* on sufficient cause being apparent on the face of the record; but the court must be satisfied that such is the fact before it will grant an arrest of judgment.

A motion for judgment *non obslante veredicto* is made in respect to some objection also apparent on the face of the record. This can only be made by a *plaintiff,* and the same rule applies as to satisfying the court.

A motion for a *repleader* is where, through misconduct or inadvertence of the pleader, the issue has been joined on a fact totally insufficient to determine the right, so that the court cannot know upon the finding for whom judgment ought to be given. This, however, is very seldom resorted to, as the point may be raised more conveniently by *demurrer.*

IX. Error.

Error lies after final judgment has been obtained to reverse a judgment on the ground of some defect in the proceedings, which renders it erroneous. Error *in fact* relates only to the case where some fact not appearing on the record invalidates the judgment on grounds of a technical character, which rarely occurs. Error *in law* is where, on the face of the record, it appears that the judgment was given on insufficient grounds, as that the allegations in the declaration were insufficient in law to maintain the action, and that judgment ought to have been given for the defendant, and not for the plaintiff.[125]

X. Execution.

Final judgment in the action having been signed, *execution* may ensue.

The ordinary writs of *execution* by which the recovery of money is enforced on a judgment are: —

1. *Fieri facias,* [fi. fa.]

2. *Elegit.*

These writs issue out of the court in which the record is, and are directed to the sheriff of the county in which the execution is to be put in force.

The writ *of fieri facias* commands the sheriff "that he cause to be made of the goods and chattels of the judgment debtor in his bailiwick the amount of such judgment with 4 per cent. interest from the day on which judgment was entered up."

The writ of *elegit* — *so* called because the person suing out the execution is said to have chosen or elected to have that remedy, in addition to the proceeding by *fieri facias,* where that remedy is supposed to be insufficient to satisfy the judgment — by which the sheriff is commanded "that he cause to be delivered to the judgment creditor the lands and tenements of the judgment debtor,

---

[125] For proceedings *in Error, see* Common Law Procedure Acts already referred to.

which he or any person in trust for him held at the time when judgment was entered up." On delivery of possession of the lands to the judgment creditor he enters upon these lands and into the receipt of the rents and profits; and when from this source he has received sufficient to satisfy the debt for which judgment was entered up, he is bound to redeliver the lands and tenements to the judgment debtor.[126]

A *writ of capias ad satisfaciendum* might, until lately, be issued, under which the body of the judgment debtor was taken to satisfy the amount of the judgment; but this *writ* is now abolished, provisions being substituted for obtaining a judge's order for payment by instalments, and for commitment to prison in case of wilful neglect.

Having stated the ordinary course of an Action at Law as remodelled by the Common Law Procedure Acts, explain the proceedings on "Interpleaders" which are sometimes incidental to, or follow upon, an Action at Law.

Interpleader, which is a motion for relief from adverse claims, is a mode of relief to a party who has in his possession money or goods which are claimed by two or more opposite parties, each requiring him to pay a certain sum of money, or to deliver certain goods; and, in order to obtain relief from these adverse claims, the holder applies to the court or a judge in chambers for an order to be served upon the adverse claimants to show cause why they should not interplead together; and, when the judge makes such an order, the responsibility is removed from the party having such money or goods in his possession, and the adverse parties proceed to try their respective rights by an

[126] Formerly only a moiety was delivered to the judgment creditor, but by 1 & 2 Vict., c. 110, the sheriff is commanded to deliver execution upon *all* the lands of the judgment debtor.

action at law, or in such other manner as the judge shall direct. If money, the amount is usually ordered to be brought into court.

By *interpleader,* relief and protection are also afforded to sheriffs and other officers when placed in a difficulty arising out of the execution of process against goods and chattels by reason of adverse claims made to such goods and chattels by assignees of bankrupts and other persons.[127]

CHAPTER XI
EQULITY JURISPRUDENCE

Let us briefly consider *matters of Equity,* which belong to the peculiar jurisdiction of the Court of Chancery; such as the *relief* which cannot be afforded by Courts of Law, but which Courts of Equity can appropriately give.

Explain Equity and the general "Equitable Principles" acted upon in the Court of Chancery.

Equity is said to be "synonymous with natural justice."

From the difficulty of framing general rules, many matters of natural justice are left to be disposed of *in foro conscientiœ* by Equity Jurisprudence; but where it is clear that the courts of law can afford adequate relief without circuity of action or multiplicity of suits and are able to do justice to all parties, equity will not interfere.

---

[127] For further information as to "Interpleader," see Interpleader Acts, 1 & 2 Wm. IV., c. 58; 1 & 2 Vict., c. 45; 9 & 10 Vict., c. 95; 11 & 12 Vict., c. 83; 19 & 20 Vict., c. 108; 23 & 24 Vict., c. 126.

Equity, then, in its true and genuine meaning, is the soul and spirit of all law. *Positive* law is construed and *rational* law is administered by it.

Natural justice is the rule by which, where positive law is either silent, defective, or not clearly defined, the decisions of courts of equity are guided. Whore the will of the legislature has been clearly pronounced with regard to all the circumstances which belong to a case, as a *general rule,* equity "can neither take it up where the law leaves it, nor extend the remedy further than the law allows."

The general maxims peculiar to equity are: —

1. That equity will not suffer a wrong to be without a remedy.

2. Equity will administer a due remedy where it cannot be had at law without circuitry of action or multiplicity of suits.

3. Equity corrects the imperfections of common law whenever there are relations existing between the parties of which the common law is unable to take cognizance. For instance, in the case of accounts between partners, a court of common law will not entertain an action by a man against his partner. Equity supplies the omission. Similar cases arise between co-executors and corporators.

4. Equity determines according to the *spirit* of the rule, and not the strictness of the letter.

5. *Fraud, accident,* and *trust* are the peculiar objects of a, court of equity.

6. Whenever possible, equity takes care that a right shall be actually enjoyed, and will interfere to prevent a violation of that right; it will anticipate the probable event, and restrain, by injunction, a person who merely shows an intention to do an injury, or to break his covenant. The

court will also restrain the infringement of a patent of invention, the counterfeiting of a trade-mark, and the piracy of a copyright.

7. Equity will often enforce the *specific performance* of a contract, whereas courts of common law can only give damages for the breach thereof.

8. It is a maxim that *de vigilantibus, et non dormientibus, æquitas subvenit,* the meaning of which is, that equity discountenances *ladies,* or delay; and, independently of any *statutes of limitation,* refuses to interfere where there has been *lâches* in prosecuting rights; or where there has been long and unreasonable acquiescence in the assertion of adverse rights.

9. In regard to *mistakes* in matter of *law,* it is a maxim that "*ignorantia legis now excusat;*" as where the mistake is one of title, arising from ignorance of a point of law of such constant occurrence as to be understood by the community at large; this is considered, in equity, sufficient to afford such a presumption, so as to disentitle the party to relief.

10. *Misrepresentation is* a ground of relief, whether the party who made the assertion or intimation knew it to be false, or made it without knowing whether it was true or false.

11. A person cannot avail himself of what has been obtained by the fraud of another, unless he not only is innocent of the fraud, but has given some valuable consideration.

12. If a person conceals facts and circumstances which he is under some legal or equitable obligation to communicate to the other, it amounts to a fraud, for which equity will grant relief; but a purchaser is not bound to communicate his knowledge of the *value* of the property

to the vendor; for it is the business of the vendor to know and sufficiently to estimate the worth of his own property. Mere inadequacy of price or any other inequality in the bargain does not constitute by itself a ground to avoid it. Still in such cases as gross inadequacy, amounting to conclusive evidence of imposition or undue influence, courts of equity will interfere on the ground of fraud.

In all cases of any complication or difficulty, whether it he in matters of *accident, mistake, fraud, trusts, accounts, mortgages;* and in cases of infants, of persons of unsound mind, and of *married women,* the Court of Chancery has thus, practically speaking, exclusive jurisdiction.[128]

CHAPTER XII
A SUIT IN CHANCERY

The practice and procedure in the Court of Chancery are now regulated and governed by certain rules and orders which were promulgated from time to time by the proper authorities, and are now consolidated by virtue of 15 & 16 Vict., c. 86 (1860), and are called "Consolidated Rules and Regulations of the Court of Chancery," These,

[128] For cases of *trust,* see Trustee Acts, 13 & 14 Vict., c. 60; and 15 & 16 Vict., c. 55.
For control which the Court of Chancery exercises over Solicitors, see Attorneys and Solicitors Acts, C & 7 Vict., c. 73; and 23 Vict., c.127.
For Charitable Trust Acts, 16 & 17 Vict., c. 187; 18 & 19 Vict., c. 124; and 23 & 24 Vict., c. 134.
For Lunacy Regulation Act, 16 & 17 Vict, c. 70; and the Amendment Act, 25 & 26 Vict., c. 85; 32 & 33 Vict., c. 110.
By the Companies Act (25 & 26 Vict., c, 89), the Court of Chancery entertains in a summary way applications by petition to wind up joint-stock companies, and the collection and distribution of the assets are made under the direction of the court. See also 30 & 31 Vict., c. 131; for Joint-Stock Companies Acts, see 21 & 22 Vict, c. 60; and 25 & 26 Vict, c. 89; for Limited Liability Act, 18 & 19 Vict., c. 133; 20 & 21 Vict, c. 14.

with a few subsequent orders, now constitute the law of the Court as to its proceedings.

Explain briefly the Proceedings in a Suit in Chancery.

The first step in a *Suit in Chancery* is what is technically called *filing a bill.* This is done by the party — who considers himself aggrieved, stating shortly the facts of the case, asking for the particular relief he thinks himself entitled to, and praying for general necessary relief at the hands of the court.

The *bill* sets forth the circumstances of the case, as *fraud, trust,* or *hardship,* and praying relief. If the bill be to stay *waste* or other injury, or to stay proceedings at law, an *injunction* is also prayed.

The bill must charge all necessary parties to appear in court to answer the statements therein. It must be signed by counsel, printed, and a copy filed.

If the defendant, having been duly served with the bill, do not enter an appearance within the prescribed time, the plaintiff may enter an appearance for him, so as to be able to proceed with the suit.

To this *bill* the defendant must enter an appearance, and if interrogatories are filed with it, he must answer them *seriatim.* Should the defendant be advised that he has a good ground of defence by *demurrer* — which is apparent on the bill itself, either from the matter contained in it or from some defect in its form — the defendant may, instead of *answering, demur* to it. This, like a demurrer at common law, is argued before the court, and disposed of as the court shall think fit. Instead of a demurrer, the defendant may plead to the *jurisdiction* of the court. Pleas, however, are not favoured by the court, and are seldom resorted to.

An *answer,* which is the usual defence that is made to a plaintiff's bill, either denies or confesses all the material parts of it; and where it does not deny, it may *confess* and *avoid;* that is, justify or qualify the facts; or it may simply admit the case made by the bill, and submit to the judgment of the court. It is given in upon oath. It is the statement of the defendant as to those matters *of fact to* which the bill refers, and by means of it the plaintiff obtains a *discovery,* as it is called, of facts which it might be otherwise impossible to prove.

After an answer is filed, the plaintiff may amend his bill, either by adding new parties, or new matter, or both; such amendment being usually made in consequence of the admissions in the answer of the defendant; and the defendant, if necessary, is obliged to answer the amended bill. If the answer to the plaintiff's bill, or interrogatories, as the case may be, is considered sufficient; that is, a full answer to the facts of the bill, and there is ground for a final order or decree, the plaintiff proceeds upon the answer without entering into evidence. In such case the cause is set down for hearing upon bill and answer, and the proper order or decree is made by the court. If, however, the plaintiff is advised that he must prove his case, he files what is called a *traversing note,* which is a declaration of his intention to proceed with his cause, as if the defendant had filed an answer traversing, that is denying, the facts of the case made by the bill.[129]

When the cause is ripe for hearing, it is set down to be heard in its turn before the Master of the Rolls or one of the three Vice-Chancellors to whose court the bill was originally attached. After having heard counsel on both sides, the court proceeds to pronounce the decree, adjusting every point in debate according to equity and good conscience. The minutes of the decree are taken down by the registrar in open court, copies of which are given out to the various parties interested in the suit, and settled before the registrar; or in cases of difficulty by the court itself, the decree taking various forms to suit the particular circumstances of the case.

During the suit the court permits the parties at any stage to make applications to it. Such applications are for subordinate and interlocutory purposes, and may be made in several ways, either by summons obtained at the judges' chambers to whose court the cause is attached; or by motion in court, or by a formal petition addressed to the court.

The most common of the important orders asked, for on motion are orders for *injunctions.* An injunction is a writ issuing out of the Court of Chancery commanding the person to whom it is addressed to abstain from doing some specified thing, upon pain of imprisonment for contempt of court. It is either *provisional* or *temporary,* until the coming in of the defendant's answer, or until the hearing of the cause. This is decided by the court on the hearing of the motion for an injunction.

If at the hearing of the cause the court shall consider that the plaintiff has not established his case by the evidence, the bill is dismissed, with such costs to be paid by the plaintiff as the court shall think fit.

If, however, a decree is made in the cause, and either party be dissatisfied with the terms, he may present his petition of appeal to the Lords Justices or the Lord Chancellor, upon giving security for, or payment of, the costs already incurred in the suit. The appeal comes on for hearing and discussion by counsel on both sides, and the

---

[129] See 26 & 26 Vict., c. 42.

court either reverses the decree, or affirms it, or makes such order varying the decree as the court may deem just.

An appeal from this decision, if *duly enrolled,* may be made to the House of Lords.

BOOK IV
PUBLIC WRONGS

CHAPTER I
THE NATURE OF CRIMES AND THEIR PUNISHMENTS

We have now arrived at the fourth and last branch, which treats of *Public Wrongs,* or *Crimes* and *Misdemeanors.* Let us, in the first place, consider the general nature of crimes and their punishments. — Secondly, the persons capable of committing crimes. — Thirdly, their several *degrees* of guilt, as *principals* or *accessories.* — Fourthly, the several *species* of crimes, with the punishment annexed to each by the laws of England. — Fifthly, the means of *preventing* their perpetration. — Sixthly, the method of *inflicting* those punishments which the law has annexed to each several crime and misdemeanor.

Explain the nature of "Crime" in general, and state the distinction between "Public" and "Private" Wrongs.

A *Crime is* an act committed or omitted in violation of a public law, either *forbidding* or *commanding* it.

In English law offences are technically divided into *felonies* and *misdemeanors. Felony (felonia,* of feudal origin) comprised every species of crime which occasioned at common law the forfeiture of lands and goods. A *misdemeanor,* by our common law, is deemed to be inferior in degree to felony; and the indictment for a felony must set forth that the act charged was done *feloniously.* By 14 & 15 Vict., c. 100, it is provided that if, upon the trial of any person for a *misdemeanor,* the evidence amounts to a *felony,* such person shall not by reason thereof be acquitted.

The distinction of *public wrongs* from *private* — of *crimes* and *misdemeanors* from *civil injuries* — seems principally to consist in this: that *private wrongs,* or civil injuries, are an infringement or privation of the civil rights which belong to individuals, considered merely as individuals; *public wrongs,* or crimes, are a breach and violation of the public rights and duties due to the whole community, considered as a community in its social aggregate capacity. As if I detain a field from another man, to which the law has given him a right, this is a civil injury, not a crime; for here only the *right* of an individual is concerned, and it is immaterial to the public which of us is in possession of the land; but treason, murder, and robbery are properly ranked among crimes; since, besides the injury done to individuals, they strike at the very being of society, which cannot possibly subsist, where actions of this sort are suffered to escape with impunity.

In all cases *crime* includes an injury. Every public offence is also a private wrong, and somewhat more; it affects the individual, and it likewise affects the community. Thus treason in imagining the sovereign's death involves in it conspiracy against an individual, which is also a *civil* injury; but as this species of treason in its consequence principally tends to the dissolution of government, and the destruction thereby of the order and peace of society, this makes it a crime of the greatest magnitude. Murder is an injury to the life of an individual; but the law of society considers principally the loss which the State sustains by being deprived of a member, and the pernicious example thereby set for others to do the like. Robbery may be considered in the same view; it is an injury to *private* property; but were that all, a civil satisfaction in damages might atone for it. The *public* mischief is the thing, for the prevention of which our laws have made this offence a felony.

There are crimes of an inferior nature, in which the public punishment is not so severe, which afford room for a private compensation also; and herein the distinction of *crimes* from *civil injuries* is very apparent. For instance, in the case of battery, or beating another, the aggressor may be indicted for this at the suit of the Crown for disturbing the public peace, and be punished criminally by fine and imprisonment; and the party beaten may also have his *private remedy* by action of *trespass* for the injury which he in particular sustains, and recover a civil satisfaction in damages. So also, in case of a *public nuisance,* as digging a ditch across a highway; this is punishable by indictment, as a common offence to the whole kingdom and all her Majesty's subject; and if any individual sustains any special damage thereby, as laming his horse, breaking his carriage, or the like, the offender may be compelled to make ample satisfaction, as well for *the private injury,* as for the *public wrong.*

What Persons "are" or "are not" capable of committing Crimes?

The GENERAL RULE is, that no person shall be excused from punishment for *disobedience* to the laws of his country, excepting such as are expressly defined and exempted by the laws themselves, which may be reduced to this single consideration — THE *want* OR *defect* OF WILL. There must be a vicious *will,* and an *unlawful* act consequent thereon.

An *involuntary act,* as it has no claim to merit, cannot induce any guilt. To make a complete crime cognizable by human laws, there must be both a *will* and an *act;* for though, *in foro conscientiæ,* a fixed design or *will* to do an unlawful act is almost as heinous as the commission of it; yet, as no temporal tribunal can search the heart or fathom the intentions of the mind, it cannot punish for what it cannot know. Therefore, to *constitute a crime* against human laws there must be, first, a *vicious will;* and secondly, an *overt* and unlawful act, or some open evidence consequent upon such vicious *will.*

There are THREE CASES in which the *will* does not cooperate with the *act:* —

1. Where there is a *defect* of understanding; for where there is *no* discernment there is *no* choice; and where there is no choice, there can be no *act* of the *will.* He, therefore, that has no understanding can have no will to guide his conduct; as in cases of *infancy, idiocy,* and *lunacy.*

2. Where there are *understanding* and *will* sufficient residing in the party, but not called forth and exerted at the time of the act done; which is the case of all offences committed by *mischance* or *ignorance.* Here the *will* is neutral; and neither concurs with the act nor disagrees with it.

3. Where the action is *constrained* by some outward force and violence. Here the WILL *counteracts the deed;* and is so far from concurring with, that it totally disagrees with, what the man is obliged to perform.

First, then, INFANCY, or *nonage,* is *assumed* in law a *defect of* the understanding.

The law of England, does, in some cases, privilege an infant, under the age of twenty-one, as to common misdemeanors, so as to escape fine, imprisonment, and the like; and, particularly in cases of *omission,* as not repairing a bridge, or a highway, and other similar offences; for it holds that, not having the means till twenty-one, he wants the capacity to do those things which the law requires. But where there is any notorious breach of the peace — a riot, battery, or the like (which infants, when full grown, are as able as others to commit), for these an infant, above the age of fourteen, is equally liable to suffer, as a person of the fall age of twenty-one.

With regard to the more serious crimes, the law is minute and circumspect; distinguishing with great nicety the several degrees of ago and discretion. By the ancient Saxon law, the age of twelve years was established for the age of possible discretion, when first the understanding might awaken; and from thence till the offender was fourteen, it was *œtus pubertati proxima,* in which he might or might not be guilty of a crime, according to his natural capacity or incapacity. By the law, as it now stands, and has stood at least ever since the time of Edward III., the capacity of doing ill, or contracting guilt, is not so much measured by years and days as by the strength of the delinquent's understanding and judgment; for one lad of eleven years old may have as much cunning as another of fourteen; and in these cases our maxim is, that "*malitia supplet œtatem.*" The evidence of that malice which is to supply age ought to be strong and clear beyond all doubt and contradiction.

Under seven years of age an infant cannot be guilty of felony; for then a felonious discretion is almost an impossibility in nature; also under fourteen, though an infant shall be *primâ facie* adjudged to be *doli incapax,* yet if it appears that he was *doli capax,* he may be convicted. After fourteen he is presumably *doli capax.*

The second case of a deficiency in *will,* which excuses from the guilt of crime, arises also from a defective or vitiated understanding, caused by *idiocy* or *lunacy.* For the rule of law as to the latter, which may easily be adapted also to the former, is that "*furiosus furore solum punitur.*" In criminal cases, therefore, idiots and lunatics are not chargeable for their own acts, if committed when under these incapacities; not even for treason itself. By the common law, if a man in his sound memory commits a capital offence, and before arraignment for it he becomes mad, he ought not to be arraigned for it, because he is not able to plead to it with requisite advice and caution; and if, after arraignment and plea, a prisoner becomes mad, he shall not be tried; for how can he make his defence? If, after he be tried and found guilty, he loses his senses before judgment, judgment shall not be pronounced; and if, after judgment, he becomes insane, execution shall be stayed; for the humanity of the English law presumes that had the prisoner been of sound memory, he might have alleged something in stay of judgment or execution.[130]

Thirdly, as to artificial, voluntarily-contracted madness by drunkenness or intoxication, depriving men of their reason, it is looked upon by our laws as an aggravation of the offence, rather than as an excuse for any criminal misbehaviour. "A. drunkard," says Sir Edward Coke, "who is *voluntarius dœmon,* hath no privilege thereby; but what hurt or ill soever he doth, his drunkenness doth aggravate it; *nam omne crimen ebrictas, et incendit, et detegit.*" Nevertheless, though drunkenness cannot excuse the commission of crime, yet the material question, whether the act was done by accident, or premeditated, or done from sudden bent and impulse, may be held proper to be taken into consideration; for *malice,* or a particular intent, is an essential ingredient in a crime.

A fourth deficiency of WILL, is where a man commits an unlawful act by *misfortune* or *chance,* and not by design. Here the *will* observes a total neutrality, and does not co-operate with the deed; which, therefore, wants one

[130] See 3 & 4 Vict., c. 54, s. 1; 23 & 24 Vict., c. 75; 27 & 28 Vict., c. 29.

main ingredient of a crime. When it affects the life of another, if any accidental mischief happens to follow from the performance of a *lawful* act with due caution, the party stands excused from all guilt; but if a man be doing anything *unlawful,* and a consequence ensues which he did not foresee or intend, as the death of a man or the like, his want of foresight shall be no excuse; for, being guilty of one offence, in doing accidentally what is in itself unlawful, he is criminally guilty of whatever consequence may follow the first misbehaviour.

Fifthly — *Ignorance* or *mistake* is another defect of WILL; when a man, intending to do a lawful act, does that which is unlawful. For here the *deed* and the *will* acting separately, there is not that conjunction between them which is necessary to form a criminal act; but this must be an ignorance or mistake *of fact,* and not an error in point of *law.* As if a man, intending to kill a thief or housebreaker in his own house, by mistake kills one of his own family, this is no criminal action; but if a man thinks he has a right to kill a person excommunicated or outlawed, wherever he meets him, and does so, this is wilful murder. For a mistake in point of law, which every person of discretion not only may, but is bound and presumed to know, is in criminal cases no sort of defence. *Ignorantia juris, quod quisque tenetur scire, nemine excusant,* is as well a maxim of our own law, as it was of the Roman law.

A sixth species of defect of WILL is that arising from *compulsion* and inevitable *necessity;* from a *constraint* upon the *will,* whereby a man is urged to do that which his judgment disapproves; and which, it is to be presumed, his *will,* if left to itself, would reject.

Compulsion, or *necessity,* is what the law calls *duress per minas;* or threats and menaces which induce a fear of death or bodily harm, and which take away for that reason the guilt of many crimes and misdemeanors; but that fear which compels a man to do an unwarrantable act, must be just and well grounded.

As to persons in *private relations,* the principal case where constraint by a superior is allowed as an excuse for criminal misconduct, is with regard to the matrimonial subjection of the wife to her husband; for neither a son nor a servant is excused for the commission of any crime, whether capital or otherwise, by the command or coercion of the parent or master; but the authority of the husband, either express or implied, will exempt the wife from punishment. This rule admits of an exception in cases that are *mala in se,* and prohibited by the law of nature, as murder and the like. In treason, also, no plea of coverture shall excuse the wife; and where the wife offends alone, without the company or coercion of her husband, she is responsible for her offence as much as any *feme sole.*

CHAPTER II
PRINCIPALS AND ACCESSORIES

Having described. what persons are or are not capable of committing crime, let us now examine the different degrees of guilt among persons that are capable of offending.

Explain the Degrees of Guilt in Criminals, first as "Principal," then as "Accessory," and the Punishment.

A man may be *principal* in an offence in either of two degrees. A principal, in the *first degree,* is he that is the actor or absolute perpetrator of the crime; and he who is present, aiding and abetting the fact to be done, is in the *second* decree, which *presence* need not always be an actual standing by, within sight or hearing of the fact; but there may be also a constructive presence, as when one commits a robbery or murder, and another keeps watch or guard at some distance. In the case of *rape,* a person present aiding and abetting may be charged as principal either in the first or second degree. In murder by poisoning, a man may be a principal felon by preparing and laying the poison, or persuading another to drink it who is ignorant of its poisonous quality; or giving it to him for that purpose, and yet not administer it himself, nor be present when the very deed of poisoning is committed. And the same reasoning will hold, with regard to other murders committed in the absence of the murderer, by means which he had prepared beforehand, and which probably could not fail of their mischievous effect.

In general the punishment inflicted upon either class of offenders in the first and second degree is the same.[131]

An *Accessory* is he who is not the chief actor in the offence, nor present at its performance, but is in some way concerned therein, either therein, *before* or *after* the fact committed.

In *high treason* there are no accessories, but all are principals; the same acts that make a man accessory in felony, make him a principal in high treason, upon account of the heinousness of the crime. Besides it is to be considered, that the bare intent to commit treason is many times actual treason; as imagining the death of the Sovereign, or conspiring to take away the Crown. And, as no one can advise and abet such a crime without an intention to have it done, there can be no accessories before the fact; since the very advice and abetment amount to treason.

In *murder* and other felonies there may be accessories; except only in those offences which by judgment of law are sudden and unpremeditated, as *manslaughter,*

---

[131] See Accessories and Abettors Act (1861), 24 & 25 Vict., c. 94.

chance-medley, and the like; which therefore cannot have any accessories before the fact. So, too, in crimes under the degree of felony; there are no accessories either before or after the fact, for all persons concerned therein, if guilty at all, are principals.

An *accessory before* the fact is one who, being absent at the time of the crime committed, doth yet procure, counsel, or command another to commit a crime. Herein absence is necessary to make him an accessory; for if such procurer, or the like, be present, he is guilty of the crime as principal. If A., then, advises B. to kill another, and B. does it in the absence of A., then B. is principal, and A. is accessory in the murder; and now, by statutes 24 & 25 Vict., c. 94, an accessory *before* the fact may be indicted, tried, convicted, and punished as if he were a principal felon.

An *accessory after* the fact may be where a person, knowing a felony to have been committed, receives, relieves, comforts, or assists the felon. Therefore, to make an accessory *ex post facto,* it is in the first place requisite that he knows of the felony committed, and the felony must be *complete* at the time of the assistance given; for if a man wounds another mortally, and after the wound given, but before death ensues, a person assists or receives the delinquent, this does not make him accessory to the homicide, for till death ensues there is no felony committed. But so stringent is the law to attain the ends of justice where a felony is complete, that the *nearest relations* are not suffered to aid or receive one another: if a parent receives his son, or a husband his wife, the receiver becomes an accessory *ex post facto.* A *feme-covert* cannot become an accessory by receiving or concealing her husband; for she is presumed to act under his coercion, and "she is not bound to discover her lord." Generally, any assistance whatever given to a felon, to hinder his being apprehended, tried, or suffering punishment, makes the assistor an accessory, and the statute enacts that every accessory after the fact shall be liable to be imprisoned for a term not exceeding two years, with or without hard labour.

As to accessories generally; if any principal offender be convicted of felony, it shall be lawful to proceed against any *accessory,* either before or after the fact, in the same manner as if such principal felon had been attainted thereof, notwithstanding the principal felon dies, or is pardoned; and every such accessory shall, upon conviction, suffer the same punishment as he would have suffered if the principal had been attainted.[132]

CHAPTER III
OFFENCES PUNISHABLE BY THE MUNICIPAL LAW

Let us now inquire into the several crimes and misdemeanors, which are either directly, or by consequence, injurious to civil society, and therefore punishable by the laws of England, with the punishments annexed to each. These offences may be distributed under the following general heads: — 1. Those which are more immediately injurious to religion. — 2. Such as violate and transgress the law of nations. — 3. Such as more especially affect the Sovereign and the Government. — 4. Such as more directly infringe the rights of the public or commonwealth. — 5. Such as derogate from those rights and duties which are owing to particular individuals, and in the preservation and vindication of which the community is deeply interested.

---

[132] See 24 & 25 Vict., c. 94, s. 5

First, then, Explain those Offences that transgress against Religion, with the Punishment.

Of this species, the first is that of APOSTASY, or a total renunciation of Christianity, by embracing either a false religion or no religion at all. For a long time the offence of apostasy was cognizable only by the ecclesiastical courts, which corrected the offender *pro salute animæ;* but about the close of the seventeenth century the civil liberties to which we were then restored being used as a cloak of maliciousness, and doctrines subversive of all religion being publicly avowed both in discourses and writings, it was thought necessary for the civil power to interpose by not admitting those *mescroyans* to the privileges of society who maintained such principles as destroyed all moral obligation. To this end it was enacted by stat. 9 & 10 Wm. III., c. 32, that if any person educated in, or having made profession of the Christian religion, shall by writing, printing, teaching, or advisedly speaking, deny the Christian religion to be true, or the Holy Scriptures to be of Divine origin, he shall upon the first offence be rendered incapable to hold any office or place of trust; and for the second offence, be rendered incapable of bringing any action, or of being guardian, executor, legatee, or donee, and shall suffer three years imprisonment without bail. To give room. however, for repentance if, within four months after the first conviction, the delinquent will in open court publicly renounce his error, he is discharged from all disabilities. Prosecutions for offences of this nature have now become practically extinct.

II. HERESY, which consists, not in a total denial of Christianity, but in a denial of some of its principal doctrines, publicly and obstinately avowed, is no longer cognizable by courts temporal.[133] The Tests and Corporation Acts were repealed by the stat. of 9 Geo. IV., c. 17. which has been supplemented by various very liberal enactments — 9 & 10 Vict., c. 59; and 29 & 30 Vict., c. 22, passed to prevent the exclusion from corporate and other offices of Protestant Nonconformists on the ground of their religious convictions. An Act has also been recently passed, 34 & 35 Vict., c. 26, to alter the law respecting *religious tests* in the Universities of Oxford, Cambridge, and Durham, and in the Halls and Colleges of those Universities.

III. BLASPHEMY against the Almighty, or jestingly or profanely scolling at the Holy Scriptures, is punishable at common law by fine and imprisonment, or corporal punishment; for Christianity forms part of the laws of England.

IV. RELIGIOUS IMPOSTORS, or persons who pretend an extraordinary commission from Heaven, or terrify the ignorant with false denunciations of judgments, are punishable by tine and imprisonment.

V. PROFANATION of the Lord's Day is an offence against religion, and is punishable by the municipal law of England. By 21 Geo. III., c. 49, any house opened for public entertainment or debate on the Lord's Day shall be deemed a disorderly house, and the owner punishable as such; and by 35 & 36 Vict., c. 94, no person licensed or authorized to sell fermented or distilled liquors shall, during certain specified hours on Sundays, *except for travellers,* open his house for sale of such liquors, or sell the same, under a penalty of £10 for every such offence, to be recovered before a justice of the peace; and every separate

[133] For writ *De hæretico comburendo,* and the sanguinary penal enactments that were formerly in force against heretics, see "Blackstone," vol. IV., chap. 5.

sale shall be deemed a separate offence. Other restrictions are. also provided.[134]

VI. Any person who is guilty of riotous, violent, or indecent behaviour in church, or any place of religions worship duly certified under 18 & 19 Vict., c. 81, or who shall molest the clergyman or minister, is liable to fine and imprisonment.

CHAPTER IV
OFFENCES AGAINST THE LAW OF NATIONS

Let us next consider the offences, more immediately repugnant to the universal law of society, which regulate the mutual intercourse between one State and another; or at all events, such of them as are particularly animadverted on by English law.

Explain the Offences against the Law of Nations cognizable by the Laws of England.

The Law of Nations is a *system of rules,* deducible by natural reason, and established by universal consent among the civilized inhabitants of the world, in order to decide all disputes, to regulate all ceremonies and civilities, and to insure the observance of justice and good faith in that intercourse which must frequently occur between two or more independent states, and the individuals belonging to each. This general law is founded upon the principle — that different nations ought, in the time of peace, to do one another all the good they can; and, in time of war, as little harm as possible, without prejudice to their own real interests. And, as none of these states will

[134] See Licensing Act (1872); 35 & 36 Vict, c. 94.

allow a superiority in the other, therefore neither can dictate nor prescribe the rules of this law to the rest; but such rules must necessarily result from those principles of natural justice, in which the learned of every nation agree, and to which all civilized States have assented; or they depend upon mutual compacts or treaties between the respective communities, in the construction of which there is no judge to resort to, but the law of nature and reason, being the only one with which the contracting parties are equally conversant, and to which they are equally subject.

In arbitrary states this law, whenever it contradicts or is not provided for by the municipal law of the country, is enforced by the royal power; but since in England no royal power can introduce a new law, or suspend the execution of the old, therefore the law of nations, wherever any question arises which is properly the object of its jurisdiction, is here adopted in its fall extent by the common law, and is held to be a part of the law of the land. And those acts of Parliament, which have from time to time been made to enforce this universal law, or to facilitate the execution of its decisions, are not to be considered as introductive of any new rule, but merely as declaratory of the old fundamental constitutions of the kingdom, without which it must cease to be a part of the civilized world. Thus in mercantile questions, such as bills of exchange and the like; in all marine causes, relating to freight, average, demurrage, insurances, bottomry, and others of a similar nature; the law-merchant, which is a branch of the law of nations, is regularly and constantly adhered to; so when even international questions arise, there is no ether rule of decision but this universal law collected from history and usage, and such writers of all nations and languages whose authority is generally acknowledged and established.

Offences against this law are principally incident to whole states or nations, in which case, if arbitration or treaty fail, recourse can only be had to war; but where the individuals of any state violate this general law, it is then the interest as well as the duty of the government under which they live, to animadvert upon them with a becoming severity, that the peace of the world may be maintained; for in vain would nations in their collective capacity observe these universal rules, if private subjects were at liberty to break them at their own discretion, and involve the two states in a war. It is therefore incumbent upon the nation injured, first to demand satisfaction and justice to be done on the offender, by the state to which he belongs; and, if that be refused or neglected, the sovereign then avows himself an accomplice or abettor of his subject's crime, and may draw upon his community the calamities of foreign war.[135]

The principal offences against the law of nations are of three kinds: —

I. As to the first, *violation* of *safe-conducts* or *passports* expressly granted by the Crown or its ambassadors to the subjects of a foreign power in time of mutual war; or committing acts of hostilities against such as are in amity, league, or truce with us, and are here under a general implied safe-conduct; these are breaches of the public faith, without the preservation of which there can be no intercourse or commerce between one nation and another; and such offences may, according to the writers upon the law of nations, constitute a just ground of war; since it is not in the power of the foreign prince to cause justice to be done to his subjects by the very individual delinquent, but he must require it of the whole community. And, as during the continuance of any safe-conduct, either express or im-

---

[135] See Serving in a Foreign State, fitting out vessels, &c.

plied, the foreigner is under the protection of the sovereign and the law; and, more especially, as it is one of the articles of *Magna Charta,* that foreign merchants should be entitled to safe-conduct and security throughout the kingdom, there is no question but that any violation of either the person or property of such foreigner may be punished by indictment in the name of the sovereign, whose honour is more particularly engaged in supporting his own safe-conduct.

II. The rights of *Ambassadors* are also established by the law of nations. The common law of England recognizes them in their full extent by immediately stopping all legal process sued out through the ignorance or rashness of individuals, which may trench upon the immunities of a foreign minister or the members of his embassy. And the more effectually to enforce the law of nations in this respect, when violated through wantonness or insolence, severe penalties have been attached to any breach of it by the statute law.

III. The crime of *Piracy,* or robbery and depredation upon the high seas, is an offence against the universal law of society; a pirate being, according to Sir Edward Coke, *hostis humani generis.* As, therefore, he has renounced all the benefits of society and government, and has reduced himself afresh to the savage state of nature, by declaring war against all mankind, all mankind is presumed to have declared war against him: so that every community has a right, by the rule of self-defence, to inflict that punishment upon him, which every individual would in a state of nature have been otherwise entitled to do, for any invasion of his person or personal property. By stat. 18 Geo. II., c. 30, any natural-born subject or denizen who in time of war shall commit hostilities at sea against any of his fellow-subjects, or shall assist an enemy on that element, is liable to be tried and convicted as a pirate; and by 1 Vict., c. 88, whosoever with intent to commit the crime of piracy, shall assault, with intent to murder, any person being on board or belonging to any vessel, or stab, cat, or wound any person, or unlawfully do any act by which his life may be endangered, shall be sentenced to suffer death.[136] The ordinary punishment of piracy under the statute law is penal servitude for life; or any term not less than five years; or imprisonment, with or without hard labour, for not more than three years.

Treaties with many foreign countries have been entered into for extending similar enactments to the ships and subjects of those countries.

CHAPTER V
OFFENCES AGAINST THE SOVEREIGN AND THE GOVERNMENT

The third *general division* of *Crimes* consists of such as more especially affect the supreme executive power, amounting either to a total renunciation of allegiance; or, at least, to a criminal neglect of that duty which is due from every subject to his Sovereign. Every offence, therefore, more immediately affecting the Royal person, his crown or dignity, maybe referred to two classes: — 1. Treason and other offences and contempts against the Sovereign. — 2. Offences against the Government.

Explain these Offences.

Treason (proditio), in its very name, imports a betraying, treachery, or breach of faith. *Alta proditio,* high treason, is the highest civil crime which any man can pos-

[136] See Piracy Act, 7 Wm. IV. & 1 Vict.. c. 88; also 12 & 13 Vict., c. 96; and 23 & 21 Vict., c. 88.

sibly commit. It is where one attacks Majesty itself, as killing or attempting to kill the Sovereign.

Treason may be classed under several heads: — I. "When a man doth compass or imagine the death of our lord the King, of our lady the Queen, or of the eldest son and heir." Under this description it is held that a queen regnant (such as Queen Elizabeth, Queen Anne, and her present most gracious Majesty, Queen Victoria), is within the words of the Act, being invested with royal power and entitled to the allegiance of her subjects; but the husband of such a queen is not comprised within these words, and therefore no treason can be committed against him. The king here intended is the king in possession, without any respect to his title; for it is held that a king *de facto* and not *de jure;* or, in other words, a usurper that hath got possession of the throne is a king within the meaning of the statute, as there is a temporary allegiance due to him for the administration of the government and protection of the public. The distinction seems to be, that the stat. 11 Henry VII, c. 1, does by no means command any opposition to a king *de jure,* but excuses the obedience paid to a king *de facto.* When therefore a usurper is in possession, the subject is *excused* and *justified* in obeying and giving him assistance; otherwise under a usurpation no man could be safe, if the lawful prince had a right to hang him for obedience to the powers in being, as the usurper would certainly do for disobedience to the powers in being.

Compassing or *imagining* the death of the King are synonymous terms; the word *compass* signifying the purpose or design of the mind or will. An accidental stroke which may mortally wound the sovereign *per infortunium,* without any traitorous intent, is no treason; as was the case of Sir Walter Tyrrel, who, shooting at a hart, the arrow glanced against a tree, and killed the king upon the spot. As the compassing or imagining is an act of the mind, it cannot possibly fall under any juridical cognizance, unless it be demonstrated by some open or *overt* act. Mere *words* spoken by an individual amount only to a high misdemeanor; for they may be spoken without any intention; or, be mistaken, perverted, or misremembered by the hearers.

II. The SECOND species of treason is — "If a man do violate the king's companion, or the king's eldest daughter unmarried, or the wife of the king's eldest son and heir." By the king's companion is meant his wife; and by violation is understood carnal knowledge, as well without force, as with it: and this is treason in both parties, if both be consenting. The plain intention of the law is to guard the blood royal from any suspicion of bastardy whereby the succession to the Crown might be rendered dubious.

III. The THIRD species of treason is — "If a man do levy war against our lord the King in his realm." This may be done by taking arms, not only to dethrone the Sovereign, but under pretence to reform religion, or the laws, or to remove evil counsellors, or other grievances, whether real or pretended. For the law does not, neither can it, permit any private man, or get of men, to interfere forcibly in matters of such high importance, the law having established a sufficient power for these purposes in the High Court of Parliament.

IV. If a man be adherent to the King's enemies in his realm, giving them aid and comfort in the realm or elsewhere, he is also declared guilty of treason. This must likewise be proved by some overt act, as by giving them intelligence, by sending them money or provisions, by selling them arms, by treacherously surrendering a fortress, or the like. By enemies are here understood the subjects of foreign powers with whom we are at open war; but to relieve a rebel, fled out of the kingdom, is no treason; for the statute is taken strictly, and a *rebel* is not an *enemy;* an enemy being always the subject of some foreign prince, and one who owes no allegiance to the Crown of England.[137]

V. To counterfeit the Great or Privy Seal is also treason.

VI. If a man slay the Chancellor, Treasurer, or the Queen's Justices in one Bench or the other; or Justices of Assize, he is guilty of treason.

The judgment for high treason, according to statute, is very solemn and terrible: — That the offender be drawn on a hurdle to the place of execution — That he be hanged by the neck until he be dead — That his body be divided into four quarters. — That his head and quarters shall be at the disposal of the Crown. But the Sovereign may, after sentence, by warrant under his sign manual, countersigned by a principal Secretary of State, change the whole sentence into beheading, or may even remit the capital punishment altogether. The sentence upon women is — to be drawn to the place of execution, and hanged by the neck until they be dead.

The punishment for counterfeiting the Seals is not capital, but penal servitude for life, or for not less than seven years.

Explain the Offences which, though they fall short of Treason, are, like it, injurious to the Person, Prerogative, or Government of the Sovereign, and state the punishment.

I. MISPRISIONS OF TREASON (a term derived from the old French, *mespris,* contempt) are high misdemeanors. Misprisions are generally divided into two sorts: *negative,*

[137] For other offences amounting to treason, see 1 Wm. IV., c. 66; and 11 & 12 Vict., c. 12.

which consists in the concealment of something that *ought* to be revealed; and *positive,* which consists in the commission of something that *ought not* to be done. Misprision of treason consists of the bare knowledge and concealment of treason, without any degree of assent thereto; for any assent makes the party a principal traitor. This concealment becomes criminal if the party apprised of the treason does not, as soon as conveniently may be, reveal it to some judge of assize or justice of the peace; but if there be any probable circumstances of assent, as if one goes to a treasonable meeting, knowing beforehand that a conspiracy is intended against the Crown; or being in such company once by accident, and having heard such treasonable conspiracy, meets the same company again, and hears more of it and conceals it; this is an *implied* assent in law, and makes the concealer guilty of actual treason.

The punishment of misprision of treason is fine and imprisonment.

II. MISDEMEANORS AGAINST THE SOVEREIGN. — Another offence against the Sovereign has been constituted by 5 & 6 Vict., c. 51, which enacts "that if any person shall wilfully discharge, or point, aim, or present at the person of the Queen any gun, pistol, or any other description of fire-arms, or other arms, whether containing any explosive or destructive material or not; or shall discharge, or cause to be discharged, or attempt to discharge any explosive substance or material near to the Queen's person, with intent to injure or alarm her, or to break the public peace, the offender shall be guilty of a high misdemeanor," and be liable to penal servitude for seven years, or not less than five years, or imprisonment for not more than three years, and whipping.

In the event of a verdict of *insanity* being found, confinement during the Queen's pleasure is usually awarded.

III. TREASON FELONY, as it is termed, is another offence against the Sovereign; and it is enacted by 11 & 12 Vict., c. 12, "That if any person shall — within the United Kingdom or without — compass, imagine, invent, devise, or intend to deprive or depose the Queen, her heirs or successors, from the style, honour, or Royal name of the Imperial Crown of the United Kingdom, or of any of her Majesty's dominions and countries; or to levy war against her Majesty, her heirs, or successors, within any part of the United Kingdom, in order, by force or constraint, to compel her or them to change her or their measures or counsels, or to intimidate or overawe both Houses, or either House of Parliament, or to move or stir any foreigner or stranger with force to invade the United Kingdom, or any other of her Majesty's dominions; and shall express, utter, or declare such compassings, imaginations, inventions, devices, or intentions, or any of them, by publishing any printing or writing, or by open and advised speaking, or by any overt act or deed, the person so offending shall be guilty of felony; and on conviction be liable to be sentenced to penal servitude for life, or for any term not less than seven years; or to be imprisoned for any term not exceeding two years, with or without hard labour, as the court shall direct."

IV. PRÆMUNIRE was another species of offence against the Sovereign, in his character as head of the Church Established, which is now obsolete. It was so called from the words of the writ — *pœmunire facias* — to be forewarned that he appear before us to answer the contempt wherewith he stands charged, and which contempt was set out in the writ.

The statutes of *pœmunire* were framed to encounter papal usurpation in the reign of Edward III. and subsequent reigns.

V. *Contempts* against the Sovereign's title, not amounting to treason, are punished by fine and imprisonment.

Explain the Offences against the Government.

The first and principal in the *mal-administration* of such high officers as are in the public trust and employment. This is usually punished by the method of Parliamentary impeachment, followed by imprisonment, fines, or perpetual disabilities. Also the offence of *embezzling* the *public money,* which is punishable with fine and imprisonment, at the discretion of the court, and the person rendered for ever incapable of holding any office under the Crown.

Larceny by persons employed in the public service of her Majesty, or by a constable employed, in the police of any county, city, borough, or district, is punishable by penal servitude for any term of years not exceeding fourteen nor less than five, or imprisonment for two years with or without hard labour. — Concealing *treasure trove,* which belongs to the Sovereign or his grantees by prerogative royal, is now punishable by fine and imprisonment. — Persons buying or selling *public offices* in the gift of the Crown, or soliciting, or obtaining any such office, or making any negotiation or pretended negotiation thereto, shall respectively be deemed guilty of a misdemeanor, and such bargain or sale is declared to be void. — To *gild, colour, or falsely* make or counterfeit any coin intended to resemble or pass for the Queen's current gold or silver coin, or any coin of foreign States, is now punishable by penal servitude for life, or for any term not less than five years; or imprisonment for any term not more than two years with or without hard labour and solitary confinement. — To falsely *make,* or *impair, diminish,* or *lighten* any of the current gold or silver coin, with intent that the coin so altered may pass for the current gold or silver coin, is felony. — Any person having in his custody or possession filings, clippings, dust, or solution produced or obtained by injuring, diminishing, or lightening any of the Queen's current gold or silver coin, knowing the same to have been so produced, shall be guilty of felony. — Whoever shall tender, utter, or put off any false or counterfeit coin, knowing the same to be false or counterfeit, shall be guilty of a misdemeanor, and may be imprisoned for any term not exceeding one year with or without hard labour and solitary confinement; and, upon a second conviction, he shall be deemed guilty of felony. —

Whoever shall deface any of the Queen's current gold, silver, or copper coin by stamping thereon any names or words shall be guilty of a misdemeanor, and is punishable by imprisonment for any term not exceeding one year, with or without hard labour.

Serving a foreign state, which service is generally inconsistent with the allegiance to one's natural prince, is restrained by the Foreign Enlistment Act,[138] which enacts that any natural-born subject of her Majesty who, without licence from the Crown, shall take, or accept, or agree to take or accept any military commission, or shall enter into the military or naval service of any foreign prince, state, or potentate; or shall, without leave and licence, go to any foreign country, or to any place beyond the seas, with intent to enlist, or endeavour to procure any other person so to enlist, to serve in any warlike operation whatever, whether by land or by sea, shall be guilty of a misdemeanor; and further, that if any person whatever, in any part of her Majesty's dominions, shall, without leave and licence from the Crown, equip, fit out, or arm any vessel for the service of any foreign state, as a transport, or with

[138] See 59 Geo. III., c. 69; also 33 and 34 Vict., c. 90.

intent to cruise, or commit hostilities against any state at peace with this country, such offender shall also be guilty of a misdemeanor, and may be punished by fine or imprisonment, or both.

Offences of *desertion* or *seducing* to *desert* from the Army or Navy are placed under the jurisdiction of courts-martial, and punished by those courts according to the Annual Mutiny Acts and the Articles of War promulgated in pursuance thereof.[139]

Setting on fire, or destroying any of her Majesty's ships of war, whether built, building, or repairing; or any of the royal arsenals, magazines, dockyards, &c.; or causing, or assisting in such offence, is punishable with death.

CHAPTER VI
OFFENCES AGAINST PUBLIC JUSTICE

The order of distribution will next lead us to take into consideration such crimes and misdemeanors as more especially affect the *Commonwealth,* or public polity of the kingdom; offences which are peculiarly pointed against the lives and security of private subjects, and also against the Sovereign, as the *paterfamilias* of the nation.

Explain the Crimes and Misdemeanors that more especially affect the Commonwealth; and state the Punishment inflicted by Law for each of them.

Crimes more especially affecting the COMMONWEALTH may be divided into four heads: — 1.

[139] See 35 & 36 Vict., c. 3, an Act for punishing mutiny and desertion, and for the better payment of the Army, and their quarters; see also c. 4, an Act for the regulation of her Majesty's Royal Marine Forces while on shore.

Offences against public justice. — 2. Offences against the public peace. — 3. Offences against public trade. — 4. Offences against public health and safety, morals and economy.

First, then, of *offences* against *Public Justice,* several of which are felonies, and punishable even to the extent of penal servitude for life; others only *misdemeanors.*

I. *Stealing, injuring, falsifying,* or *embezzling* records or other proceedings of a court of judicature is a felonious offence against public justice. By 24 & 25 Vict., c. 98, it is enacted — "that whosoever shall forge, or counterfeit the above, or shall utter the same, knowing them to be forged or counterfeited, shall be declared guilty of felony, punishable by penal servitude for any term not exceeding seven years, or for not less than five years; or for imprisonment for any term not exceeding two years, with or without solitary confinement."

II. *Injuring* records, and *falsifying* proceedings of a court of judicature is an offence against public justice, and by stat. 24 & 25 Vict., c. 96, it is enacted "that whosoever shall steal, or shall for any fraudulent purpose take from its place of deposit for the time being, or from any person having the lawful custody thereof, or shall unlawfully and maliciously cancel, obliterate, injure, or destroy any record, writ, rule, order, or original document of any court of record, shall be guilty of felony, and be punishable by penal servitude for five years, or imprisonment for any term not exceeding two years, with or without hard labour, and with or without solitary confinement."

It is also enacted by stat. 24 & 25 Vict., c. 98, s. 27, "that whosoever shall forge or fraudulently alter, or shall offer, utter, dispose of, or put off, knowing the same to be forged or fraudulently altered, any record, writ, process, rule, answer, decree, or original document of or belonging to any Court of Equity or Court of Admiralty, used or intended to be used as evidence in any such court as aforesaid, shall be guilty of felony, and punishable by penal servitude for any term not exceeding seven years and not less than five years; or imprisonment for any term not exceeding two years with or without hard labour, and with or without solitary confinement."

III. *Striking,* or any outrage in the Courts at Westminster, or at the assizes, or in any inferior court of jurisdiction, is also an offence against public justice, and formerly punishable with great severity. It may now be punished by the judges on the spot by imprisonment.

Intimidation towards the parties or witnesses in a cause in a court of justice is also an offence against public justice, and punishable by fine and imprisonment.

Obstructing the execution of lawful process is an offence of a very high and presumptuous nature; and more particularly so when it is an obstruction of an arrest upon criminal process. It is held that the party opposing such arrest becomes thereby *particeps criminis;* that is, an accessory in felony and a principal in treason, and is highly penal.

Dissuading witnesses from giving evidence and *contempts* of court are high misprisions, and punishable by fine and imprisonment. The wilful refusal to aid a peace officer in the execution of his duty, in order to preserve the peace, is an indictable misdemeanor at common law.

IV. An *escape* of a person arrested upon criminal process is an offence against public justice. The party so escaping is punishable by fine or imprisonment; and the officer permitting such escape, either by negligence or connivance, subjects himself to be fined and imprisoned for a misdemeanor.

Breach of prison by the offender himself, when committed for any treason or felony, is punishable by penal servitude for not more than seven nor less than five years; or imprisonment for not more than two years with or without hard labour. When confined upon an inferior charge, it is punishable as a misdemeanor.

Rescue is the forcibly and knowingly freeing another from an arrest or imprisonment. A rescue of one apprehended for felony is felony; for treason, treason; for a misdemeanor, a misdemeanor. The party rescuing may be punished for a misdemeanor, although the principal, or person rescued, be not convicted.

V. Another offence against public justice was the returning from transportation, or being at large in Great Britain before the expiration of the term for which the offender was transported renal servitude is now substituted for transportation, and to escape and be at large is punishable by penal servitude for life, or for not less than five years, with previous imprisonment for any term not exceeding four years; or imprisonment with or without hard labour for not more than two years.[140]

VI. *Taking a reward,* under pretence of helping the owner to stolen goods, or any chattel, money, valuable security, or other property which has by any felony or misdemeanor been stolen, taken, obtained, extorted, embezzled, or disposed of, is punishable by penal servitude for seven or for not less than five years, or imprisonment, with or without hard labour and solitary confinement, for any term not exceeding two years; and if a male under the age of eighteen years, with or without hard labour and whipping.

---

[140] See stats. 16 & 17 Vict., c. 99; 20 & 21 Vict., c. 3; see also 27 & 28 Vict., c. 47, an Act to amend the Penal Servitude Acts.

VII. *Compounding of felony* [*theft-bote*] *is* whore the party robbed takes his goods again, or other amends, upon agreement not to prosecute. This was held to make a man accessory to the theft; but is now punished only with fine and imprisonment.

To *advertise* a *reward* for the return of property stolen or lost, with words purporting that no questions will be asked, subjects the advertiser, the printer, and the publisher to a forfeiture of £50 each.

VIII. *Common barratry* is the offence of *frequently* inciting and stirring up suits and quarrels between her Majesty's subjects either at law or otherwise. The punishment for this offence, in a common person, is by fine and imprisonment; but if the offender belongs to the profession of the law, a barrator who is thus able as well as willing to do mischief may, besides the punishment, be disabled from practising for the future. Stat. 30 & 31 Vict., c. 59, enacts that if any one who has been convicted of forgery, perjury, subornation of perjury, or common barratry shall practise as an attorney, solicitor, or agent in any suit, the court, upon complaint, shall examine it in a summary way, and if proved, the offender shall subject himself to penal servitude for seven, or not less than live years.

Another offence of equal malignity is *suing* a party in the name of a fictitious plaintiff. Tins offence is punishable by six months imprisonment and treble damages to the party injured.[141]

IX. *Maintenance* is an offence that bears a near relation to common barratry, being an officious intermeddling in a suit that in no way belongs to one; by maintaining or assisting either party with money or otherwise, to prose-

---

[141] See Larceny Acts, 24 & 26 Vict., c. 96; and 31 & 33 Vict., c. 116.

cute or defend it. This is an offence against public justice, as it keeps alive strife and contention, and perverts the remedial process of the law into an engine of oppression. A man may, however, maintain the suit of his kinsman, servant, or poor neighbour, out of charity and compassion, with impunity. The punishment by common law is fine and imprisonment.

X. *Champerty* [*campi-partitio*] *is* a species of maintenance, being a bargain with a plaintiff or defendant to divide the land or other matter sued for between them, if they prevail at law, whereupon the champertor is to carry on the party's suit at his own expense. It in fact signifies the purchasing of a suit or right of suing, a practice so much abhorred by our law, that it is one main reason why a *chose in action,* or thing of which one hath the right, but not the possession is not assignable at common law; because no man should purchase any pretence to sue in another's right. Stat. 32 Henry VIII., c. 9, provides that no one shall sell or purchase any pretended right or title to land, unless the vendor has received the profits thereof for one whole year before such grant or has been in actual possession of the land, or of the reversion or remainder; on pain that both purchaser and vendor shall each forfeit the value of such land to the Crown and to the prosecutor.

XI. *Compounding of information* is an offence against public justice. It is enacted by 18 Eliz., c. 5, s. 4, that if; my person informing makes any composition without leave of the court, or takes any money or promise from the defendant to excuse him which demonstrates his intent in commencing the prosecution to be merely to serve his own ends and not for the public good, he shall, *inter alia,* forfeit £10, and shall be for over disabled to sue on any popular or penal statute.

XII. *Conspiracy* is a combination or agreement between two or more persons to carry into effect an unlawful purpose, hurtful to some individual, or the community or public at large. Thus a conspiracy to indict an innocent man of felony falsely and maliciously, who is accordingly indicted and acquitted, is an abuse and perversion of public justice, for which the party injured may have a civil action for damages; or the conspirators may be indicted at the suit of the Crown, and the delinquents sentenced to imprisonment and fine.

XIII. *Wilful and corrupt perjury is* defined by Sir Edward Coke to be a crime committed when a lawful oath is administered in some judicial proceeding to a person who swears wilfully, absolutely, and falsely in a matter material to the issue or point in question. The false oath must be taken either in a judicial proceeding, or in some other public proceeding of a like nature. It must be taken before persons lawfully authorised to administer an oath; for a mere voluntary oath, that is, an oath administered in a case for which the law has not provided, is not one in which perjury can be assigned; for such a proceeding is not required, and therefore it is not protected by law.

Subornation of perjury is the offence of procuring another to take such a false oath as would constitute perjury in the principal. Perjury and subornation of perjury are both misdemeanors, and the punishment by common law is fine and imprisonment; but by statute, the offender may be sentenced to penal servitude for not more than seven nor less than five years.

XIV. *Bribery* is an offence against public justice, as when a judge or other person concerned in the administration of justice takes any undue reward to influence his behaviour in his office. This offence has always been looked upon as one of a very serious nature. Stat. 11 Henry IV. enacts that all judges and officers of the king convicted of bribery should forfeit treble the bribe, be punished at the king's will, and be discharged from the king's service for ever.[142]

XV. *Embracery* is an attempt to influence a jury corruptly to one side by promises, persuasions, entreaties, money, entertainments, and the like, and is punishable by fine and imprisonment.

XVI. *Extortion is* an abuse of public justice, which consists in any officer's unlawfully taking, by colour of his office, from any man any money or thing of value that is not due to him, or more than is due, or before it is due. The punishment is fine and imprisonment, and sometimes a forfeiture of office.

XVII. *Negligence* of officers intrusted with the administration of justice; as a sheriff, coroner, constable, and the like, is punishable by fine, and may entail a forfeiture of office.

CHAPTER VII
OFFENCES AGAINST THE PUBLIC PEACE

Let us now consider the offences against the public peace, the preservation of which is entrusted to the Sovereign and the Executive.

---

[142] As to bribery at elections of Members of Parliament, see 22 & 23 Vict., c. 48; also 32 & 33 Vict., c. 55, an Act to shorten the term of resilience required at a qualification for the Municipal Franchise, and to make provision for other purposes.

Explain those Offences which are either an actual Breach of the Peace, or "constructively" so, by tending to make others break it?

I. *Riotous assembling* of twelve persons or more, and not dispersing on proclamation, is a crime against the peace. The Riot Act[143] enacts generally that if any twelve persons are unlawfully assembled to the disturbance of the peace, and any one justice of the peace, sheriff, under-sheriff, or mayor of a town shall think proper to command them by proclamation to disperse, if they contemn his orders and continue together for one hour afterwards, such contempt shall be felony. The Act contains a clause indemnifying the officers and their assistants in case any of the mob be unfortunately killed in the endeavour to disperse them.

Besides the Riot Act various enactments have been made with the view of checking the destruction of property by rioters and others. The punishment is penal servitude for life, or for not less than five years; or imprisonment for any term not exceeding two years, with or without hard labour and with or without solitary confinement.

II. *Sending, delivering,* or *uttering,* directly or indirectly causing to be received, knowing the contents thereof, any letter or writing threatening to kill or murder any person, or to burn or destroy property, or threatening to accuse any person, of a crime with a view to extort money, are felonies, and punishable by penal servitude for seven years, or imprisonment with or without hard labour.[144]

III. An *affray* (from *effrayer, to* frighten), is the fighting of two or more persons in some public place, to the terror of her Majesty's subjects; for if the fighting be in

[143] See 1 Geo. I., stat. 2, c. 5, materially amended by 24 & 25 Vict., c. 97.
[144] See 24 & 25 Vict., cc. 96, 97,100.

private it is no affray, but an assault. This is a misdemeanor, and the punishment is fine or imprisonment, or both.

IV. *Riots, routs,* and *unlawful assemblies* Two persons may be guilty of an affray, but three persons at least must have to constitute them. A *riot is* where three or more actually do an unlawful act of violence, either with or without a common cause or quarrel; as if they beat a man, or hunt and kill game in another's park, chase, warren, or liberty; or do any other unlawful act with force and violence; or even do a lawful act, as removing a nuisance, in a violent and tumultuous manner. — A *rout is* where three or more persons meet to do an unlawful act upon a common quarrel, as forcibly breaking down fences upon a right claimed of common or of way; and make some advances towards it. — An *unlawful assembly is* when three or more persons do assemble themselves together to do an unlawful act, as to pull down enclosures, to destroy a warren or the game therein; and part without doing it, or making any motion towards it.

The punishment of unlawful assemblies, if to the number of twelve, as stated by the provisions of the Riot Act, may extend to penal servitude; but from the number of three to eleven, by fine and imprisonment, with or without hard labour.

An assembly of persons to witness a fight is an unlawful assembly, and every one present and countenancing the fight is guilty of an offence, which is punishable by fine and imprisonment.

Nearly related to this head of riots is the offence of *tumultuous petitioning,* which was carried to an enormous height in the times preceding the Grand Rebellion. Wherefore by stat. 13 Gar. II., c. 5, it is enacted that not more than twenty names shall be signed to any petition to the

Crown or either House of Parliament for any alteration of matters established by law in Church or State, unless the contents thereof be previously approved, in the country, by three justices, or the majority of the grand jury at the assizes or quarter-sessions; and, in London, by the Lord Mayor, aldermen, and common council; and that no petition shall be delivered by a company of more than ten persons, on pain in either case of incurring a penalty not exceeding £100 and three months' imprisonment.[145] By stat. 57 Geo. III., c. 19, no meeting of more than fifty persons within the distance of one mile from Westminster Hall, for the purpose or on the pretext of petitioning the Grown or Parliament during the sitting of Parliament or of the Courts at Westminster, is legal.

Besides actual breaches of the peace, anything that tends to provoke or excite others to break it is an offence, therefore a *challenge* to fight, either by word or letter; or the bearing of such challenge, is punishable by fine and imprisonment, according to the circumstances of the offence.

V. Another offence against the public peace is that of a *forcible entry* or *detainer;* which is committed by violently taking or keeping possession of lands and tenements, with menaces, force, and arms, and without the authority of law.[146]

VI. A *libel, libellus famosus,* taken in its largest sense, signifies any writing, picture, or the like, of an immoral or illegal tendency; but, in the sense now under consideration, it is a malicious defamation of any person, made public by printing, writing, a sign, or a picture, in order to provoke him to wrath, or expose him to public hatred,

---

[145] Several of the provisions of these Acts are nearly obsolete.

[146] See Forcible Entry Acts, 8 Hen. VI., c. 9; 31 Eliz., c. 11; and 21 Jac. I., c. 15.

contempt, and ridicule. The direct tendency of these libels is the breach of the public peace by stirring up the objects of them to revenge, and perhaps to bloodshed. The communication of a libel to any one person is a publication in the eye of the law; and therefore the sending an abusive private letter to a man is as much a libel as if it were openly printed, for it equally tends to a breach of the peace, and it is now enacted by 6 & 7 Vict., c. 96, that if any person shall maliciously publish any defamatory libel, *knowing the same to be false,* ho shall be liable on conviction to imprisonment for any term not exceeding two years, and to pay such fine as the court shall award;[147] and, by sec. 5, if any person shall *maliciously* publish any defamatory libel, any such person being convicted thereof shall be liable to fine or imprisonment, such imprisonment not to exceed the term of one year.

CHAPTER VIII
OFFENCES AGAINST PUBLIC TRADE

Offences against *public trade,* like those of the preceding classes, are either felonies or misdemeanors.

What are the Offences against Public Trade; and state those that are Felonies and those that are Misdemeanors, with the punishment?

I. *Smuggling,* which belongs to the former, is the offence of importing or exporting goods without paying the duties imposed thereon by the laws of the customs and excise. This is restrained by a variety of statutes,[148] which inflict pecuniary penalties and seizure of the goods for

---

[147] See "Publication of *Libel.*"

[148] See 8 & 9 Vict., c. 87, entitled, an Act for the Prevention of Smuggling.

clandestine smuggling, and in aggravated cases, a penalty is inflicted and imprisonment for twelve months.

By stat. 16 & 17 Vict, c. 107 (the Customs' Consolidation Act, 1853), persons assaulting or obstructing any officer in the performance of his duty may be sentenced to penal servitude for not more than seven or less than five years, or to imprisonment, with hard labour, for not more than three years.

II. *Fraudulent bankruptcy* is an offence against public trade, and by 32 & 33 Vict., c. 62, a bankrupt who defrauds or wilfully defeats the rights of his creditors, is guilty of a misdemeanor, and liable to imprisonment for any term not exceeding two years, with or without hard labour.[149]

III. *Cheating is* another offence against public trade, as trade cannot be carried on without a punctilious regard to common honesty and faith between man and man. The general punishment for all cheating, forging or counterfeiting trade-marks, or for aiding and abetting any such offence, is by fine and imprisonment, to which hard labour may now be added.

IV. TRADE-MARKS. — By 25 & 26 Vict., c. 88, any person *forging* or *counterfeiting* trade-mark to any article not being the manufacture, production, or merchandise of any person denoted by such trade-mark, so as to pass it off as genuine when in fact it is spurious, is guilty of a misdemeanor, and punishable by line and imprisonment; but the usual remedy is by application to the Court of Chancery for an injunction to restrain the sale of the article of trade to which the trade-mark was attached and the future publication of the trade-mark, as well as for the amount of loss sustained by the applicant.

---

[149] See Court of Bankruptcy.

The same statute enacts that every person who aids, abets, counsels, or procures the commission of any such offence shall be guilty of a misdemeanor, and punished accordingly.

V. A *monopoly* was a licence or privilege allowed by the Crown for the sole buying and selling, making, working, or using of anything whatsoever, whereby the subject was restrained from that liberty of manufacturing or trading which he had before. The granting of exclusive privileges had been carried to an enormous height during the reign of Queen Elizabeth, but was remedied by 21 Jac. I., c. 3, which declares such monopolies, except as to patents, to be contrary to law and void.

VI. *Combinations* amongst persons to effect illegal objects, such as molesting parties engaged in the exercise of a lawful trade, or by threats and intimidation, subject the offenders, on conviction, to imprisonment for three months. By a recent statute it is enacted that any person wilfully committing an assault in pursuance of an unlawful combination or conspiracy to raise the rate of wages shall be guilty of a misdemeanor, punishable by imprisonment with or without hard labour for any term not exceeding two years.[150]

CHAPTER IX
OFFENCES AGAINST THE PUBLIC HEALTH, SAFETY, AND ECONOMY

Let us now consider another species of offences affecting the Commonwealth, for the preservation of which

[150] For the law relating to combinations amongst workmen, see 6 Geo. IV., c. 129, amended by 22 Vict., c. 34; also 34 & 35 Vict., c. 32, an Act to amend the criminal law relating to violence, threats, and molestation.

magistrates and police are appointed and charged with specific duties by the Legislature, viz., Offences against the *public health, safety* and *economy.*

Explain Offences prejudicial to the Public Health and Safety, and state the Punishments that are inflicted on Conviction.

I. First, then, amongst offences prejudicial to the public health is that of infringing the *quarantine laws;* which impose a probation on, or detention of, ships coming from infected ports; and by stat. 6 Geo. IV., c. 78, amended by 29 & 30 Vict., c. 90. it is enacted that if any officer of customs or other person charged, with the execution of orders concerning quarantine desert from his duty when so employed, or knowingly or willingly permit any person, vessel, or goods, or merchandise to depart, or be conveyed out of the lazaret, or place appointed for the performance of quarantine, unless under authority from the Crown; or, shall knowingly give a false certificate that a vessel has duly performed quarantine, he shall be guilty of felony, and in minor infringements be liable to fine or imprisonment.

II. Offences against the Vaccination Acts[151] are also punishable by fine and imprisonment.

It is indictable to expose in a public thoroughfare a person labouring under a contagious disease, or to bring a glandered horse into a public place at the risk of causing infection to the Queen's subjects; and it is a misdemeanor at common law to sell unwholesome provisions, or to give to any person injurious food to eat, whether the offender be a public contractor or otherwise. By stat. 11 & 12 Vict., c. 107, heavy penalties are imposed on persons who offer

[151] See 34 & 35 Vict., c. 98, an Act to amend the Vaccination Act, 1867.

for sale in any market or other public place any meat unfit for human food.[152]

III. A *Common Nuisance* is an offence against the public order, and consists in *doing* a thing to the annoyance of all the Queen's subjects or the *neglecting* to do a thing which the common good requires. These are distinguishable from nuisances affecting private persons, for which damages may be sued for. They are — 1. Annoyances in or closely adjoining *highways,* or affecting *bridges*, and *public rivers,* by rendering the same inconvenient or dangerous to pass, either positively by actual obstructions, or negatively by want of reparations. The person so obstructing, or such individuals as are bound to repair them, may be indicted for a nuisance, and fined. — 2. All kinds of nuisances, such as dangerous and offensive trades and manufactures, which, when injurious to a private man, are actionable; when detrimental to the public, are punishable by fine and imprisonment. — 3. All *disorderly inns,* houses of ill-fame, gambling-houses, play-houses improperly conducted, unlicensed booths and stages, and the like, are either at common law or by statute public nuisances, and may, upon indictment, be suppressed, and their keepers fined and imprisoned.[153]

Explain those offences which especially affect the Commonwealth, viz., those against public economy.

1. Offences relating to marriage. Any person who, falsely pretending to be in holy orders, solemnizes matrimony according to the rites of the Church of England, and knowingly and wilfully so offends, is guilty of felony.[154]

---

[152] See 35 & 36 Vict., c. 74, an Act to amend the law for the Prevention of Adulteration of food and drink, and of drugs.

[153] See 8 & 9 Vict., c. 109; 16 & 17 Vict., c. 38; 22 & 23 Vict., c. 17; and 30 & 31 Vict., c. 134.

[154] See 6 & 7 Wm. IV., c. 85; also 23 & 24 Vict., c. 18.

2. Whoever shall forge or fraudulently alter any licence of or certificate of marriage, or shall unlawfully destroy or injure any register of marriages, shall be guilty of felony.

3. Another offence against the commonwealth is called *bigamy;* that is, a second marriage by one having a former husband or wife living. Such second marriage is void, and being a great violation of the public economy, is a felony; and the offender is liable to penal servitude for five or seven years, or imprisonment with or without hard labour for two years.

4. *Selling* or exposing indecent prints for sale is indictable as a misdemeanor, and is punishable by fine or imprisonment, or both, and with hard labour.

5. *Drunkenness* is punishable by a pecuniary penalty. Idleness and vagrancy are deemed offences against the public order and economy.

6. *Wanton* or furious driving is also an offence against public order, and punishable by fine and imprisonment.

7. *Cruelty* to animals is also a like offence, and punishable by fines according to the circumstances.[155]

8. *Concealment* of birth is also a crime against public economy and punishable by imprisonment, with or without hard labour, for not more than two years.

9. *Refusing* to serve a public office, as constable or overseer, without lawful excuse or exemption, is also a misdemeanor at common law, and punishable by line and imprisonment.

---

[155] See 12 & 13 Vict., c. 92; 17 & 18 Vict., c. 60; 24 & 25 Vict, c. 97.

CHAPTER X
OFFENCES AGAINST THE PERSON

In the preceding chapters we have considered such crimes and misdemeanors as are more immediately injurious to religion; secondly, such as violate or transgress the law of nations; thirdly, such as more especially affect the Sovereign; fourthly, such as more directly infringe the rights of the public or commonwealth; and now we have to consider those crimes which, in a more particular manner, affect and injure individuals or private subjects — crimes which cannot be committed without a violation of the laws of nature — of the moral as well as political rules of right; and, for which, the Government calls upon the offender to submit to public punishment for the public crime.

Explain Offences against the Person, which are considered both as "public" and "private" wrongs.

Were these *injuries* confined to individuals, and did they affect none but their immediate objects, they would fall absolutely under the head of *private wrongs,* for which a satisfaction would be due only to the party injured; but the wrongs now in question affect the entire community: — 1. Because it is impossible they can be committed without a violation of the laws of nature — of the moral as well as political rules of right. — 2. Because they include ill them almost always a breach of the public peace. — 3. Because, by their example and evil tendency, they threaten and endanger the subversion of all civil society.

Upon these accounts, besides the private satisfaction due and given in many cases to the individual by action for the private wrong, the Government also calls upon the offender to submit to public punishment for the public crime; and the prosecution of these offences is always at the suit and in the name of the Sovereign, in whom, by the texture of our constitution, the executory power of the law entirely resides.

These crimes and misdemeanors against private subjects are principally of two kinds — 1. Against their PERSONS.[156] — 2. Against their PROPERTY.

Of crimes injurious to the *persons* of private subjects, the principal and most important is the offence of taking away life, which is the immediate gift of the great Creator, and of which, therefore, no man can be entitled to deprive himself or another.

FIRST, then, as to the offence of *homicide,* or destroying the life of man, in its several stages of guilt, arising from the particular circumstances of mitigation or aggravation which attend it.

Homicide, or the killing of any human creature, is of three kinds: — 1. *Justifiable.* — 2. *Excusable.* — 3. *Felonious.* The first has no share of legal guilt at all; the second very little; but the third is the highest crime against the law of nature that man is capable of committing.

Justifiable homicide is of divers kinds: — 1. Such as is owing-to some unavoidable necessity, without any will, intention, or desire, and without any inadvertence or negligence in the party killing, and therefore without any shadow of blame; as, for instance, by virtue of such an office as obliges one, in the execution of public justice, to put a malefactor to death who has forfeited his life by the laws of his country. Again, where au officer, in the exercise of his duty, attempts to take a man charged with fel-

[156] The Acts of Parliament relating to these crimes have recently been consolidated by 24 & 25 Vict., c. 100, entitled, "An Act to consolidate and amend the laws of England and Ireland, relating to offences against the person."

ony, and is resisted, and in the endeavour to take him, kills him. In case of a riot, or rebellious assembly, the officers endeavouring to disperse the mob are justifiable, both at common law and by the Riot Act, 1 Geo. I., c. 5. Where the prisoners in a, gaol, or going to a gaol, assault the gaoler or officer, and he in his defence kills any of them, it is justifiable, for the sake of preventing an escape. There must be, however, an apparent *necessity* on the part of the officer, for without such it is not justifiable.

In the next place, homicide committed for the *prevention* of any forcible and atrocious *crimes* is *justifiable.* If any person attempts a robbery or murder of another, or attempts to break open a house *in the night time,* and be killed in such attempt, the slayer shall be acquitted and discharged. But this does not extend to any crime unattended by force, as picking-pockets, &c.

The law justifies a woman killing a mail who attempts to ravish her; and so, too, the law justifies a husband or father killing a man who attempts a rape upon his wife or daughter; but not if he takes a man in adultery by consent, for the one is forcible and felonious, but not the other.

II. *Excusable homicide* is of two sorts: either *per infortunium,* by misadventure; or *se defendendo,* upon a principle of self-preservation.

Homicide *per infortunium* is where a man doing a lawful act, without any intention of hurt, unfortunately kills another; as where a man is at work with a hatchet, and the head thereof flies off and kills a bystander; or where a person shooting at a mark undesignedly kills a man; for the act is lawful, and the effect is merely *accidental.* So where a parent is moderately correcting his child, a master his apprentice or scholar, or an officer punishing a criminal, and happens to occasion his death, it is only misadventure, for the act of the correction is lawful; but if he exceeds the bounds of moderation, either in the manner, the instrument, or the amount of punishment, and death ensues, it is manslaughter at least, and may, according to the circumstances, be murder; for immoderate correction is unlawful.

Boxing and sword-playing, which have succeeded our ancestors' martial diversions of tilt and tournament, are, when they descend to prize-fighting, unlawful; for if a man so engaged chance to kill his opponent, he will be guilty of manslaughter. — Likewise to whip another man's horse, whereby he runs over a person, and kills him, is held to be accidental in the rider, but manslaughter in the party who whipped the horse; for the act was a trespass, and, at least, a piece of idleness of dangerous consequence. In general, if death ensues in consequence of an idle, dangerous, and unlawful sport, as shooting or casting stones in a town, in such and similar cases the slayer is guilty of manslaughter, and not misadventure only, for these are unlawful acts.

Homicide in *self-defence* or *se defendendo,* upon a sudden affray, is also excusable; but to excuse homicide by the plea of self-defence, it must appear that the slayer had no other possible, or at least probable, means of escaping from his assailant. Men cannot legally exercise the right of preventive defence but in sudden and violent cases. The *time* of the defence is also to be considered, for if the person assaulted does not fall upon the aggressor till the affray is over, or when he is running away, this is *revenge,* and not defence. There must be a *necessity* to justify the defence.

III. *Felonious homicide* is the killing a human creature of any age or sex without justification or excuse. This may be done by either killing one's self or another person.

Self-murder which the law of England wisely and religiously ranks among the highest crimes, is a peculiar species of felony — a felony committed on one's self. This crime admits of accessories before the fact; for if one persuades another to kill himself, and he does so, the adviser is guilty of murder; and if two persons agree to commit suicide, and both attempt to destroy themselves together, but only one dies, it has been held murder in the survivor. A *felo de se,* therefore, is he who deliberately puts an end to his own existence; or commits any *unlawful* malicious act, the consequence of which is his own death; as if attempting to kill another, he runs upon his antagonist's sword; or shooting at another, the gun bursts, and kills himself. The party must be of years of discretion, and in his senses, otherwise it is no crime.

Now the question follows, what punishment can human laws inflict on one who has withdrawn himself from their reach? They can only act upon what he has left behind him, his reputation and fortune. Accordingly, by stat. 4 Geo. IV. c. 52, it is enacted that the remains of persons against whom a finding of *felo de se* is returned are to be privately buried; the interment to take place within twenty-four hours after verdict of the inquisition, between nine and twelve at night, and without performance of the rites of Christian burial; and that his goods and chattels be forfeited to the Crown; but the letter of the law may in this respect be mitigated, for the Sovereign is bound by the oath of his office to execute judgment in mercy.

IV. The other species of *criminal homicide* is that of killing another person; but in this offence there are also degrees of guilt, which divide it into *manslaughter* and *murder.*

Manslaughter is the felonious killing of another *without* malice, *express* or *implied.* It may be either *voluntary,* upon a sudden heat, as killing a man in a chance medley; or *involuntarily,* in the commission of some unlawful act. Hence it follows that in manslaughter there can be no accessories before the fact, because it must be done without premeditation.

As to the *voluntary* branch, if upon a sudden quarrel two persons fight, and one of them kills the other, this is manslaughter; and so it is, it they upon such an occasion go out and fight in a field; for this is one continued act of passion; and the law pays that regard to human frailty, as not to put a hasty and deliberate act upon the same footing with regard to guilt. So also if a man greatly provokes another, as by pulling his nose, or other like indignity, and the person aggrieved *immediately* kills the aggressor; though this is not excusable *se defendendo,* since there is no absolute necessity for doing it to preserve himself, yet neither is it murder, for there is no previous malice; but it is manslaughter. Yet in this, and in every other case of homicide upon provocation, if there be a sufficient cooling-time for passion to subside and reason to interpose, and the person so provoked afterwards kills the other, this act is deliberate revenge, not heat of blood, and accordingly amounts to murder. So if a man takes another in the act of adultery with his wife, and kills him directly upon the spot, it is not absolutely ranked in the class of justifiable homicide, as in the case of a forcible rape; but it is manslaughter. Manslaughter, therefore, on a sudden provocation differs from excusable homicide, *se defendendo,* in this: that in one case there is an apparent necessity for self-preservation to kill the aggressor; in the other, no necessity at all, being only a sudden act of revenge.

The second branch, or *involuntary* manslaughter, differs also from homicide excusable by misadventure, in this; that *misadventure* always happens in consequence of a *lawful act,* but this species of manslaughter ill consequence of an unlawful one. As where a person does an act, lawful in itself, but in an unlawful manner, and without due caution and circumspection; as when a workman flings down a stone or piece of timber into the street and kills a man; this may be either misadventure, manslaughter, or murder, according to the circumstances under which the original act was done. If it were in a country village, where few passengers are, and he calls out to all people to have a care, it is misadventure only; but if it were in London, or in any other populous town where people are continually passing, it is manslaughter, though he gives loud warning; and murder, if he knows of their passing, and gives no warning at all, for then there is evidence of malice against all mankind. And, in general, when an involuntary killing happens in consequence of an unlawful act, it will be either murder or manslaughter, according to the nature of the act which occasioned it. If it be in prosecution of a felonious intent, or in its consequences naturally tended to bloodshed, it will be murder; but if no more was intended than a mere civil trespass, it will only amount to manslaughter.

All struggles in anger are clearly forbidden by law, and should death result to one of the parties engaged in such a contest, the survivor will at least be guilty of manslaughter, perhaps even of murder.

The punishment of felonious homicide is thus set forth by stat. 24 & 25 Vict., c. 100 — that whosoever shall be convicted of felonious manslaughter shall be liable to be kept in penal servitude for life, or for a term of not less than five years; or imprisonment with or without hard labour for any term not exceeding two years; or to pay such fine as the Court shall award with or without such other discretionary punishment.

Define and explain that crime at which human nature revolts, and which is punished almost universally throughout the world with death.

The crime of *deliberate* and *wilful murder* is thus defined by Sir Edward Coke: — "When a person of *sound memory* and *discretion* unlawfully killeth any *reasonable creature* in being, and under the King's peace, with *malice aforethought,* either *caress* or *implied.*"

First, then, it must be committed by a person of *sound memory* and discretion, for *lunatics,* and *infants,* as formerly stated, are incapable of committing crime, unless in cases where they show a consciousness of doing wrong; and, of course, a discretion, or capacity of discerning between good and evil.

The *unlawfulness* arises from the killing without *warrant* or *excuse*; and there must be an actual killing to constitute murder — which may be by poisoning, striking, starving, drowning, and various other forms of death by which human nature may be overcome.

Further, the person killed must be a *reasonable creature* in *being,* and under the King's peace at the time of the killing; therefore, to kill an alien or an outlaw, for both are under the King's peace and protection, is as much murder as to kill the most regular-born Englishman. To kill a child in its mother's womb is no murder, but felony; but if the child be born alive, and die by reason of the potion or bruises it received in the womb, it may be murder in the wrong-doer. With regard to child-murder, unfortunately common and difficult of detection, it is especially enacted, that if any woman shall be delivered of a child, every person who shall, by any secret disposition of the dead body of the said child, whether such child died before, at, or after the birth, endeavour to conceal the birth thereof, shall be guilty of a misdemeanor.

Lastly, the *killing* must be committed with "*malice aforethought*" to make it the crime of murder; and this is the criterion which now distinguishes *murder* from other *killing.* This *malice prepense,* the dictate of a wicked, depraved, and malignant heart, may be either *express* or *implied* in law. Express malice is when one, with a deliberate mind and formed design, doth kill another, which *formed* is evidenced by external circumstances discovering the inward intention; as lying in wait, antecedent menaces, former grudges, and concerted schemes to do him some bodily harm. This takes place in the case of deliberate duelling, where both parties inert with an intent to commit homicide, the principals and seconds in which are, if the duel terminates fatally, alike guilty or murder.

Where no *malice* is expressed, the law will *imply it;* as where a man wilfully poisons another, the law presumes malice, though no particular enmity call be proved; and if a man kills another suddenly, without any or without considerable provocation, the law *implies* malice, for no person, unless of an abandoned heart, would be guilty of such an act upon a slight or no apparent cause. Also, if one intends to commit a felony and undesignedty kills a man, this is murder. Thus, if one shoots at A, and misses him, but kills B, this is murder, because of the previous felonious *intent,* which the law transfers from one to the other. The same is the case where one lays poison for A; and B, against whom the *poisoner* had no malicious intent, takes it, and it kills him, this is likewise murder.

It may be taken as a general rule that all homicide is malicious, and consequently amounts to murder, unless where *justified* by the command or permission of the law; *excused,* on the account of accident or self-preservation in sudden quarrel; or *alleviated* into manslaughter, by being either the involuntary consequence of some act not strictly lawful; or if voluntary, occasioned by some sudden and sufficiently violent provocation.

Attempts to Murder, until very recently, amounted to a capital felony; but it is now provided by 21 Vict., c. 100, that whoever shall administer to, or cause to be administered to, or taken by, any person, any poison or other destructive thing, or shall by *any means whatsoever* wound or cause any grievous bodily harm to any person, with intent to commit murder, shall be guilty of felony, and on conviction may be sentenced to penal servitude for life, or for not less than three years, or imprisonment for any term not exceeding two years, with or without hard labour and solitary confinement.

Explain the Felonies that cause or tend to cause Danger to Life or Bodily Harm.

I. *Mayhem* (to maim) is a *civil* injury, but it is also looked upon in a *criminal* light, being an atrocious breach of the peace, for mayhem *(mayhemium)* is properly defined to be the violently depriving another of the use of such of his members as may render him the less able in fighting either to defend himself or to annoy his adversary. By the ancient law of England, he that maimed any man, whereby he lost any portion of his body, was sentenced to lose the like part — *membrum pro membo.* The Act now in force is 24 & 25 Vict.. c. 100. which enacts that whosoever shall unlawfully and maliciously, by *any means whatsoever,* wound or cause any grievous bodily harm to any person, or shoot at any person, or by drawing a trigger, or in any other manner attempt to discharge any kind of loaded arms at any person, or with intent to maim disfigure, or disable, or to do some grievous bodily harm to any person; or with intent to resist or prevent the lawful apprehension or detainer of any person, he shall be guilty of felony, and on conviction may be sentenced to penal servitude for life, or for not less than five years, or imprisonment for any term not exceeding two years, with or without hard labour. And in cases of garrotting or robbery with violence, flogging is added to the punishment.

II. The *second offence* more immediately affecting the personal security of individuals relates to the female part of Her Majesty's subjects, being that of their *forcible abduction* and *marriage.* Formerly it was a capital offence, but these enactments are repealed, and by 24 & 25 Vict., c. 100, it is enacted that where any woman, of *any age,* shall have any interest in any real or personal estate, or shall be an heiress presumptive, or co-heiress, it shall be *felony* in any person who shall take away or detain her against her will, with intent to marry her or carnally know her; or who shall cause her to be married or carnally known by any other person, and the offender is punishable by penal servitude for fourteen years, or not less than five; or by imprisonment for not less than two years, with or without hard labour. The same punishment is awarded to whomsoever shall *by force* take away or detain against her will a woman of *any age* with a similar intent.

Unlawfully taking, or causing to be taken, any unmarried girl, under the age of sixteen years, out of the possession and against the will of her father and mother, or of any other person having the lawful care or charge of her, is punishable by imprisonment for not more than two years, with or without hard labour.

Rape, *raptus mulierum,* is the gravest offence against the female portion of Her Majesty's subjects, and by the civil law was punished with death and confiscation of goods, and continued to be punishable with death until the year 1841. Now, by stat. 24 & 25 Vict., c. 100, it is enacted that "whosoever shall be convicted of the crime of rape shall be guilty of felony, and liable to be kept in penal servitude for life, or imprisoned for any term not exceeding two years, with or without hard labour." A person present, aiding and abetting, may be charged as principal either in the first or second degree.

Abusing any girl under the age of twelve years, or an indecent assault upon a female, or attempt to have carnal knowledge of a girl under twelve years of age is punishable with imprisonment for not more than two years, with or without hard labour.

A *male* infant, under the age of fourteen years, is presumed by law to be physically incapable of committing a rape, and therefore cannot be found guilty of it.

Assaults, batteries, wounding, false imprisonment, and *kidnapping* were previously considered as *civil injuries,* being PRIVATE WRONGS, for which a satisfaction or remedy is given to the party aggrieved; but taken in a public light, these offences are broaches of the peace, and are also indictable and punishable with fine and imprisonment.

CHAPTER XI
OFFENCES AGAINST PROPERTY

The next species of offences against private subjects are such as more immediately affect their property, and are chiefly made punishable by statute: — 1. *Maliciously setting fire* to buildings and. other things. — 2. *Burglary* and *housebreaking.* — 3. *Larceny — embezzlement — fraud-obtaining property by false pretences,* and other offences injurious to the "Rights of Property."

What are the Two Offences that more immediately affect the Habitations of Individuals, and explain them?

I. *Arson* and *Burglary*[157] Arson, *ab ardendo,* is the malicious and wilful burning of the house or outhouse of another man, which is an offence of very great malignity, and may be more destructive than murder itself; for murder, atrocious as it is, seldom extends beyond the felonious act designed, whereas fire may involve in a common calamity persons unknown to the incendiary. In order to constitute the crime of arson, the burning must be *malicious,* and the punishment by our ancient Saxon laws was death. Now, by stat. 24 & 25 Vict., c. 97, it is felony to attempt by any overt act to *maliciously* burn an outhouse, barn, or stable, or setting fire to a crop of hay, corn, plantation, or other vegetable produce, whether standing or cut down; and punishable by penal servitude for not more than seven, nor less than five years, or imprisonment for not more than two years with or without hard labour, and with or without solitary confinement; and if a male under the age of sixteen, with or without whipping. And the same statute enacts that setting fire to any dwelling-house is punishable by penal servitude for life, or not less than five years; or imprisonment for not more than two years, with or without hard labour, and with or without solitary confinement; and if a male under the age of sixteen years, with or without whipping.

II. *Burglary,* or nocturnal housebreaking, *burgi latrocinium,* is a very heinous offence, not only by the terror that it carries with it, but also as it is a forcible invasion and disturbance of that right of habitation which the law of England will never suffer to be violated with impunity.

---

[157] See 24 & 25 Vict., cc. 96-98, Acts to consolidate and amend the Statute Law of England and Ireland relating to *larceny malicious injuries* to property, *forgery,* and other similar offences.

The definition of a burglar, as given by Sir Edward Coke, is "he that by *night* breaketh and entereth into a *mansion-house* with intent to commit a felony."

In this definition there are four things to be considered: — the *time,* the *place,* the *manner,* and the *intent.* The *time* must be by night, for in the daytime there is no burglary; and stat. 24 & 25 Vict., c. 96, enacts "that night shall be deemed to commence at nine o'clock in the evening, and to conclude at six o'clock in the morning."

As to the *place.* It must be in a mansion or dwelling-house, or in some building communicating with such a dwelling-house. A chamber in a college, or an inn of court, where each inhabitant has a distinct property, is to all purposes the mansion-house of the owner; so is a room or lodging in any private house; but if I hire a shop, parcel of another man's house, and work or trade in it, but never sleep there, it is no dwelling-house, nor can burglary be committed therein; neither can burglary be committed in a tent or booth erected in a market or fair, though the owner may lodge therein, for the law regards only permanent edifices.

As to the *manner* of committing burglary, there must be both a breaking and an entry to complete it; not a mere legal *clausum fregit* — an ideal boundary which may constitute a civil trespass; but a substantial and forcible irruption, as at least by breaking or taking out the glass of or otherwise opening, a window, picking a lock, or opening it with a key; by lifting the latch of a door, or unloosing any other fastening which the owner has provided. If a person, however, leaves his door or window open, and if a man enters therein, it is no burglary; but if the man afterwards unlocks an inner or chamber door, it is so. If a servant opens and enters his master's chamber door with a felonious design, or if any other person lodging in the same house, or in a public inn, opens the door and enters with such evil *intent,* it is burglary. In fact, any forcible entry at night, with a felonious intent, is burglary; but such breaking and entry must be with a felonious *intent,* otherwise it is only a trespass. Should a man enter a house and hide himself therein and break out at night, that also constitutes burglary.

Burglary is now punishable with penal servitude for life, or for any term not less than five years; or with imprisonment for not more than two years with or without hard labour, and with or without solitary confinement.

Housebreaking is closely allied to the crime of *burglary.* Breaking and entering any dwelling-house, shop, warehouse, or place of divine worship with intent to commit a felony therein is punishable by penal servitude for not more than fourteen, nor less than five years; or imprisonment for not more than two years with or without hard labour, and with or without solitary confinement.

It is further provided, that any one found by night, having in his possession, without *lawful excuse,* any dangerous or offensive weapon, or found in any dwelling-house or other building with an unlawful intent, shall be guilty of a misdemeanor, and punishable by penal servitude for five years, or imprisonment for not more than two years with or without hard labour.

Explain Larceny.

Larceny, or theft *(latrocinium),* is the unlawful taking and carrying away things personal, with intent to deprive the right owner of the same.

To constitute *larceny* there must be an unlawful *taking* and *carrying-away (cepit et asportavit).* This implies the consent of the owner to be wanting; therefore no delivery of the goods from the owner to the offender, *upon trust,* can ground a larceny. If A lends B a horse, and B rides away with it; or, if I send goods by a carrier and he carries them away, these are no larcenies; but if the carrier opens a bale or pack of goods, or pierces a vessel of wine, and takes away part thereof; or if he carries it to the place appointed, and afterwards takes away the whole, these are larcenies, for here the *animus furandi* is manifest; but bare non-delivery will not, of course, be imputed to arise from a felonious design, as that may happen from a variety of accidents.

Where the sale of a horse or any other article is complete, and possession delivered to the buyer, who rides away with the horse or carries off the article without paying for it, no felony is committed; for the property as well as possession is parted with, and the owner is defrauded, not of the horse or article, but only of its price, and he has his own remedy by an action to recover it.

A removal of the goods from the place in which the offender found them, though he does not quite make off with them, is a sufficient asportation or carrying-away to constitute larceny. As if a man be leading another's horse out of a close, and be apprehended in the fact; or if a guest, stealing goods out of an inn, has removed them from his chamber downstairs; or if a thief, intending to steal plate, takes it out of a chest in which it was, and lays it down upon the floor, but is surprised before he can make his escape with it, those have also been adjudged sufficient carrying-away to constitute larceny.

The ordinary discovery of a felonious intent is where the party does it clandestinely; or, being charged with the fact, denies it. But this is by no means the only criterion of criminality; for in cases that may amount to larceny the variety of circumstances is so great, and the complications thereof so mingled, that it is impossible to recount all those which may evidence a felonious intent, or *animum furandi;* therefore they must be left to the due and attentive consideration of the court and jury.

In order to satisfy the definition of *larceny,* the felonious. taking and carrying-away must be of the *personal* goods of another; for of things *real,* or savouring of the realty, larceny at common law cannot be committed. In virtue, however, of statutory provisions, larceny may now be committed by stealing, cutting, severing, or breaking, with intent to steal, glass or woodwork, lead, metal, trees, shrubs, or underwood; or anything fixed in land, being private property; or in any place dedicated to public use or ornament.

Bonds, bills, and notes, which concern mere *choses* in action, were at the common law held not to be such goods whereof larceny might be committed, being of no intrinsic value, and not importing any property in possession of the person from whom they are taken; but by statute they are now put upon the same footing with respect to larceny as the money they were meant to secure.

If, upon the trial of any person for a misdemeanor, it shall appear that the facts given in evidence amount in law to a felony, such person shall not by reason thereof be entitled to be acquitted of such misdemeanor; in which case such person may be dealt with in all respects as if he had not been put upon his trial for such misdemeanor.

It is now lawful to insert several counts in the same indictment against the same person for any number of distinct acts of stealing, not exceeding three, which may have been committed by him against the same person within the space of six months from the first to the last of such acts, and to proceed thereon for all or any of them.

Where any prisoner shall be convicted, either summarily or otherwise, of larceny or other offence, and it shall appear to the court by the evidence that the prisoner has sold the stolen property to any person, and that such person has had no knowledge that the same was stolen, and that money has been taken from the prisoner on his apprehension, it is lawful for the court, on the application of such purchaser, and on the restitution of the stolen property to the prosecutor, to order that out of such moneys a sum not exceeding the proceeds of the sale be delivered to the said purchaser.

Any constable or peace officer may take into custody, without warrant, any person whom he shall find lying or loitering in any highway, yard, or other place, during the night, and whom he shall have good cause to suspect of having committed or being about to commit any felony, and shall take such person as soon as reasonably may be before a justice of the peace, to be dealt with according to law. If such justice be of opinion that the charge is fit to be made the subject of prosecution by indictment rather than to be disposed of summarily, the case may be sent for trial by a jury at the sessions or assizes.

In every case of summary proceeding, the person accused, shall be allowed to make his full answer and defence, and to have all witnesses examined and cross-examined by counsel or attorney.

What are the Larcenies that are punishable by Summary Jurisdiction.

Persons charged before justices of the peace with having committed larceny, where the value of the whole of the property alleged to have been stolen does not, in the judgment of such justices, exceed five shillings; or, with having attempted to commit larceny from the person, are punishable by summary jurisdiction.[158]

[Statute 24 & 25 Vict., c. 96, an Act to consolidate and amend the Statute Law of England and Ireland relating to *larceny* and other similar offences, abolishes the distinction between grand and petty larceny. Every larceny, whatever the value of the property stolen, is now deemed to be of the same nature, and subject to the same incidents in all respects, as grand larceny was before the 21st June, 1827; and every court whose power as to the trial of larceny was before that time limited to petty larceny, shall have power to try every case of larceny and all accessories to such larceny.]

Stealing trees, shrubs, underwood, wherever growing, or fruit or vegetable productions in a garden, is punishable, on conviction before a justice of the peace, by imprisonment, with or without hard labour, for any term not exceeding six months; or by the forfeit over and above the value of the articles stolen and injured, of such sum of money not exceeding £20 as to the justice shall seem meet. A second offence, against this or any other Act of Parliament, makes the offender guilty of felony, and punishable as in the case of larceny.[159]

---

[158] See explanation of "Summary proceedings in Criminal Courts."

[159] *Punishment for Common-Law Misdemeanors* — The punishment of all common-law misdemeanors; that is, of all those crimes which do not amount to felony, and the punishment of which has not been regulated by statute, is fine and imprisonment. The court may also require the defendant to find sureties to keep the peace and be of good behaviour.

Commitment of Juvenile Offenders to Reformatory Schools — Whenever any offender who, in the judgment of the court, justices, or magistrate, before whom ho is charged, is under the age of sixteen years, is convicted on indictment or in a summary manner of an offence punishable with penal servitude or imprisonment, and is sentenced to be imprisoned for the term of ten days or a longer term, the court, justices, or magistrate may also sentence him to be sent, at the expiration of imprisonment, to a certified reformatory school, and to be there detained for a period of not less than two years and not more than five years.

Dog-stealing is punishable by imprisonment for six months, and after a previous conviction for such offence, the offender may be indicted for a misdemeanor, and punished by imprisonment for not more than eighteen months with or without hard labour. It is also enacted that whosoever shall unlawfully have in his possession or on his premises any stolen dog, or the skin of any stolen dog, knowing such dog to have been stolen, or such skin to be the skin of any stolen dog, shall, on summary conviction, be liable over and above the value of the dog, to a penalty not exceeding £20, and after a previous conviction for such offence may be indicted for a misdemeanor. Also, if any one corruptly take a reward, directly or indirectly, under pretence or upon account of aiding any person to recover any dog which has been stolen, or in possession of any person not being the owner, ho is guilty of a misdemeanor, and punishable by imprisonment for not more than eighteen months with or without hard labour.

Stealing any bird, beast, or animal ordinarily kept in a state of confinement or for any domestic purpose, not being the subject of larceny at the common law; or the wilful killing any such bird, beast, or animal with intent to steal the same, subjects the offender, on conviction before a justice of the peace, to imprisonment for any term not exceeding six months, or to the forfeiture over and above the value of such bird, beast, or animal of such sum of money, not exceeding £20, as the justices may think fit; a second offence of this kind is punishable by imprisonment for not more than twelve months.

Punishment for Larceny— Penal servitude for five years; or, imprisonment for not more than two years, with or without hard labour, and after a previous conviction, penal servitude for any term not exceeding seven years and not less than three; or imprisonment for any term not exceeding two years, with or without hard labour, and with or without solitary confinement; and, if a male under sixteen with or without whipping.

Unlawfully and willfully taking, or destroying *fish,* is a misdemeanor; and stealing oysters, or oyster brood, from any oyster bed or fishery, sufficiently marked out and known as the property of another person, is a felony, punishable as simple larceny; and whosoever shall unlawfully and wilfully use any dredge or net within the limits of any such oyster bed or fishery for the purpose of taking oysters or oyster brood shall be guilty of a misdemeanor, and be liable to imprisonment for three months with or without hard labour, and with or without solitary confinement.

Unlawfully hunting, coursing, waring, carrying away, killing, or wounding deer, being in the unenclosed part of any forest, chase, or purlieu, is punishable on summary conviction before a justice of the peace, by a penalty not exceeding £50; and the unlawfully hunting, killing, or wounding deer in the enclosed part of any forest, chase, or purlieu, is constituted a felony, and is punishable by imprisonment for any term not exceeding two years; and, if a male under sixteen years, with whipping.

Summary punishment may also be imposed by fine, not exceeding £20, upon any person who shall have in his possession, or upon his premises with his knowledge, any deer, or the head, skin, or other part thereof, or any snare or engine for the taking of deer, without satisfactorily accounting for such possession. To take or kill hares or rabbits in any warren is punishable by fine or imprisonment, also stealing any beast or bird ordinarily kept in a state of confinement, or knowingly being in possession thereof, or of the skin or plumage thereof, is in like manner punishable on summary conviction.[160]

A *trespass* during the daytime in pursuit of game subjects the offender to civil proceedings for the trespass;

---

[160] In cases where the value or price of the articles or goods is not of the essence of the offence, no statement or price is necessary in the indictment.

and by 24 & 25 Vict., c. 96, s. 17, "whoever shall unlawfully and wilfully, between the beginning of the last hour before sunrise and the expiration of the first hour after sunset, take or kill any hare or rabbit in a warren, enclosed, or not; or shall at any time set or use therein any snare or engine for the taking of hares or rabbits, shall, on conviction thereof before a justice of the peace, forfeit and. pay a sum of money, not exceeding £5; and after two convictions, may be indicted, for a misdemeanor, and punished by penal servitude for not more than seven nor less than five years, or imprisonment with hard labour for not more than two years."

Opening or delaying letters. — Every person employed by or under the post office who shall, contrary to his duty, open or suffer to be opened a post letter, or who shall wilfully detain or delay, or suffer to be detained or delayed, a post letter, shall be guilty of a misdemeanor, and punishable by fine or imprisonment, or both; and every person stealing or embezzling letters, or stealing money, &c., out of letters, shall be guilty of felony.

Ripping, cutting, severing, or breaking, with intent to steal any glass or wood-work belonging to any building whatsoever, or any lead, iron, copper, brass, or other metal, is felony, and on conviction is punishable, as in the case of simple larceny.

As to *larceny of cattle* or other animals, whoever shall steal any horse, mare, gelding, colt, or filly; or any bull, cow, ox, heifer, or calf; or any ram, ewe, sheep, or lamb, shall be guilty of felony; and whoever shall wilfully kill any animal with intent to steal the carcase, skin, or any part of the animal, and being convicted thereof, shall be liable to the same punishment as if he had been convicted of feloniously stealing the same, provided the offence of stealing the animal so killed would have amounted to felony.

II. *Larceny by tenants or lodgers.* — Stealing any chattel or fixture let to be used by him or her or with any house or lodging is felony, and being convicted thereof the offender shall be liable, at the discretion of the court, to be imprisoned for any term not exceeding two years, with or without hard labour, and with or without solitary confinement; and, if a male under the age of sixteen years, with or without whipping. If the value of such chattel or fixture exceeds £5, the person convicted shall be liable, at the discretion of the court, to be kept in penal servitude for any term not exceeding five years and not less than three years; or imprisonment for any term not exceeding two years with or without hard labour, and with or without solitary confinement; and if a male under the age of sixteen, with or without whipping.

Larceny from the person is either by privately stealing, or by open and violent assault. It is enacted by stat. 27 & 28 Vict., that whosoever shall rob any person, or shall steal any chattel, money, or valuable security from the person of another, is punishable with penal servitude for not more than five years, nor less than two years; or by imprisonment for not more than two years, with or without hard labour, and with or without solitary confinement; and that whosoever shall assault any person with intent to rob, and at the time of, or immediately after such robbery, shall wound, beat, strike, or use any other personal violence to any person, shall be guilty of felony, and punishable with penal servitude for life or not less than five yeas; or imprisonment for not more than two years, with or without lend labour, and with or without solitary confinement, to which the lash may now be added.

If upon the trial of any person upon any indictment for robbery it shall appear to the jury upon the evidence that the defendant did not commit the crime of robbery, but that he did commit an assault with intent to rob, he shall be liable to be punished as in the case of larceny.

III. *Embezzlement* is a theft by clerks, servants, or agents, and is distinguished from *larceny* as being committed in respect of property which is not at the time in the actual or legal possession of the owner. By 24 & 25 Vict., c. 96, ss. 67 & 68, it is enacted that if a person fraudulently embezzle any chattel, money, or *valuable security* delivered to, received, or taken into possession by him for, or in the name, or on account of his master or employer, he shall be deemed to have feloniously stolen the same, and be punishable by penal servitude for not more than fourteen, nor less than five years, or imprisonment for not more than two years, with or without hard labour, and with or without solitary confinement; and, if a male under the age of sixteen years, with or without whipping.

The same Act also provides that any person entrusted with any money or security, as a banker, merchant, broker, attorney, or other agent, with a written direction to apply the same in a, specified manner, who shall, in violation of good faith and contrary to such direction, convert the same to the use or benefit of any one other than the person by whom he was so entrusted, shall be guilty of a misdemeanor, and may be sentenced to penal servitude for a term not exceeding seven years, nor loss than five years; or imprisonment not exceeding two years, with or without hard labour and solitary confinement.

A *bailee* of any chattel, money, or valuable security who shall fraudulently take or convert the same to his own use or to the use of any person other than the owner thereof, although he shall not break bulk or otherwise determine the bailment, shall be guilty of larceny, and may be convicted thereof upon an indictment of larceny. This provision does not extend to any offence punishable on summary conviction.

IV. *False pretence.* — By the Larceny Act, 24 & 25 Vict., c. 98, it is enacted that whosoever, by any false pretence, obtains from any other person any chattel, money, or valuable security with *intent to defraud,* shall be guilty of a misdemeanor, and be punishable as in cases of larceny, *ante* p. 320. The *pretence* may be evidenced by the acts and conduct of the offender, without any verbal misrepresentation. This offence is closely allied to *larceny,* and is mainly distinguishable from it, that in larceny the property in the thing taken does not pass, whereas in *false pretences* it is meant to do so.

Obtaining property by *false personation* — personating owners of stock, seamen, sailors, &c., is punishable by penal servitude for five years, or not less than two years, or imprisonment for two years with or without hard labour. False personation of voters at an election of a member of Parliament is punishable by fine and imprisonment.

It is also enacted that whosoever, by any false pretences, fraudulently causes or induces another to execute, make, accept, endorse, or destroy the whole or any part of any valuable security, or to write, impress, or affix his name, or the name of any other person, or of any company, or the seal of any body corporate, with a view to defraud, is guilty of a misdemeanor, and punishable as in the case of larceny.

Cheating at play. — Every person who shall by any fraud or unlawful device or ill-practice in playing at, or with cards, dice, tables, or other game, win from any other person to himself, or any other person or persons, any sum of money or valuable thing, shall be deemed guilty of obtaining such money or valuable thing from such other person by a *false pretence,* and shall be punished accordingly.

Forgery, or the *crimen falsi,* is an offence which was punished by the civil law, and formerly by our laws almost invariably with death. It may be defined to be the *fraudulent making* or *alteration* of a writing or seal, to the prejudice of another man's right. Forgery, to be punishable, must show an *intent* to defraud, for the very essence of forgery is fraudulent intention. The mere imitation of another's writing, the assumption of a name, or the alteration of a written instrument, where no person can be injured, does not come within the definition of this offence.[161]

By stat. 24 & 25 Vict., c. 98, forging any transfer of stock, whether public or of any body corporate, or any power of attorney relating thereto, is felony. — Also personating an owner of stock, and transferring or receiving, or endeavouring to transfer or receive, the dividends thereupon — Forging an attestation to a power of attorney for the transfer of stock, or receipt of dividends — Making false entry in the books of the public funds — Making false dividend warrants for the payment of money by clerks — Forging an East-India bond or Exchequer bill — Making plates or paper in imitation of those used for Exchequer bills — Having without lawful authority in possession paper, plates, or dies to be used for Exchequer bills — Forging or uttering bank-notes, knowing the same to be forged — Purchasing, receiving, or having forged banknotes — Forging or uttering deeds, bonds, wills, bills

[161] The forging and counterfeiting of any writing, or the uttering and publishing it as true, knowing it to be forged and counterfeited with a fraudulent intent, is a misdemeanor at common law, in all cases where it has not been made felony by statute. A false testimonial to character in order to attain an appointment or situation, false recommendation, and the like, are forgeries at common law.

of exchange, or promissory notes — Obliterating crossings on cheques — Forging debentures — Forging proceedings of Courts of Record or Courts of Equity, and similar offences.

Forgery, though amenable to punishment at common law, is now mainly regulated by stat. 24 & 25 Vict., c. 98, which contains provisions applicable to almost every conceivable kind of forgery, with the punishment, which in most cases is penal servitude for five years and upwards; or imprisonment for not more than two years, with or without hard labour, and with or without solitary confinement.

VI. *Stolen goods.* — To buy or receive *stolen goods,* knowing them to be stolen, was formerly a mere misdemeanor; but now, by stat. 24 & 25 Vict., c. 96, all such receivers are made accessories, where the principal felony admits of accessories, and may now be indicted either as accessories after the fact, or for substantive felony, and on conviction be punished by imprisonment or penal servitude.

By recent legislation, the law, with regard to receivers of stolen property, has been made more stringent.[162] Now, in certain cases evidence may be given before verdict of a previous conviction; or, of other stolen goods having been found in the prisoner's possession. Powers of search for and seizure of stolen goods are also given to the police.

VII. *Sending letters* demanding money, with *menaces* or *by force, is* felony; also sending letters threatening to *accuse, of crime,* with intent to extort; or sending letters threatening to burn, or destroy, or to murder any person, is felony, and the party on conviction shall be liable, at the discretion of the court, to be kept in penal servitude for

---

[162] See 32 & 33 Vict., c. 99, on Act for the more effectual prevention of crime.

any term not exceeding ten years, and not less than five years; or imprisonment for any term not exceeding two years with or without hard labour.

VIII. *Lost property.* — *It* a man finds goods that have been actually lost, or are reasonably supposed by him to have been lost, and appropriates them with the intent to take the entire dominion over them, *really believing* when he takes them that the owner *cannot* be found, it is not larceny; but if he takes them with the like intent, though lost, or reasonably supposed to be lost, but *reasonably believing* the owner can be found, it is larceny.

CHAPTER XII
THE MEANS OF PREVENTING OFFENCES

We are now arrived at a very important branch or head of this work, viz., — the *means of preventing the commission of crimes and misdemeanors,* and it is an honour to our English laws that they furnish a title of this sort, since "preventive justice" is, upon every principle of reason, of humanity, and of sound principle, preferable in all respects to "punishing justice," the execution of which, though necessary, and in its consequences a species of mercy to the commonwealth, is attended with many harsh and disagreeable circumstances.

In what does Preventive Justice consist?

Preventive Justice consists in obliging those persons whom there is a probable ground to suspect of future misbehaviour to find pledges or securities (commonly called *bail*) for keeping the peace, or future good behaviour. It may he divided into foul-heads: —

I. In the apprehending persons at whom suspicious circumstances point as likely to commit crime.

II. In requiring persons to find sureties for keeping the peace, or for their good behaviour.

III. In making criminal the having in possession certain things presumably for the commission of crime.

IV. In searching for the evidences of guilt, and seizing weapons or instruments, the use or possession of which may scarcely be deemed compatible with innocence of unlawful intent.

Explain the Procedure of Preventive Justice.

First, then, a *constable,* or even a private person, seeing another on the point of committing felony, may lawfully lay hold. of the individual thus acting; and detain him until it can be presumed that he has changed, his purpose; and when a felony is committed, it is the duty of a bystander to arrest the offender. By 24 & 25 Vict., c. 100, s. 66, a constable or peace officer may take into custody, without a warrant, any person whom he shall find lying or loitering in any highway, yard, or other place during the night, whom he shall have good cause to suspect of having committed, or being about to commit, a felony; and shall take such suspected person, as soon as reasonably may be, before a justice of the peace, to be dealt with according to law.

Secondly, *preventive justice* obliges those persons whom there is a probable ground to suspect of future misbehaviour to find *pledges* or *bail* for keeping the peace, or for their future good behaviour. This security consists in being bound, with one or more sureties, in a recognizance or obligation to the Crown entered on record, whereby the parties acknowledge themselves to be indebted to the Crown in the sum therein stated, with a *condition,* to be void and of none effect if the party shall appear in court on such a day, and in the meantime shall keep the peace either generally towards the sovereign and all his liege people, or particularly also with regard to the person who craves the security. Or, if it be for good behaviour, then on condition that he shall behave himself well, or be of good behaviour, either generally or specially for the time therein limited; and if the condition of such recognizance be broken, the recognizance becomes forfeited, and the party and his sureties become the Crown's absolute debtors for the several sums in which they are respectively bound.

The third head renders illegal, unless satisfactorily accounted for, the possession of certain things presumably for the commission of crime.

Fourthly, a *search warrant,* with a view to the prevention of crime and the detection of criminals, may be granted, by a justice of the peace. Also a warrant may be granted to send for and seize property suspected to have been stolen, sufficient ground for suspicion having been shown.[163]

Justices of the peace, by virtue of their commissions, or those who are *ex officio* conservators of the peace, may bind all those to keep the peace who make any affray, or threaten to kill or beat another, or contend together with angry words or menaces, or go about with unusual weapons or followers, to the terror of the people.

The justices are also empowered to bind over to good behaviour towards the Queen and her people all who are not of *good fame,* wherever they are found. "Good fame"

---

[163] For the several cases in which *search warrants* maybe granted for the discovery and seizure of paper and implements employed for forgery, &c., see 24 & 25 Vict., c. 98, s. 46; 24 & 25 Vict., c. 99, s. 27; 24 & 25 Vict., C. 100, s. 65.

is an expression of great latitude, which leaves much to be determined by the discretion of the magistrate himself.

In default of finding sureties when required, the party may be sent to prison, subject to the restriction imposed by stat. 16 & 17 Vict., c. 30, s. 3, which enacts that no person committed to prison under any warrant or order, on account of not entering into recognizances, or finding sureties to keep the peace, or to be of good behaviour, shall be detained under such warrant or order for more than twelve calendar months from the time of such commitment.

A recognizance may be discharged by the death of the party bound thereby; or by order of the court, on sufficient cause being shown.

CHAPTER XIII
COURTS OF CRIMINAL JURISDICTION

The next and last object of our inquiries will he the method of inflicting *punishments* which the law has annexed to these particular offences; in the discussion of which let us briefly mention the several Courts of criminal jurisdiction wherein offenders may be prosecuted, and explain the proceedings therein respectively.

Mention briefly the several Courts of Criminal Jurisdiction, and Explain the Proceedings.

I. The High Court of Parliament.

The High Court of Parliament is the Supreme Court in the Kingdom for the trial of great offenders, whether Lords or Commoners, by a method called Parliamentary impeachment. The articles of impeachment are prepared and agreed to by the House of Commons, and afterwards tried by the Lords, who are in such cases of misdemeanor considered, not only as their own Peers, but as the Peers of the whole nation. A *commoner* cannot be impeached before the Lords for any capital offence, but only for high misdemeanor; a *peer* may be impeached for any crime. Our Constitution deems it proper in such cases that the nobility should judge, to insure justice to the accused, and that the people should accuse, to insure justice to the Commonwealth.

II. Court of the Lord High Steward.

This is a court instituted for the trial of peers indicted for treason or felony, or for misprision of either. When, therefore, such an indictment is found by a grand jury of freeholders in the Queen's Bench, or at the Assizes before the justices of *oyer* and *terminer,* it has to he removed by a writ of *certiorari* into the Court of the Lord. High Steward, which only has power to determine it. When the indictment is regularly removed, by writ of *certiorari,* the Lord High Steward, who is appointed *pro hâc vice,* by commission under the great seal, directs a precept to the serjeant-at-arms, to summon the lords to attend and try the indicted peer. The decision is by the majority; but a majority cannot convict unless it consist of twelve or more.

During the Session of Parliament, the trial of an indicted peer or peeress is not properly in the Court of the Lord High Steward, but before the Court of our Lady the Queen in Parliament.

Upon conviction for felony or misdemeanor, a peer is now liable to the same punishment as any other subject of the Crown.

III. The Court of Queen's Bench.

This court, which was noticed in a former chapter, is divided into a Crown side and a plea side. On the Crown side or Crown office it takes cognizance of criminal causes, from high treason down to the most trivial misdemeanor or breach of the peace. Into this court also indictments from all inferior courts may be removed by writ of *certiorari,* and tried either at *bar,* which rarely happens, or at *nisi prius* by a jury out of the county of which the indictment is brought. The removal, however, of an indictment by *certiorari* into this court can only take place where the indictment is against a body corporate, not authorized to appear by attorney in the court below; or else where it is made to appear to the court or to a judge thereof by the party applying for the writ, that a fair and impartial trial cannot be had in the court below; or that a question of law of more than usual difficulty and importance is likely to arise upon the trial; or that a special jury may be required for the satisfactory trial of the case.

IV. The High Court of Admiralty.

The High Court of Admiralty, held before the Lord High Admiral, or his deputy, styled the Judge of the Admiralty, is a court not only of civil, but also of criminal jurisdiction, but this latter branch is now usually exercised by other criminal courts, pursuant to divers statutes. By a recent statute, all offences alleged to have been committed on the high seas and other places within the jurisdiction of the Admiralty of England, may be inquired of, heard, and determined by the justices of assize, oyer and terminer, and general gaol delivery, who may deliver the gaol in every county and franchise within the limits of their several commissions of every person committed to or imprisoned therein for any offence alleged to have been committed upon the high seas.

V. Court for Crown Cases Reserved.

This court was constituted by stat. 11 & 12 Vict., c. 78, for the further amendment of the administration of the Criminal Law, which enacts that when a person has been convicted of any treason, felony, or misdemeanor before any court of oyer and terminer, or gaol delivery, or court of quarter-sessions, the judge, or commissioner, or justice of the peace before whom the case was tried, may reserve any question of law for the consideration of the judges, and thereupon may respite execution of the judgment on such conviction, or postpone judgment until such question shall have been decided.[164]

VI. Courts of Oyer and Terminer.

The Courts of *Oyer* and *Terminer* and *general gaol delivery* are held before the Queen's commissioners, among whom are usually two judges of the Courts at Westminster, twice at least in the year in every county of the kingdom, with an exception as to the metropolis and parts of the adjacent counties. The judges sit by virtue of four several authorities, viz., the commission of the peace, the commission of *oyer* and *terminer,* the commission of general gaol delivery, and the commission of *nisi prius.* All the justices of the peace of the county wherein the assizes are held are bound by law to attend them, or else are liable to a fine, in order to return recognizances, &c., and. to assist the judges in such matters as lie within their knowledge and jurisdiction, and in which, some of them have most probably been concerned in their committal of prisoners. The commission of *oyer* and *terminer* gives the judges authority to hear and determine all treasons, felonies, and misdemeanors committed within the county. They have besides a commission of general *gaol delivery,*

---

[164] See Criminal Law Consolidation and Amendment Acts, 24 & 25 Vict, cc. 96-100.

which empowers them to try and deliver every prisoner who shall be in the gaol when they arrive at the circuit town, whenever or before whomsoever indicted, or for whatever crime committed. So that, one way or other, the gaols are in general cleared, and all prisoners tried, punished, or delivered, at least *twice in every year.* Sometimes, upon urgent occasions, the Crown issues a *special* or *extraordinary* commission of *oyer* and *terminer* and gaol delivery confined to the offences therein particularly mentioned.

VII. Central Criminal Court.

This is another important court of criminal jurisdiction, established by stat. 4 & 5 Wm. IV., c. 36. It must sit at least twelve times a year, and oftener if need be, and has cognizance of all offences committed in London and Middlesex, and in certain specified portions of the adjacent counties of Essex, Kent, and Surrey, and now by statute has criminal jurisdiction in Admiralty cases for offences committed on the high seas. An indictment for felony or misdemeanor committed out of the jurisdiction of the Central Criminal Court, and removed into the Queen's Bench by *certiorari,* may by the latter court be ordered to be tried there.[165]

VIII. Court of Quarter Sessions.

The Court of *General Quarter Sessions of the Peace* is a court that must be held in every county once in each quarter of the year. By stat. 1 Wm. IV., c. 70, s. 35, the quarter sessions are appointed to be held in the first week after the 11th of October, the 28th of December, the 31st of March, and the 24th of June in every year. They are held before two or more justices of the peace, one of

---

[165] See 19 & 20 Vict., c. 16, an Act to empower the Court of Queen's Bench to order certain offenders to be tried at the Central Criminal Court.

whom must be of the Quorum. The jurisdiction is not circumscribed, but it is expressly provided by stat. 5 & 6 Vict., c. 38, that neither the justices for any county, nor the recorder of any borough at any general or quarter sessions, shall try any prisoner for treason, murder, or capital felony, nor for any of the particular offences enumerated in the Act. They are also restrained from trying persons charged with fraudulent practices as agents, trustees, bankers, or factors under the Larceny Act of 1861.

There are also, in most municipal boroughs. Courts of Quarter Sessions of the Peace, having in general the same authority in cases arising within the limits of the borough as the Quarter Sessions within the county. Of these the several Recorders are the presiding judges.

IX. Middlesex Sessions.

For the county of Middlesex it has lately been enacted by 7 & 8 Vict., c. 71, amended by 22 & 23 Vict., c. 4, that there shall be holden for that county two sessions or adjourned sessions of the peace in every calendar month; and that the first sessions, in January, April, July, and October respectively, shall be the general quarter sessions of the county; and that the second sessions in January, April, July, and October shall be adjournments of the general quarter sessions.

X. The Court of the Coroner.

The *Court of the Coroner* is also a Court of Record to inquire, when any one dies in prison or comes to a violent or sudden death, by what manner he came to his end; and this the coroner and the jury must do *super visum corporis*.

XI. Chancellors' Courts of Oxford and Cambridge.

The *Chancellors'* Courts of Oxford and Cambridge, already mentioned, have also criminal jurisdiction over persons having the privileges of the University for offences or misdemeanors under the degree of *treason, felony, or mayhem.* By 17 & 18 Vict., c. 45; and 25 & 26 Vict., c. 26, the Chancellors' Court of the University of Oxford is governed by the statute law of the realm, and no longer by the rules of the civil law. As to Cambridge, the privilege is now practically obsolete.

CHAPTER XIV "SUMMARY" AND "REGULAR" CONVICTIONS

We have next to take into consideration the *proceedings* of Criminal Courts for the punishment of offenders. These proceedings are divisible into two kinds — *summary* and *regular.*

Explain briefly "Summary" proceedings in Criminal Courts; then the "Regular" proceedings.

By a *summary proceeding is* meant principally such as is directed by several Acts of Parliament for the conviction of offenders, and infliction of certain penalties created by those Acts. In these there is no intervention of a jury; but the party accused is acquitted or condemned by the judgment of such person only as the statute has appointed for his judge, an institution designed professedly for the greater convenience of the subject, by doing him speedy justice, and by not harassing a jury with frequent and troublesome attendances to try every minute offence.[166]

Of this summary nature are trials of offences and frauds against the laws of the *excise,* the *customs,* and other branches of the revenue, which are determined by the commissioners of revenue or before justices of the peace in the country.

Another branch of summary proceedings is that which takes place before justices of the peace in respect of a variety of minor offences.[167] The practice of proceeding upon summary convictions in general is regulated by stat. 11 & 12 Vict., c. 43, which consolidates and amends the previous provisions on the subject.

By stat. 20 & 21 Vict., c. 43 — (an Act to improve the administration of the law respecting summary proceedings before justices of the peace) — after the hearing and determination of any information or complaint by a justice in a summary way, either party dissatisfied with the decision, as being erroneous in — *point of law,* may apply for the opinion thereon of one of the superior courts of law. To prevent the abuse of such privilege, security for costs will have to be given by the appellant.

Explain briefly the "Regular" and "Ordinary" Methods of proceedings in Courts of Criminal Jurisdiction, where the offence charged amounts to a felony or indictable misdemeanor.

This subject may be distributed under these general heads: — 1. Arrest. — 2. Commitment and bail. — 3. Prosecution. — 4. Process and Arraignment. — 5. Plea

[166] A summary conviction is a bar to all further or other proceedings for the same cause.

[167] See Summary Jurisdiction Act, 13 & 14 Vict., c. 37; also 24 & 25 Vict., cc. 96, 100.

and issue. — 6. Trial and conviction. — 7. Proceedings after the Trial. — 8. Judgment. — 9. Reprieve or pardon. — 10. Execution.

I. Arrest.

First, then, of an *arrest,* which is apprehending or restraining a person, in order that he shall be forthcoming to answer an alleged or suspected crime. To this *arrest* all persons are, without distinction, equally liable in criminal cases, and it may be made either with or without a *warrant.*

Warrants are ordinarily issued by justices of the peace out of sessions; but a warrant may be granted, in cases of treason or other offence affecting the Government by the Privy Council or one of the Secretaries of State, and. by any judge of the Court of Queen's Bench, to bring before him for examination a person charged, with felony.

A warrant of the Chief Justice or other Justice of the Court of Queen's Bench extends all over the kingdom; but a warrant of a justice of the peace in one county must be endorsed by a justice of the peace of the county in which it is intended, to be executed.

Arrests by officers *without warrant* may be executed by a justice of the peace, by the sheriff, the coroner, or by the constable, on witnessing any person committing a felony or breach of peace. Also ripen a reasonable charge of treason or felony, or of a dangerous wounding, whereby felony is likely to ensue; or upon reasonable suspicion that any of such offences have been committed, the constable may, without warrant, be justified in arresting the party so charged or suspected. He is also authorized in these cases to break open doors.

A private person, and, *a fortiori,* a peace officer, who is present when any felony is committed, is bound by law to arrest the felon, on pain of fine and imprisonment.

II. Commitment and Bail.

When a delinquent is arrested, he ought to be taken before a justice of the peace; and the justice or justices are bound immediately to examine the circumstances of the crime alleged. When all the evidence against the accused person shall have been heard on oath, which must be put in writing and signed by the witnesses and the justice, it is then read over to the accused, who shall be asked if he wishes to say anything in answer to the charge, after a caution that what he may say will be taken down, and may be read in evidence against him. If the justice is of opinion that the offence is not sufficient to put the accused upon his trial, he shall forthwith order him to be discharged; but, if of the opposite opinion, the justice or justices shall either commit him to prison to take his trial, or admit him to bail; that is, allow him to be discharged on entering into a recognizance, with sufficient surety or sureties, to appear and surrender himself to take his trial in respect of the charge in question at the next assizes or quarter-sessions of the peace. Supposing the offence is such that no bail is allowed,[168] or if allowed and the accused cannot find bail, he is then committed to prison by the warrant of the justice, to be there safely kept until delivered by due course of law.

III. Prosecution.

The next step is the *prosecution,* or the manner of the formal accusation; and this is either by a previous finding

---

[168] See 11 & 12 Vict., c. 42, which, *inter alia,* gives a discretionary power to the justices to commit to prison or hold to bail in the particular cases there enumerated.

of the fact by an inquest or a grand jury; or without such previous finding, by *presentment* or *indictment.*

Where the coroner's *inquisition* is taken concerning the death of a man, and a verdict of murder or manslaughter is returned, the offender may he arraigned and tried without the intervention of a grand jury; and if an indictment be found for the same offence, and the defendant be acquitted on the one, he may be arraigned on the other, to which he may, however, effectually plead his former acquittal.

A *presentment* is the notice taken by a grand jury of an offence from their own knowledge or observation, without any bill of indictment laid before them, as of a nuisance or a libel, upon which the officer of the court must frame an indictment before the party presented can be put to answer.

They may also make presentment of any circumstance relative to criminal proceedings which, in their opinion, the judge should be made acquainted with.

An *indictment* is a written accusation of one or more persons. of a felony or misdemeanor, preferred to and presented upon oath to a grand jury. The indictment must state the facts of the offence with as much certainty as the nature of the case will admit.

When the *grand jury* have heard the evidence, if they think it a groundless accusation, they now intimate "*not found*" — not a *true bill;* and then the bill is said to be "thrown out," and the party is discharged; on the other hand, if they are satisfied of the *primâ facie* truth of the accusation, they indorse upon it — "a true bill." As many as appear upon the panel are sworn upon the grand jury, to the number of twelve at least, and not more than twenty-three, that twelve may be a majority. The indictment is then said to be *found,* and the party stands indicted; but to find a true bill twelve at least of the jury must agree, for so tender is the law of England of the life or liberty of the subject, that no man can be convicted at the suit of the Crown of any indictable offence, unless by the unanimous voice of twenty-four of his equals and neighbours; that is, by twelve at least of the grand jury assenting to the accusation, and afterwards by twelve more, called the petty jury, finding him guilty upon his trial.

IV. Process and Arraignment.

The *indictment* having been found by the grand July, the offender, if in custody, is immediately *arraigned* thereon,[169] that is, called to the bar of the court to answer the matter charged upon him in the indictment.

After the indictment has been read to the prisoner, it is demanded of him whether he be *guilty* of the crime whereof he stands indicted, or *not guilty.*

Upon a simple and plain confession of *guilty,* the court necessarily awards judgment; but it is usually slow in receiving and recording such confession; and, in capital cases, will generally advise the prisoner to retract it and plead "not guilty" to the indictment.

V. Plea and Issue.

The plea or *demurrer* of the prisoner is the defensive matter alleged by him on his arraignment, if he does not confess or stand mute. This is either: — 1. A plea to the jurisdiction. — 2. A demurrer. — 3. A plea in abatement. — 4. A special plea in bar. — 5. The general issue.

[169] For the mode of compelling the appearance of a defendant against whom an indictment has been found, see 11 & 12 Vict., c. 42, s. 3.

1. A plea to the *jurisdiction* is where an indictment is taken before a court which has no cognizance of the offence, as if a man be indicted for a rape at the sheriff's tourn, or for treason at the quarter-sessions. In these or similar cases he may take exception to the jurisdiction of the court, without answering to the crime alleged.

2. A plea in *abatement* is founded on some matter of fact extraneous to the indictment, tending to show that it is defective in point of form; in the case of *misnomer,* a wrong name or a false addition; but now, by 14 & 15 Vict., c. 100, s. 24, no indictment for any offence shall be held *insufficient* "for want of, or imperfection in, the *addition* of any defendant."

3. A *demurrer.* This is incident to criminal cases as well as civil; where the fact as alleged is allowed to be true, but the person accused takes exception to the sufficiency of the charge on the face of it. Stat. 14 & 15 Vict., c. 100, ss. 24 & 25, has rendered such and some other imperfections amendable and immaterial.

4. A *special plea* in *bar,* which goes to the merits of the indictment, gives a reason why the prisoner ought not to answer it at all, nor put himself upon his trial for the crime alleged. Special pleas are principally of three kinds: — 1. A former acquittal. — 2. A former conviction. — 3. A pardon.

The plea of *autrefois acquit,* or a former acquittal, is grounded on the universal maxim of the common law of England, "that no man is to be brought into jeopardy more than once for the same offence."

The plea of *autrefois convict* is a good plea in bar, and this depends upon the same principle as the former.

A *pardon* may be pleaded in bar, as at once destroying the end and purpose of the indictment.

5. By the plea of *not guilty,* the prisoner puts himself upon the trial by jury, and various formalities which were formerly observed subsequent to this plea have fallen into disuse.

VI. Trial and Conviction.

When the trial[170] is called on, the jurors, to the number of twelve, are sworn, or required to make the affirmation or declaration permitted by 30 & 31 Vict., c. 35, s. 8, by persons who are unwilling from alleged conscientious motives to take an oath.

Challenges are made as on a civil trial.

When the jury are sworn, the indictment is usually opened, and the evidence marshalled, examined, and enforced by the counsel for the Crown or prosecution.

Evidence may be either *direct* and *positive,* or *presumptive* and *circumstantial.* Hearsay evidence is not admissible.

A *presumption* is where some facts, being proved, another follows as a very natural or very probable conclusion from them, so as readily to gain assent from the mere probability of its having occurred without further proof. The fact thus assented to is said to be *presumed;* that is, taken for granted until the contrary be proved by the opposite party.

These presumptions are of three kinds: — 1. Violent presumptions, where the facts and circumstances proved, *necessarily* attend the fact presumed. As if upon an indictment for murder it were proved that the deceased was murdered in a house, and that the defendant was immediately afterwards seen running out of it with a bloody

[170] For an account of various ordeals, purgations, trials by battle, &c., long since abolished, see Blackstone, Vol. IV.

sword in his hand. — 2. *Probable* presumptions, where the facts and circumstances proved *usually* attend the fact presumed. As upon an indictment for *arson,* proof that property which was in the house at the time it was burnt was afterwards found in the possession of the defendant raises a probable presumption that the defendant was present and concerned in the arson. — 3. *Light* or *rash presumptions,* which, however, should have no weight or validity at all.

The doctrine of evidence is in most respects the same as that recognized in civil actions. No proof is admissible which in its very nature indicates the existence of some better proof. Depositions, however, of a witness taken by the committing magistrate, and purporting to be signed by him, may, under certain circumstances, be read as evidence. Also the statement of a person dangerously ill, taken by a justice and signed by him, may be read in evidence either for or against the accused.

A witness cannot be compelled to answer a question the reply to which might tend to criminate himself. A witness may, however, be questioned as to whether he has been convicted of any felony or misdemeanor, and if he either denies or does not admit the fact, or refuses to answer, the cross-examiner may prove such conviction. The character of a witness for habitual veracity is an essential ingredient in his credibility. An accomplice is admissible as a witness, but his testimony is acted upon with a scrupulous consideration as to its merit and value, and in general some corroboration of it is required.

After the witnesses have been sworn, the counsel for the party who calls them proceeds to examine them; and two things are to be strictly observed; first, that the questions be pertinent to the matter immediately in issue; secondly, that they be not *leading* questions; in other words, questions framed in such a manner as to suggest to the witness the answers required of him. If an irrelevant question be put, the counsel on the other side should immediately interpose and object to it, and the admissibility of the question is decided by the judge. When the direct examination is finished, the witness may then be cross-examined by the counsel for the opposite party. If any new fact arises out of the cross-examination, the witness maybe re-examined by the counsel who examined him.

The right to reply, where *evidence is given* for the prisoner or defendant, is vested in the counsel for the prosecution, though not *usually exercised* where witnesses are called merely to speak to the character of the accused.

When the evidence and speeches of counsel on both sides are closed, it is for the court to instruct the jury as to matters of law, to read, sum up, and comment upon the evidence, to clear any difficulties, and remove obstacles towards a satisfactory conclusion.

The jury then give in their verdict. If the jury find the prisoner not *guilty,* he is then for ever quit and discharged of the accusation, and immediately set at liberty; but if the jury find him *guilty,* he is then said to be *convicted* of the crime whereof he stands indicted.

Under the Larceny Act, 24 & 25 Vict., c. 96, the court is empowered to award restitution to the owner of the property stolen, or wrongfully got from him; and by 30 & 31 Vict., c.35, s. 9. in the case of stolen property sold by the prisoner to some person who had no knowledge that the property was stolen, on restitution of such property to the prosecutor the court may, on application of such purchaser, order that out of any money which may have been taken from the prisoner on his apprehension, a sum, not exceeding the proceeds of the said sale, be delivered to the purchaser.

VII. Proceedings after the Trial. — Judgment.

When, upon a charge of felony, the jury have brought in their verdict *guilty,* in the presence of the prisoner, he is either immediately or soon after asked by the court if he has anything to offer why judgment should not be awarded against him. At this period he may offer any exceptions to the indictment in *arrest of judgment;* as for some defect apparent on the face of the record, or now only in respect of some substantial objection. By 11 & 12 Vict., c. 78, the court is now empowered to *reserve* the question, and in the meantime to postpone the judgment, or respite the execution of it, as may be thought fit.

VIII. Reprieve or Pardon.

The only other remaining ways of avoiding the execution of the judgment are by a *Reprieve;* or a *Pardon;* the former being temporary only, the latter permanent.

A *reprieve,* from *reprendre,* to take back, is the withdrawing of a sentence for an interval of time, whereby its execution is suspended. This may be, first, *ex mandate regis;* that is, the mere pleasure of the Crown, where the Crown has that power; and secondly, *ex arbitrio judicis,* as where the judge is not satisfied with the verdict, or the evidence is suspicious, or the indictment is insufficient, or sometimes, if it be a petty felony, or any favourable circumstances appear in the criminal's character, in order to give room to apply to the Crown for either an absolute or conditional pardon.

Reprieves may also be *ex necessitate legis:* as, where a woman is capitally convicted, and pleads her pregnancy; though this is no cause to stay the judgment, yet it is to respite the execution till she be delivered. In case this plea be made in stay of execution, the judge must direct a jury of twelve matrons, assisted by a medical man, to inquire into the fact; and if they bring in their verdict *quick with child,* execution will be stayed generally till either she is delivered; or proves, by the course of nature, not to have been with child at all.

Another cause of regular reprieve is, if the offender become *non compos mentis* between the judgment and the award of execution; for if a man be *compos* when he commits a capital crime, yet if he becomes *non compos* after, he shall not be indicted; if after indictment, he shall not be convicted; if after conviction, he shall not receive judgment; if after judgment, he shall not be ordered for execution: for "*furiosus solo furore punitur,*" and the law knows not but he might have offered some reason, if in his senses, to have stayed, these respective proceedings.

If no special reason can be adduced to avoid the judgment, and stay the execution consequent thereupon, the last resort is to the Crown for *pardon,* the granting of which is its merciful prerogative.

A *pardon* may either be *absolute* or *conditional;* that is, the Queen may extend her mercy upon what terms she pleases, and may annex to her bounty a condition either precedent or subsequent. This prerogative is exercised, through the Home Secretary, in the pardon of felons or misdemeanants.

IX. Execution.

When sentence of death has, in due course, been pronounced upon a person convicted of murder or other capital offence, *execution,* the completion of human punishment, follows, and this must be performed by the legal officer, the sheriff, or his deputy, whose warrant for so doing was anciently by precept under the hand and seal of the judge; but now the usage is, for the judge to sign the calendar, or list of all the prisoners' names, with their separate judgments in the margin, which is left with the sheriff as his warrant and authority, and if he receives no order to the contrary, he executes the judgment of the law accordingly. As, for a capital felony, it is written to the prisoner's name, "let him be hanged by the neck; formerly, in the days of Latin and abbreviations, "*sus.* per *coll.,*" for "*suspendatur per collum.*" And this is the only warrant the sheriff has for so material an act as taking away the life of another.

By stat. 31 & 32 Vict., c. 24, a recent and salutary statute, it is enacted, *inter alia,* that judgment of death shall henceforth be executed on any prisoner within the walls of the prison in which the offender is confined, in the presence of the sheriff or his deputy and certain other persons. That, after execution, the fact of death is to be certified by the prison surgeon, and that a coroner's inquest is to be held upon the body.

Made in the USA
Monee, IL
04 November 2026

67387293R00203